P9-DMB-643

Praise for Pamela Druckerman's
bringing up bébé

"Marvelous . . . Like Julia Child, who translated the secrets of French cuisine, Druckerman has investigated and distilled the essentials of French child rearing. . . . Druckerman provides fascinating details about French sleep training, feeding schedules, and family rituals. But her book's real pleasures spring from her funny, self-deprecating stories. Like the principles she examines, Druckerman isn't doctrinaire."   —NPR

"*Bringing Up Bébé* is a must-read for parents who would like their children to eat more than white pasta and chicken fingers."   —Fox News

"On questions of how to live, the French never disappoint. . . . Maybe it all starts with childhood. That is the conclusion that readers may draw from *Bringing Up Bébé*."   —*The Wall Street Journal*

"French women don't have little bags of emergency Cheerios spilling all over their Louis Vuitton handbags. They also, Druckerman notes, wear skinny jeans instead of sweatpants. . . . The world arguably needs more kids who don't throw food."   —*Chicago Tribune*

"I've been a parent now for more than eight years, and—confession—I've never actually made it all the way through a parenting book. But I found *Bringing Up Bébé* to be irresistible."   —*Slate*

"Engaging work . . . Ms. Druckerman, meanwhile, is easy to like as she relays her insights with stylish humor."   —*Pittsburgh Post-Gazette*

"Self-deprecating, witty, informative . . . But however much she admires the 'easy, calm authority' French parents seem to possess, will Druckerman manage it herself? Her efforts to do so add a compelling narrative to this fascinating study of French parenting."   —*The Guardian* (London)

"In recounting how her three children went native, Druckerman is engagingly self-deprecating. . . . This book is worth its price for the crucial information it reveals about how to win the sleep wars."   —*Daily Mail* (London)

"Fascinating . . . gripping . . . extremely funny . . . A desperately needed corrective to received wisdom about child rearing and what having children is supposed to do to a woman's sense of self. I loved it."

—*The Sunday Times* (London)

"I couldn't put *Bringing Up Bébé* down! It's smart, funny, and fascinating, insightful, provocative, and genuinely eye-opening. I love Pamela Druckerman's honesty, rueful humor, and her premise that parents of all cultures should be able to learn from one another."

—Amy Chua, author of *The Triple Package*
and *Battle Hymn of the Tiger Mother*

"In engaging storytelling prose, American Druckerman describes a French 'society of good little sleepers, gourmet eaters, and relaxed parents,' and with her bicultural glasses sees a few telling contrasts, for better or worse, with how she is doing things the American way."

—Mireille Guiliano, author of *French Women Don't Get Fat*

"Living in Paris has allowed American journalist Druckerman a riveting glimpse into a calmer, rational, sage way of raising children. . . . Ever engaging and lively to read." —*Publishers Weekly*

"Druckerman neither sneers at nor fawns over the French way, but approaches the topic with high interest, prodding the advice with the curiosity of a great journalist, then writing it all down with the humor and detail of a great storyteller." —*Minneapolis Star Tribune*

"This is not a shrill or preachy book. It's a carefully observed memoir tied into a larger conversation about how a less intense—but still structured—parenting style may deliver happier parents and children."

—*Houston Chronicle*

"Druckerman's epiphanies include how months-old French babies sleep through the night via the 'pause' technique and, soon after, are taught the art of patience. She demystifies the day care 'crèche' and preschool 'maternelle,' and how French mothers return to top physical shape (and their jobs) following childbirth. The author is a delightfully droll storyteller with an effortless gift of gab that translates well to the page. She backs up assumptions and associated explorations with historical parenting examples and comparisons that temper her skepticisms with an authoritative air."

—*Kirkus Reviews*

"Druckerman, a former *Wall Street Journal* reporter, set out to determine just what French parents are doing right. . . . Written in a winningly chatty style."

—Associated Press

"*Bringing Up Bébé* is a fun read."

—*Entertainment Weekly*

"Druckerman embarked on a painstaking study of parenting *à la française*. The result is amusing, helpful, and charmingly self-effacing. . . . Pamela Druckerman is a charming narrator. . . . A natural neurotic, she has produced an important guide to staying calm, and if half of what she says about Anglophone parents is true, her book should be dispensed on prescription."

—*The Spectator* (London)

"Druckerman is right in that the key to enjoying our kids is educating them on how to be more enjoyable."

—*Redbook*

"Written with verve and humor."

—*The Bookseller* (London)

PENGUIN BOOKS

bringing up bébé

Pamela Druckerman is a contributing opinion writer for the *International New York Times* and a former staff reporter for *The Wall Street Journal*, where she covered foreign affairs. She has also written for *The Washington Post* and *Marie Claire*. Her books have been translated into twenty-two languages. She lives in Paris.

bringing
up
bébé

· · · · · · • · • · · · · ·

One American Mother
Discovers the Wisdom of
French Parenting

· · · ·

NOW WITH
bébé day by day
100 Keys to French Parenting

Pamela Druckerman

A PENGUIN BOOK

PENGUIN BOOKS
Published by the Penguin Group
Penguin Group (USA) LLC
375 Hudson Street
New York, New York 10014

USA | Canada | UK | Ireland | Australia
New Zealand | India | South Africa | China

penguin.com
A Penguin Random House Company

Bringing Up Bébé first published in the United States of America by
The Penguin Press, a member of Penguin Group (USA) Inc., 2012
Bébé Day by Day first published by The Penguin Press 2013
Published in Penguin Books 2014

Copyright © 2012, 2013 by Pamela Druckerman
Penguin supports copyright. Copyright fuels creativity, encourages diverse
voices, promotes free speech, and creates a vibrant culture. Thank you for
buying an authorized edition of this book and for complying with copyright
laws by not reproducing, scanning, or distributing any part of it in any form
without permission. You are supporting writers and allowing Penguin to
continue to publish books for every reader.

Illustrations © 2012 by Margaux Motin

LIBRARY OF CONGRESS CATALOGING-IN-PUBLICATION DATA:
Druckerman, Pamela.
Bringing up Bébé : one American mother discovers the wisdom of French
parenting / Pamela Druckerman.
pages cm
"Including Bébé day by day: 100 keys to French parenting."
ISBN 978-0-14-312296-8
1. Child rearing—France.   2. Parent and child—France.   3. Child rearing—
United States.   4. Parent and child—United States.   I. Druckerman,
Pamela. Bébé day by day. II. Title.
HQ769.D78 2014
649'.10944—dc23
2014016158

Printed in the United States of America
1 3 5 7 9 10 8 6 4 2

Set in Goudy Old Style MT Std

Penguin is committed to publishing works of quality and integrity.
In that spirit, we are proud to offer this book to our readers; however,
the story, the experiences, and the words are the author's alone.

For Simon,

who makes everything matter

note:

Some names and identifying details have
been changed to protect the privacy
of the individuals involved.

Les petits poissons dans l'eau
Nagent aussi bien que les gros.
The little fish in the water
Swim as well as the big ones do.

—French children's song

contents

bébé day by day

glossary of
french parenting terms

attend (ah-tahn)—wait, stop. A command that a French parent says to a child. "Wait" implies that the child doesn't require immediate gratification, and that he can entertain himself.

au revoir (oh-reh-vwa)—good-bye. What a French child must say when he leaves the company of a familiar adult. It's one of the four French "magic words" for kids. See *bonjour*.

autonomie (oh-toh-no-mee)—autonomy. The blend of independence and self-reliance that French parents encourage in their children from an early age.

bêtise (beh-teeze)—a small act of naughtiness. Labeling an offense a mere *bêtise* helps parents respond to it with moderation.

bonjour (bohn-juhr)—hello, good day. What a child must say when he encounters a familiar adult.

caca boudin (caca booh-dah)—literally, "caca sausage." A curse word used almost exclusively by French preschoolers.

cadre (kah-druh)—frame, or framework. A visual image that describes the French parenting ideal: setting firm limits for children, but giving them tremendous freedom within those limits.

caprice (kah-preese)—a child's impulsive whim, fancy, or demand, often accompanied by whining or tears. French parents believe it is damaging to accede to *caprices*.

classe verte (klass vehr-tuh)—green class. Beginning in about first grade, a class trip in which students spend a week or so in a natural setting. The teacher chaperones, along with a few other adults.

colonie de vacances (koh-loh-nee duh vah-kahnce)—vacation colony. One of hundreds of group holidays for kids as young as four, without their parents, usually in the countryside.

complicité (kohm-plee-see-tay)—complicity. The mutual understanding that French parents and caregivers try to develop with children, beginning from birth. *Complicité* implies that even small babies are rational beings, with whom adults can have reciprocal, respectful relationships.

crèche (khresh)—a full-time French day-care center, subsidized and regulated by the government. Middle-class French parents generally prefer crèches to nannies or to group care in private homes.

doucement (doo-ceh-mahnt)—gently; carefully. One of the words that parents and caregivers say frequently to small children. It implies that the children are capable of controlled, mindful behavior.

doudou (doo-doo)—the obligatory comfort object for young children. It's usually a floppy stuffed animal.

école maternelle (eh-kole mah-tehr-nell)—France's free public preschool. It begins in September of the year a child turns three.

éducation (eh-doo-cah-see-ohn)—upbringing. The way that French parents raise their kids.

enfant roi (an-fahnt rwa)—child king. An excessively demanding child who is constantly the center of his parents' attention and who can't cope with frustration.

équilibre (eh-key-lee-bruh)—balance. Not letting any one part of life—including being a parent—overwhelm the other parts.

éveillé/e (eh-vay-yay)—awakened, alert, stimulated. This is one of the ideals for French children. The other is for them to be *sage*.

gourmand/e (goohre-mahn)—someone who eats too quickly, too much of one thing, or too much of everything.

goûter (gew-tay)—the afternoon snack for kids, eaten at about four thirty P.M. The *goûter* is the only snack of the day. It can also be a verb: Did you already *goûter*?

les gros yeux (leh grohz yuh)—"the big eyes." The look of admonishment that French adults give children, signaling them to stop doing a *bêtise*.

maman-taxi (mah-mo tax-ee)—taxi mother. A woman who spends much of her free time shuttling her child to extracurricular activities. This is not *équilibrée*.

n'importe quoi (nemporta kwa)—whatever; anything you like. A child who does *n'importe quoi* acts without limits or regard for others.

non (noh)—no; absolutely not.

profiter (proh-feeh-teh)—to enjoy the moment and take advantage of it.

punir (pew-near)—to punish. To be *puni*—punished—is serious and important.

rapporter (ra-poor-tay)—to tell on someone; to tattle. French children and adults believe that it's very bad to do this.

sage (sah-je)—wise and calm. This describes a child who is in control of himself or absorbed in an activity. Instead of saying "be good," French parents say "be *sage*."

tétine (teh-teen)—pacifier. It's not uncommon to see these in the mouths of French three- or four-year-olds.

bringing
up
bébé

french children
don't throw food

When my daughter is eighteen months old, my husband and I decide to take her on a little summer holiday. We pick a coastal town that's a few hours by train from Paris, where we've been living (I'm American, he's British), and we book a hotel room with a crib. She's our only child at this point, so forgive us for thinking: How hard could it be?

We have breakfast at the hotel. But we have to eat lunch and dinner at the little seafood restaurants around the old port. We quickly discover that two restaurant meals a day, with a toddler, deserve to be their own circle of hell. Bean is briefly interested in food: a piece of bread or anything fried. But within a few minutes she starts spilling salt shakers and tearing apart sugar packets. Then she demands to be sprung from her high chair so she can dash around the restaurant and bolt dangerously toward the docks.

Our strategy is to finish the meal quickly. We order while we're being seated, then we beg the server to rush out some bread and bring us all our food, appetizers and main courses, simultaneously. While my husband has a few bites of fish, I make sure that Bean doesn't get kicked by a waiter or lost at sea. Then we switch. We leave enormous, apologetic tips to compensate for the arc of torn napkins and calamari around our table.

On the walk back to our hotel we swear off travel, joy, and ever having more kids. This "holiday" seals the fact that life as we knew it eighteen months earlier has officially vanished. I'm not sure why we're even surprised.

After a few more restaurant meals, I notice that the French families all around us don't look like they're in hell. Weirdly, they look like they're on vacation. French children the same age as Bean are sitting contentedly in their high chairs, waiting for their food, or eating fish and even vegetables. There's no shrieking or whining. Everyone is having one course at a time. And there's no debris around their tables.

Though I've lived in France for a few years, I can't explain this. In Paris, kids don't eat in restaurants much. And anyway, I hadn't been watching them. Before I had a child, I never paid attention to anyone else's. And now I mostly just look at my own. In our current misery, however, I can't help but notice that there seems to be another way. But what exactly is it? Are French kids just genetically calmer than ours? Have they been bribed (or threatened) into submission? Are they on the receiving end of an old-fashioned seen-but-not-heard parenting philosophy?

It doesn't seem like it. The French children all around us don't look cowed. They're cheerful, chatty, and curious. Their parents are affectionate and attentive. There just seems to be an invisible, civilizing force at their tables—and I'm starting to suspect, in their lives—that's absent from ours.

Once I start thinking about French parenting, I realize it's not just mealtime that's different. I suddenly have lots of questions. Why is it, for example, that in the hundreds of hours I've clocked at French playgrounds, I've never seen a child (except my own) throw a temper tantrum? Why don't my French friends ever need to rush off the phone because their kids are demanding something? Why haven't their living rooms been taken over by teepees and toy kitchens, the way ours has?

And there's more. Why is it that so many of the American kids I meet are on mono-diets of pasta or white rice, or eat only a narrow menu of "kids" foods, whereas most of my daughter's French friends eat fish, vegetables, and practically everything else? And how is it that, except for a specific time in the afternoon, French kids don't snack?

I hadn't thought I was supposed to admire French parenting. It isn't a *thing*, like French fashion or French cheese. No one visits Paris to soak up the local views on parental authority and guilt management. Quite the contrary: the American mothers I know in Paris are horrified that French mothers barely breastfeed and let their four-year-olds walk around with pacifiers.

So how come they never point out that so many French babies start sleeping through the night at two or three months old? And why don't they mention that French kids don't require constant attention from adults, and that they seem capable of hearing the word "no" without collapsing?

No one is making a fuss about all this. But it's increasingly clear to me that, quietly and en masse, French parents are achieving outcomes that create a whole different atmosphere for family life. When American families visit our home, the parents usually spend much of the visit refereeing their kids' spats, helping their toddlers do laps around the kitchen island, or getting down on the floor to build LEGO villages. There are always a few rounds of crying and consoling. When French friends visit, however, we grown-ups have coffee and the children play happily by themselves.

French parents are very concerned about their kids.[1] They know about pedophiles, allergies, and choking hazards. They take reasonable precautions. But they aren't panicked about their children's well-being.

This calmer outlook makes them better at both establishing boundaries and giving their kids some autonomy.

I'm hardly the first to point out that middle-class America has a parenting problem. In hundreds of books and articles this problem has been painstakingly diagnosed, critiqued, and named: overparenting, hyperparenting, helicopter parenting, and, my personal favorite, the kindergarchy. One writer defines the problem as "simply paying more attention to the upbringing of children than can possibly be good for them."[2] Another, Judith Warner, calls it the "culture of total motherhood." (In fact, she realized this was a problem after returning from France.) Nobody seems to like the relentless, unhappy pace of American parenting, least of all parents themselves.

So why do we do it? Why does this American way of parenting seem to be hardwired into our generation, even if—like me—you've left the country? First, in the 1990s, there was a mass of data and public rhetoric saying that poor kids fall behind in school because they don't get enough stimulation, especially in the early years. Middle-class parents took this to mean that their own kids would benefit from more stimulation, too.[3]

Around the same period, the gap between rich and poor Americans began getting much wider. Suddenly, it seemed that parents needed to groom their children to join the new elite. Exposing kids to the right stuff early on—and perhaps ahead of other children the same age—started to seem more urgent.

Alongside this competitive parenting was a growing belief that kids are psychologically fragile. Today's young parents are part of the most psychoanalyzed generation ever and have absorbed the idea that every choice we make could damage our kids. We also came of age during the divorce boom in the 1980s, and we're determined to act more selflessly than we believe our own parents did.

And although the rate of violent crime in the United States has plunged since its peak in the early 1990s,[4] news reports create the impression that children are at greater physical risk than ever. We feel that we're parenting in a very dangerous world, and that we must be perpetually vigilant.

The result of all this is a parenting style that's stressful and exhausting. But now, in France, I've glimpsed another way. A blend of journalistic curiosity and maternal desperation kicks in. By the end of our ruined beach holiday, I've decided to figure out what French parents are doing differently. It will be a work of investigative parenting. Why don't French children throw food? And why aren't their parents shouting? What is the invisible, civilizing force that the French have harnessed? Can I change my wiring and apply it to my own offspring?

I realize I'm on to something when I discover a research study[5] led by an economist at Princeton, in which mothers in Columbus, Ohio, said child care was more than twice as unpleasant as comparable mothers in the city of Rennes, France, did. This bears out my own observations in Paris and on trips back home to the United States: there's something about the way the French parent that makes it less of a grind and more of a pleasure.

I'm convinced that the secrets of French parenting are hiding in plain sight. It's just that nobody has looked for them before. I start stashing a notebook in my diaper bag. Every doctor's visit, dinner party, playdate, and puppet show becomes a chance to observe French parents in action, and to figure out what unspoken rules they're following.

At first it's hard to tell. French parents seem to vacillate between being extremely strict and shockingly permissive. Interrogating them isn't much help either. Most parents I speak to insist that they're not doing anything special. To the contrary, they're convinced that France is beset by a "child king" syndrome in which parents have lost their authority. (To which I respond, "You don't know from 'child kings.' Please visit New York.")

For several years, and through the birth of two more children in

Paris, I keep uncovering clues. I discover, for instance, that there's a "Dr. Spock" of France, who's a household name around the country, but who doesn't have a single English-language book in print. I read this woman's books, along with many others. I interview dozens of parents and experts. And I eavesdrop shamelessly during school drop-offs and trips to the supermarket. Finally, I think I've discovered what French parents do differently.

When I say "French parents" I'm generalizing of course. Everyone's different. Most of the parents I meet live in Paris and its suburbs. Most have university degrees and professional jobs and earn above the French average. They aren't the superrich or the media elites. They're the educated middle and upper-middle classes. So are the American parents I compare them to.

Still, when I travel around France I see that middle-class Parisians' basic views on how to raise kids would sound familiar to a working-class mother in the French provinces. Indeed, I'm struck that while French parents may not know exactly what they do, they all seem to be doing more or less the same things. Well-off lawyers, caregivers in French day-care centers, public-school teachers, and old ladies who chastise me in the park all spout the same basic principles. So does practically every French baby book and parenting magazine I read. It quickly becomes clear that having a child in France doesn't require choosing a parenting philosophy. Everyone takes the basic rules for granted. That fact alone makes the mood less anxious.

Why France? I certainly don't suffer from a pro-France bias. *Au contraire*, I'm not even sure that I like living here. I certainly don't want my kids growing up into sniffy Parisians. But for all its problems, France is the perfect foil for the current problems in American parenting. On the one hand, middle-class French parents have values that look very familiar to me. Parisian parents are zealous about talking to their kids, showing them nature, and reading them lots of books. They take them to tennis lessons, painting classes, and interactive science museums.

Yet the French have managed to be involved without becoming obsessive. They assume that even good parents aren't at the constant service of their children, and that there's no need to feel guilty about this. "For me, the evenings are for the parents," one Parisian mother tells me. "My daughter can be with us if she wants, but it's adult time." French parents want their kids to be stimulated, but not all the time. While some American toddlers are getting Mandarin tutors and preliteracy training, French kids are— by design— often just toddling around by themselves.

And the French are doing a lot of parenting. While its neighbors are suffering from population declines, France is having a baby boom. In the European Union, only the Irish have a higher birth rate.[6]

The French have all kinds of public services that surely help make having kids more appealing and less stressful. Parents don't have to pay for preschool, worry about health insurance, or save for college. Many get monthly cash allotments—wired directly into their bank accounts—just for having kids.

But these public services don't explain all the differences I see. The French seem to have a whole different framework for raising kids. When I ask French parents how they discipline their children, it takes them a few beats just to understand what I mean. "Ah, you mean how do we *educate* them?" they ask. "Discipline," I soon realize, is a narrow, seldom-used category that deals with punishment. Whereas "educating" (which has nothing to do with school) is something they imagine themselves to be doing all the time.

For years now, headlines have been declaring the demise of the current style of American child rearing. There are dozens of books offering Americans helpful theories on how to parent differently.

I haven't got a theory. What I do have, spread out in front of me, is a fully functioning society of good little sleepers, gourmet eaters, and reasonably relaxed parents. I'm starting with that outcome and working backward to figure out how the French got there. It turns out that to be a different kind of parent, you don't just need a different parenting philosophy. You need a very different view of what a child actually is.

Chapter 1

are you waiting
for a child?

It's ten in the morning when the managing editor summons me to his office and tells me to get my teeth cleaned. He says my dental plan will end on my last day at the newspaper. That will be in five weeks, he says.

More than two hundred of us are laid off that day. The news briefly boosts our parent company's stock price. I own some shares and consider selling them—for irony rather than profit—to cash in on my own dismissal.

Instead, I walk around lower Manhattan in a stupor. Fittingly, it's raining. I stand under a ledge and call the man I'm supposed to see that night.

"I've just been laid off," I say.

"Aren't you devastated?" he asks. "Do you still want to have dinner?"

In fact, I'm relieved. I'm finally free of a job that—after nearly six years—I hadn't had the guts to quit. I was a reporter for the foreign desk in New York, covering elections and financial crises in Latin America. I'd often be dispatched on a few hours' notice, then spend weeks living out of hotels. For a while, my bosses were expecting great things from me. They talked about future editorships. They paid for me to learn Portuguese.

Only suddenly they aren't expecting anything. And strangely, I'm okay with that. I really liked movies about foreign correspondents. But actually being one was different. Usually I was all alone, shackled to an unending story, fielding calls from editors who just wanted more. The men working the same beat as me managed to pick up Costa Rican and Colombian wives, who traveled around with them. At least they had dinner on the table when they finally slogged home. The men I went out with were less portable. And anyway, I rarely stayed in a city long enough to reach the third date.

Although I'm relieved to be leaving the paper, I'm unprepared to become socially toxic. In the week or so after the layoffs, when I still come into the office, colleagues treat me like I'm contagious. People I've worked with for years say nothing or avoid my desk. One work-mate takes me out for a farewell lunch, then won't walk back into the building with me. Long after I clear out my desk, my editor—who was out of town when the ax fell—insists that I return to the office for a humiliating debriefing, in which he suggests that I apply for a lower-ranking job, then rushes off to lunch.

I'm suddenly clear about two things: I don't want to write about politics or money anymore. And I want a boyfriend. I'm standing in my three-foot-wide kitchen, wondering what to do with the rest of my life, when Simon calls. We met six months earlier at a bar in Buenos Aires, when a mutual friend brought him to a foreign correspondents' night out. He's a British journalist who was in Argentina for a few days to write a story about soccer. I'd been sent to cover the country's economic collapse. Apparently, we were on the same flight from New York. He remembered me as the lady who'd held up boarding when, already on the gangway, I realized that I'd left my duty-free purchase in the departure lounge and insisted on going back to fetch it. (I did most of my shopping in airports.)

Simon was exactly my type: swarthy, stocky, and smart. (Though he's of average height, he later adds "short" to this list, since he grew up in Holland among blond giants.) Within a few hours of meeting him, I realized that "love at first sight" just means feeling immediately and extremely calm with someone. Though all I said at the time was, "We definitely must not sleep together."

I was smitten, but wary. Simon had just fled the London real-estate market to buy a cheap apartment in Paris. I was commuting between South America and New York. A long-distance relationship with someone on a third continent seemed a stretch. After that meeting in Argentina, we exchanged occasional e-mails. But I didn't let myself take him too seriously. I hoped that there were swarthy, smart men in my time zone.

Fast-forward seven months. When Simon calls out of the blue and I tell him that I've just been sacked, he doesn't emote or treat me like damaged goods. To the contrary, he seems pleased that I suddenly have some free time. He says he feels that we have "unfinished business," and that he'd like to come to New York.

"That's a terrible idea," I say. What's the point? He can't move to America because he writes about European soccer. I don't speak French, and I've never considered living in Paris. Though I'm suddenly quite portable myself, I'm wary of being pulled into someone else's orbit before I have one of my own again.

Simon arrives in New York wearing the same beat-up leather jacket he wore in Argentina and carrying the bagel and smoked salmon that he'd picked up at the deli near my apartment. A month later I meet his parents in London. Six months later I sell most of my possessions and ship the rest to France. My friends all tell me that I'm being rash. I ignore them and walk out of my rent-stabilized studio apartment in New York with three giant suitcases and a box of stray South American coins, which I give to the Pakistani driver who takes me to the airport.

And poof, I'm a Parisian. I move into Simon's two-room bachelor

pad in a former carpentry district in eastern Paris. With my unemploy-
ment checks still arriving, I ditch financial journalism and begin researching a book. Simon and I each work in one of the rooms during
the day.

The shine comes off our new romance almost immediately, mostly
because of interior design issues. I once read in a book about feng shui
that having piles of stuff on the floor is a sign of depression. For
Simon, it just seems to signal an aversion to shelves. He has cleverly
invested in an enormous unfinished wooden table that fills most of
the living room, and a primitive gas-heating system, which ensures that
there's no reliable hot water. I'm especially irked by his habit of letting
spare change from his pockets spill onto the floor, where it somehow
gathers in the corners of each room. "Get rid of the money," I plead.

I don't find much comfort outside our apartment either. Despite
being in the gastronomic capital of the world, I can't figure out what
to eat. Like most American women, I arrive in Paris with extreme food
preferences. (I'm an Atkins-leaning vegetarian.) Walking around, I feel
besieged by all the bakeries and meat-heavy restaurant menus. For a
while I subsist almost entirely on omelets and goat-cheese salads.
When I ask waiters for "dressing on the side," they look at me like I'm
nuts. I don't understand why French supermarkets stock every American cereal except my personal favorite, Grape-Nuts, and why cafés
don't serve fat-free milk.

I know it sounds ungrateful not to swoon for Paris. Maybe I find it
shallow to fall for a city just because it's so good-looking. The cities
I've had love affairs with in the past were all a bit, well, swarthier: São
Paulo, Mexico City, New York. They didn't sit back and wait to be
admired.

Our part of Paris isn't even that beautiful. And daily life is filled
with small disappointments. No one mentions that "springtime in
Paris" is so celebrated because the preceding seven months are over-
cast and freezing. (I arrive, conveniently, at the beginning of this seven-

month stretch.) And while I'm convinced that I remember my eighth-grade French, Parisians have another name for what I'm speaking to them: Spanish.

There are many appealing things about Paris. I like it that the doors of the metro open a few seconds before the train actually stops, suggesting that the city treats its citizens like adults. I also like that, within six months of my arrival, practically everyone I know in America comes to visit, including people I'd later learn to categorize as "Facebook friends." Simon and I eventually develop a strict admissions policy and rating system for houseguests. (Hint: If you stay a week, leave a gift.)

I'm not bothered by the famous Parisian rudeness. At least that's interactive. What gets me is the indifference. No one but Simon seems to care that I'm here. And he's often off nursing his own Parisian fantasy, which is so uncomplicated it has managed to endure. As far as I can tell, Simon has never visited a museum. But he describes reading the newspaper in a café as an almost transcendent experience. One night at a neighborhood restaurant, he swoons when the waiter sets down a cheese plate in front of him.

"This is why I live in Paris!" he declares. I realize that, by the transitive property of love and cheese, I must live in Paris for that smelly plate of cheese, too.

To be fair, I'm starting to think that it's not Paris, it's me. New York likes its women a bit neurotic. They're encouraged to create a brainy, adorable, conflicted bustle around themselves—à la Meg Ryan in *When Harry Met Sally* or Diane Keaton in *Annie Hall*. Despite having nothing more serious than boy troubles, many of my friends in New York were spending more on therapy than on rent.

That persona doesn't fly in Paris. The French do like Woody Allen's movies. But in real life, the ideal Parisian woman is calm, discreet, a bit remote, and extremely decisive. She orders from the menu. She doesn't blather on about her childhood or her diet. If New York is about the woman who's ruminating about her past screwups and fumbling to find herself, Paris is about the one who—at least outwardly—regrets nothing. In France "neurotic" isn't a self-deprecating half boast; it's a clinical condition.

Even Simon, who's merely British, is perplexed by my self-doubt and my frequent need to discuss our relationship.

"What are you thinking about?" I ask him periodically, usually when he's reading a newspaper.

"Dutch football," he invariably says.

I can't tell if he's serious. I've realized that Simon is in a state of perpetual irony. He says everything, including "I love you," with a little smirk. And yet he almost never actually laughs, even when I'm attempting a joke. (Some close friends don't know that he has dimples.) Simon insists that not smiling is a British habit. But I'm sure I've seen Englishmen laugh. And anyway, it's demoralizing that when I finally get to speak English with someone, he doesn't seem to be listening.

The not laughing also points to a wider cultural gulf between us. As an American, I need things to be spelled out. On the train back to Paris after a weekend with Simon's parents, I ask him whether they liked me.

"Of course they liked you, couldn't you tell?" he asks.

"But did they *say* they liked me?" I demand to know.

In search of other company, I trek across town on a series of "friend blind dates," with friends of friends from back home. Most are expatriates, too. None seem thrilled to hear from a clueless new arrival. Quite a few seem to have made "living in Paris" a kind of job in itself, and an all-purpose answer to the question "What do you do?" Many show up late, as if to prove that they've gone native. (I later learn that French people are typically on time for one-on-one meetings. They're only fashionably late for group events, including children's birthdays.)

My initial attempts to make French friends are even less successful.

At a party, I hit it off reasonably well with an art historian who's about my age and who speaks excellent English. But when we meet again for tea at her house, it's clear that we observe vastly different female bonding rituals. I'm prepared to follow the American model of confession and mirroring, with lots of comforting "me-too's." She pokes daintily at her pastry and discusses theories of art. I leave hungry, and not even knowing whether she has a boyfriend.

The only mirroring I get is in a book by Edmund White, the American writer who lived in France in the 1980s. He's the first person who affirms that feeling depressed and adrift is a perfectly rational response to living in Paris. "Imagine dying and being grateful you'd gone to heaven, until one day (or one century) it dawned on you that your main mood was melancholy, although you were constantly convinced that happiness lay just around the next corner. That's something like living in Paris for years, even decades. It's a mild hell so comfortable that it resembles heaven."

Despite my doubts about Paris, I'm still pretty sure about Simon. I've become resigned to the fact that "swarthy" inevitably comes with "messy." And I've gotten better at reading his micro-expressions. A flicker of a smile means that he's gotten the joke. The rare full smile suggests high praise. He even occasionally says "that was funny" in a monotone.

I'm also encouraged by the fact that, for a curmudgeon, Simon has dozens of devoted, longtime friends. Perhaps it's that, behind the layers of irony, he is charmingly helpless. He can't drive a car, blow up a balloon, or fold clothes without using his teeth. He fills our refrigerator with unopened canned goods. For expediency's sake, he cooks everything at the highest temperature. (College friends later tell me he was known at school for serving drumsticks that were charred on the outside and still frozen on the inside.) When I show him how to make salad dressing using oil and vinegar, he writes down the recipe and still pulls it out years later whenever he makes dinner.

Also to Simon's credit, nothing about France ever bothers him. He's in his element being a foreigner. His parents are anthropologists who raised him all over the world and trained him from birth to delight in local customs. He'd lived in six countries (including a year in the United States) by the time he was ten. He acquires languages the way I acquire shoes.

I decide that, for Simon's sake, I'll give France a real go. We get married outside Paris at a thirteenth-century château, which is surrounded by a moat. (I ignore the symbolism.) In the name of marital harmony, we rent a larger apartment. I order bookshelves from IKEA and position spare-change bowls in every room. I try to channel my inner pragmatist instead of my inner neurotic. In restaurants, I start ordering straight from the menu and nibbling at the occasional hunk of foie gras. My French starts to sound less like excellent Spanish and more like very bad French. Before long I'm almost settled: I have a home office, a book deadline, and even a few new friends.

Simon and I have talked about babies. We both want one. I'd like three, in fact. And I like the idea of having them in Paris, where they'll be effortlessly bilingual and authentically international. Even if they grow up to be geeks, they can mention "growing up in Paris" and be instantly cool.

I'm worried about getting pregnant. I've spent much of my adult life trying, very successfully, not to, so I have no idea whether I'm any good at the reverse. This turns out to be as whirlwind as our courtship. One day I'm Googling "How to get pregnant." The next, it seems, I'm looking at two pink lines on a French pregnancy test.

I'm ecstatic. But alongside my surge of joy comes a surge of anxiety. My resolve to become less Carrie Bradshaw and more Catherine Deneuve immediately collapses. This doesn't seem like the moment to go native. I'm possessed by the idea that I've got to oversee my pregnancy and do it exactly right. Hours after telling Simon the good news, I go online to scour American pregnancy Web sites and rush to buy some pregnancy guides at an English-language bookstore near the Louvre. I want to know, in plain English, exactly what to worry about.

Within days I'm on prenatal vitamins and addicted to BabyCenter's online "Is It Safe?" column. Is it safe to eat nonorganic produce while pregnant? Is it safe to be around computers all day? Is it safe to wear high heels, binge on Halloween candy, or vacation at high altitudes?

What makes "Is It Safe?" so compulsive is that it creates new anxieties (Is it safe to make photocopies? Is it safe to swallow semen?) but then refuses to allay them with a simple "yes" or "no." Instead, expert respondents disagree with one another and equivocate. "Is it safe to get a manicure while I'm pregnant?" Well, yes, but chronic exposure to the solvents used in salons isn't good for you. Is it safe to go bowling? Well, yes and no.

The Americans I know also believe that pregnancy—and then motherhood—comes with homework. The first assignment is choosing from among myriad parenting styles. Everyone I speak to swears by different books. I buy many of them. But instead of making me feel more prepared, having so much conflicting advice makes babies themselves seem enigmatic and unknowable. Who they are, and what they need, seems to depend on which book you read.

We also become experts in everything that can go wrong. A pregnant New Yorker who's visiting Paris declares, over lunch, that there's a five-in-one-thousand chance her baby will be stillborn. She says she knows that saying this is gruesome and pointless, but she can't help herself. Another friend, who unfortunately has a doctorate in public health, spends much of her first trimester cataloging the baby's risks of contracting every possible malady.

I realize this anxiety is in the British ether, too, when we visit Simon's family in London. (I've decided to believe that his parents adore me.) I'm sitting in a café when a well-dressed woman interrupts me to describe a new study showing that consuming a lot of caffeine increases the risk of miscarriage. To emphasize how credible she is, she says that she's "married to a doctor." I couldn't care less who her husband is. I'm just irritated by her assumption that I haven't read that study. Of course I have; I'm trying to enjoy my one cup a week.

With so much studying and worrying to do, being pregnant increasingly feels like a full-time job. I spend less and less time working on my book, which I'm supposed to hand in before the baby comes. Instead, I commune with other pregnant Americans in due-date-cohort chat rooms. Like me, these women are used to customizing their environments, even if it's just to get soy milk in their coffee. And like me, they find the primitive, mammalian event happening inside their bodies to be uncomfortably out of their control. Worrying—like clutching the armrest during airplane turbulence—at least makes us feel like it's not.

The American pregnancy press, which I can easily access from Paris, seems to be lying in wait to channel this anxiety. It focuses on the one thing that pregnant women can definitely control: food. "As you raise fork to mouth, consider: 'Is this a bite that will benefit my baby?' If it is, chew away . . . ," explain the authors of *What to Expect When You're Expecting*, the famously worrying—and bestselling—American pregnancy manual.

I'm aware that the prohibitions in my books aren't all equally important. Cigarettes and alcohol are definitely bad, whereas shellfish, cold cuts, raw eggs, and unpasteurized cheese are dangerous only if they've been contaminated with something rare like listeria or salmonella. To be safe, I take every prohibition literally. It's easy enough to avoid oysters and foie gras. But—since I'm in France—I'm panicked about cheese. "Is the Parmesan on my pasta pasteurized?" I ask flabbergasted waiters. Simon bears the brunt of my angst. Did he scrub the cutting board after chopping that raw chicken? Does he really love our unborn child?

What to Expect contains something called the Pregnancy Diet, which its creators claim can "improve fetal brain development," "reduce the risk of certain birth defects," and "may even make it more likely that your child will grow to be a healthier adult." Every morsel seems to represent potential SAT points. Never mind hunger: if I find myself short a protein portion at the end of the day, the Pregnancy Diet says I should cram in a final serving of egg salad before bedtime.

They had me at "diet." After years of dieting to slim down, it's thrilling to be "dieting" to gain weight. It feels like a reward for having spent years thin enough to nab a husband. My online forums are filled with women who've put on forty or fifty pounds over the recommended limits. Of course we'd all rather resemble those compactly pregnant celebrities in designer gowns or the models on the cover of *FitPregnancy*. A few women I know actually do. But a competing American message says that we should give ourselves a free pass. "Go ahead and EAT," says the chummy author of *The Best Friends' Guide to Pregnancy*, which I've been cuddling up with in bed. "What other joys are there for pregnant women?"

Tellingly, the Pregnancy Diet says that I can "cheat" with the occasional fast-food cheeseburger or glazed donut. In fact, American pregnancy can seem like one big cheat. Lists of pregnancy cravings seem like a catalog of foods that women have been denying themselves since adolescence: cheesecake, milkshakes, macaroni and cheese, and Carvel ice-cream cake. I crave lemon on everything, and entire loaves of bread.

Someone tells me that Jane Birkin, the British actress and model who built a career in Paris and married the legendary French singer Serge Gainsbourg, could never remember whether it was "un baguette" or "une baguette," so she would just order "deux baguettes" (two baguettes). I can't find the quote. But whenever I go to the bakery, I follow this strategy. Then—surely unlike the twiggy Birkin—I eat them both.

• • • • • • • • • •

I'm not just losing my figure. I'm also losing a sense of myself as someone who once went on dinner dates and worried about the Palestinians. I now spend my free time studying late-model strollers and memorizing the possible causes of colic. This evolution from "woman" to "mom" feels inevitable. A fashion spread in an American pregnancy magazine, which I pick up on a trip back home, shows big-bellied women in floppy shirts and men's pajama bottoms, and says that these outfits are worthy of wearing all day. Perhaps to get out of ever finishing my book, I fantasize about ditching journalism and training as a midwife.

Actual sex is the final, symbolic domino to fall. Although it's technically permitted, books like *What to Expect* presume that sex during pregnancy is inherently fraught. "What got you into this situation in the first place may now have become one of your biggest problems," the authors warn. They go on to describe eighteen factors that may inhibit your sex life, including "fear that the introduction of the penis into the vagina will cause infection." If a woman does find herself having sex, they recommend a new low in multitasking: using the moment to do Kegel exercises, which tone your birth canal in preparation for childbirth.

I'm not sure that anyone follows all this advice. Like me, they probably just absorb a certain worried tone and state of mind. Even from abroad, it's contagious. Given how susceptible I am, it's probably better that I'm far from the source. Maybe the distance will give me some perspective on parenting.

I'm already starting to suspect that raising a child will be quite different in France. When I sit in cafés in Paris, with my belly pushing up against the table, no one jumps in to warn me about the hazards of caffeine. To the contrary, they light cigarettes right next to me. The only question strangers ask when they notice my belly is, "Are you waiting for a child?" It takes me a while to realize that they don't think I have a lunch date with a truant six-year-old. It's French for "Are you pregnant?"

I am waiting for a child. It's probably the most important thing I've ever done. Despite my qualms about Paris, there's something nice about being pregnant in a place where I'm practically immune to other people's judgments. Though Paris is one of the most cosmopolitan cities on earth, I feel like I'm off the grid. In French I don't understand name dropping, school histories, and other little hints that, to a French person, signal someone's social rank and importance. And since I'm a foreigner, they don't know my status either.

When I packed up and moved to Paris, I never imagined that the move would be permanent. Now I'm starting to worry that Simon likes being a foreigner a bit too much. After living in all those countries growing up, it's his natural state. He confesses that he feels connected to lots of people and cities and doesn't need one place to be his official home. He calls this style "semidetached," like a London town house.

Already, several of our Anglophone friends have left France, usually when their jobs changed. But our jobs don't require us to be here. The cheese plate aside, we're really here for no reason. And "no reason"—plus a baby—is starting to look like the strongest reason of all.

Chapter 2

paris is burping

Our new apartment isn't in the Paris of postcards. It's off a narrow sidewalk in a Chinese garment district, where we're constantly jostled by men hauling trash bags full of clothes. There's no sign that we're in the same city as the Eiffel Tower, Notre Dame, or the elegantly winding river Seine.

Yet somehow this new neighborhood works for us. Simon and I each stake out our respective cafés nearby and retreat each morning for some convivial solitude. Here, too, socializing follows unfamiliar rules. It's okay to banter with the servers, but generally not with the other patrons (unless they're at the bar and talking to the server, too). Though I'm off the grid, I do need human contact. One morning I try to strike up a conversation with another regular—a man I've seen every day for months. I tell him, honestly, that he looks like an American I know.

"Who, George Clooney?" he asks snidely. We never speak again.

I make more headway with our new neighbors. The crowded sidewalk outside our house opens onto a cobblestone courtyard, where low-slung houses and apartments face one another. The residents are a mix of artists, young professionals, mysteriously underemployed people, and elderly women who hobble precariously on the uneven stones. We all live so close together that they have to acknowledge our presence, though a few still manage not to.

It helps that my next-door neighbor, an architect named Anne, is due a few months before me. Though I'm caught up in my Anglophone whirlwind of eating and worrying, I can't help but notice that Anne and the other pregnant Frenchwomen I come to know handle their pregnancies very differently.

For starters, they don't treat pregnancy like an independent research project. There are plenty of French parenting books, magazines, and Web sites. But these aren't required reading, and nobody seems to consume them in bulk. Certainly no one I meet is comparison shopping for a parenting philosophy or can refer to different techniques by name. There's no new, must-read book, nor do the experts have quite the same hold on parents.

"These books can be useful to people who lack confidence, but I don't think you can raise a child while reading a book. You have to go with your *feeling*," one Parisian mother says.

The Frenchwomen I meet aren't at all blasé about motherhood, or about their babies' well-being. They're awed, concerned, and aware of the immense life transformation that they're about to undergo. But they signal this differently. American women typically demonstrate our commitment by worrying and by showing how much we're willing to sacrifice, even while pregnant, whereas Frenchwomen signal their commitment by projecting calm and flaunting the fact that they haven't renounced pleasure.

A photo spread in *Neuf Mois* (*Nine Months*) magazine shows a heavily pregnant brunette in lacy ensembles, biting into pastries and licking jam off her finger. "During pregnancy, it's important to pamper your inner woman," another article says. "Above all, resist the urge to borrow your partner's shirts." A list of aphrodisiacs for moms-to-be includes chocolate, ginger, cinnamon, and—this being France—mustard.

I realize that ordinary Frenchwomen take these calls to arms seriously when Samia, a mother who lives in my neighborhood, offers me a tour of her apartment. She's the daughter of Algerian immigrants and grew up in Chartres. I'm admiring her soaring ceilings and chandeliers, when she picks up a stack of photographs from the mantel.

"In this one I was pregnant, and here I was pregnant. *Et voilà*, the big belly!" she says, handing me several pictures. It's true, she's extremely pregnant in the photographs. She's also extremely topless.

I'm shocked, first of all because we've been using the formal *vous* with each other, and now she's casually handed me naked pictures of herself. But I'm also surprised that the pictures are so glamorous. Samia looks like one of those lingerie models from the magazines, *sans* most of the lingerie.

Granted, Samia is always a bit dramatic. Most days she drops off her two-year-old at day care looking like she just stepped out of a film noir: a beige trench coat cinched tightly at the waist, black eyeliner, and a fresh coat of shiny red lipstick. She's the only French person I know who actually wears a beret.

Nevertheless, Samia has merely embraced the conventional French wisdom that the forty-week metamorphosis into mother shouldn't make you any less of a woman. French pregnancy magazines don't just say that pregnant women can have sex; they explain exactly how to do it. *Neuf Mois* maps out ten different sexual positions, including "horseback rider," "reverse horseback rider," "the greyhound" (which it calls "*un grand classique*"), and "the chair." "The oarsman" has six steps, concluding with, "In rocking her torso back and forth, Madame provokes delicious frictions. . . ."

Neuf Mois also weighs in on the merits of various sex toys for pregnant women (yes to "geisha balls," no to vibrators and anything electric). "Don't hesitate! Everyone wins, even the baby. During an orgasm, he feels the 'Jacuzzi effect' as if he were massaged in the water," the text explains. A father in Paris warns my husband not to stand at the "business end" during the birth, to preserve my feminine mystique.

French parents-to-be aren't just calmer about sex. They're also calmer about food. Samia makes a conversation with her obstetrician sound like a vaudeville routine:

"I said, 'Doctor, I'm pregnant, but I adore oysters. What do I do?'

"He said, 'Eat oysters!'" she recalls. "He explained to me, 'You seem like a fairly reasonable person. Wash things well. If you eat sushi, eat it in a good place.'"

The stereotype that Frenchwomen smoke and drink through their pregnancies is very outdated. Most women I meet say that they had either the occasional glass of champagne or no alcohol at all. I see a pregnant woman smoking exactly once, on the street. It could have been her once-a-month cigarette.

The point in France isn't that anything goes. It's that women should be calm and sensible. Unlike me, the French mothers I meet distinguish between the things that are almost definitely damaging and those that are dangerous only if they're contaminated. Another woman I meet in the neighborhood is Caroline, a physical therapist who's seven months pregnant. She says her doctor never mentioned any food restrictions, and she never asked. "It's better not to know!" she says. She tells me that she eats steak tartare, and of course joined the family for foie gras over Christmas. She just makes sure to eat it in good restaurants or at home. Her one concession is that when she eats unpasteurized cheese, she cuts off the rind.

I don't actually witness any pregnant women eating oysters. If I did, I might have to throw my enormous body over the table to stop them. They'd certainly be surprised. It's clear why French waiters are baffled when I interrogate them about the ingredients in each dish. Frenchwomen generally don't make a fuss about this.

The French pregnancy press doesn't dwell on unlikely worst-case scenarios. *Au contraire*, it suggests that what mothers-to-be need most is serenity. "9 Months of Spa" is the headline in one French magazine. *The Guide for New Mothers*, a free booklet prepared with support from the French health ministry, says its eating guidelines favor the baby's "harmonious growth," and that women should find "inspiration" from different flavors. "Pregnancy should be a time of great happiness!" it declares.

Is all this safe? It sure seems like it. France trumps the United States on nearly every measure of maternal and infant health. The infant mortality rate is 57 percent lower in France than it is in America. According to UNICEF, about 6.6 percent of French babies have a low birth weight, compared with about 8 percent of American babies. An American woman's risk of dying during pregnancy or delivery is 1 in 4,800; in France it's 1 in 6,900.[1]

What really drives home the French message that pregnancy should be savored isn't the statistics or the pregnant women I meet, it's the pregnant cat. She's a slender, gray-eyed cat who lives in our courtyard and is about to deliver. Her owner, a pretty painter in her forties, tells me that she plans to have the cat spayed after the kittens are born. But she couldn't bear to do it before the cat had gone through a pregnancy. "I wanted her to have that experience," she says.

Of course French mothers-to-be aren't just calmer than we are. Like the cat, they're also skinnier. Some pregnant Frenchwomen do get fat. In general, body-fat ratios seem to increase the farther you get from central Paris. But the middle-class Parisians I see all around me look alarmingly like those American celebrities on the red carpet. They have basketball-sized baby bumps pasted onto skinny legs, arms, and hips. Viewed from the back, you usually can't tell they're expecting.

Enough pregnant women have these proportions that I stop gawking when I pass one on the sidewalk or in the supermarket. This French norm is strictly codified. American pregnancy calculators tell me that with my height and build I should gain up to thirty-five pounds during my pregnancy. But French calculators tell me to gain no more than twenty-six and a half pounds. (By the time I see this, it's too late.)

How do Frenchwomen stay within these limits? Social pressure helps. Friends, sisters, and mothers-in-law openly transmit the message that pregnancy isn't a free pass to gorge. (I'm spared the worst of this because I don't have French in-laws.) Audrey, a French journalist with three kids, tells me that she confronted her German sister-in-law, who had started out tall and svelte.

"The moment she got pregnant she became enormous. And I saw her and I found it monstrous. She told me, 'No, it's fine, I'm entitled to relax. I'm entitled to get fat. It's no big deal,' et cetera. For us, the French, it's horrible to say that. We would *never* say that." She adds a jab disguised as sociology: "I think the Americans and the Northern Europeans are a lot more relaxed than us, when it comes to aesthetics."

Everyone takes for granted that pregnant women should battle to keep their figures intact. While my podiatrist is working on my feet, she suddenly announces that I should rub sweet almond oil on my belly to avoid stretch marks. (I do this dutifully, and get none.) Parenting magazines run long features on how to minimize the damage that pregnancy does to your breasts. (Don't gain too much weight, and take a daily jet of cold water to the chest.)

French doctors treat the weight-gain limits like holy edicts. Anglophones in Paris are routinely shocked when their obstetricians scold them for going even slightly over. "It's just the French men trying to keep their women slim," a British woman married to a Frenchman huffed, recalling her prenatal appointments in Paris. Pediatricians feel free to comment on a mother's postpregnancy belly when she brings her baby for a checkup. (Mine will just cast a worried glance.)

The main reason that pregnant Frenchwomen don't get fat is that they are very careful not to eat too much. In French pregnancy guides, there are no late-night heapings of egg salad or instructions to eat way past hunger in order to nourish the fetus. Women who are "waiting for a child" are supposed to eat the same balanced meals as any healthy adult. One guide says that if a woman is still hungry, she should add an afternoon snack consisting of, for instance, "a sixth of a baguette," a piece of cheese, and a glass of water.

In the French view, a pregnant woman's food cravings are a nuisance to be vanquished. Frenchwomen don't let themselves believe— as I've heard American women claim—that the fetus wants cheesecake. The *Guidebook for Mothers to Be*, a French pregnancy book, says that instead of caving in to cravings, women should distract their bodies by eating an apple or a raw carrot.

This isn't all as austere as it sounds. Frenchwomen don't see pregnancy as a free pass to overeat, in part because they haven't been denying themselves the foods they love—or secretly binging on those foods—for most of their adult lives. "Too often, American women eat on the sly, and the result is much more guilt than pleasure," Mireille Guiliano explains in her intelligent book *French Women Don't Get Fat*. "Pretending such pleasures don't exist, or trying to eliminate them from your diet for an extended time, will probably lead to weight gain."

About halfway through my pregnancy, I find out that there's a support group in Paris for English-speaking parents. I immediately recognize that these are my people. Members of the group, called Message, can tell you where to find an English-speaking therapist, buy a car with an automatic transmission, or locate a butcher who'll roast a whole turkey for Thanksgiving. (The birds don't fit in most French ovens.) Wondering how to bring cases of Kraft macaroni and cheese back from a trip to America? You ditch the elbow noodles, which you can buy in France, and put the cheese packets in your suitcase.

Message members find a lot to like about France. In online forums, they marvel at the fresh bread, the cheap prescription drugs, and at how their own toddlers now demand Camembert at the end of a meal. One member chuckles that her five-year-old plays "labor strike" with his PLAYMOBIL figures.

But the group is also a bulwark against what are seen as the darker aspects of French parenting. Members exchange the cell-phone numbers of English-speaking doulas, sell one another breastfeeding pillows, and commiserate about French medicine's penchant for giving kids suppositories. A member I know was so reluctant to subject her daughter to French public preschool that she enrolled her in a brand-new Montessori, where the little girl was—for quite a while—the only student.

Like me, these women see being pregnant as an excuse to bond, worry, shop, and eat. They fortify one another against the social pressure to lose their baby weight. "At some point I'll get around to it," one new mother writes. "I'm not going to waste precious time weighing out lettuce leaves now."

The most salient dilemma among pregnant Message members and other Anglophones I know is *how* to give birth. I meet an American in Rome who delivered her baby in an Italian wine vat (filled with water, not Pinot Grigio). A friend in Miami read that the pain of childbirth is a cultural construct, so she trained to birth her twins using only yoga breaths. In our Message-sponsored parenting class, one woman planned to fly home to Sydney for an authentic Australian delivery.

Birth, like most everything else, is something we try to customize. My obstetrician says she once received a four-page birth plan from an American patient, instructing her to massage the woman's clitoris after the delivery. The uterine contractions from the woman's orgasm were supposed to help expel the placenta. Interestingly, this woman's birth plan also specified that both of her parents should be allowed in the delivery room. ("I said 'no way.' I didn't want to be arrested," my doctor recalls.)

In all this talk about giving birth, I never hear anyone mention that the last time the World Health Organization ranked national health-care systems, France's was first, while America's was thirty-seventh. Instead, we Anglos focus on how the French system is overmedicalized and hostile to the "natural." Pregnant Message members fret that French doctors will induce labor, force them to have epidurals, then secretly bottle-feed their newborns so they won't be able to breast-feed. We've all been reading the English-language pregnancy press, which emphasizes the minute risks of epidurals. Those among us who deliver "naturally" strut around like war heroes.

Despite being the birthplace of Dr. Fernand Lamaze, epidurals are now extremely common in France. In Paris's top maternity hospitals and clinics, about 87 percent of women have epidurals, on average[2] (not counting C-sections). In some hospitals it's 98 or 99 percent.

Very few women make a fuss about this. French moms often ask me where I plan to deliver, but never how. They don't seem to care. In France, the way you give birth doesn't situate you within a value system or define the sort of parent you'll be. It is, for the most part, a way of getting your baby safely from your uterus into your arms.

In French, giving birth without an epidural isn't called "natural" childbirth. It's called "giving birth without an epidural" (accouchement sans péridurale). A few French hospitals and maternity clinics now have birthing pools and giant rubber balls for laboring women to hug. But few Frenchwomen use these. That 1 or 2 percent of nonepidural births in Paris are, I'm told, either crazy Americans like me or Frenchwomen who didn't get to the hospital in time.

The absolute earthiest Frenchwoman I know is Hélène. She takes her three kids on camping trips and breast-fed them all past age two. Hélène also had an epidural at each delivery. For her, there's no contradiction. She likes some things au naturel and some with a giant dose of drugs.

. . . .

The difference between France and America crystallizes for me when, through mutual friends, I meet Jennifer and Eric, a couple in their thirties. She's an American who works for a multinational company in Paris. He's a Frenchman with a job in advertising. They live just outside Paris with their two daughters. When Jennifer got pregnant for the first time, Eric assumed that they would find a doctor, choose a hospital, and have the baby. But Jennifer brought home a stack of baby books and pressed Eric to study them with her.

Eric still can't believe how Jennifer wanted to script the delivery. "She wanted to give birth on a balloon, give birth in a bath," he recalls. He says the doctor told her, "It's not a zoo here, or a circus. Basically you will give birth like everyone, on your back, legs open. And the reason is that if there is a problem, then I can do something."

Jennifer also wanted to deliver without anesthesia, so that she could feel what it was like to give birth. "I've never heard of a woman wanting to suffer so much to have a kid," Eric says.

What stands out for both Eric and Jennifer is what I've come to think of as the "Croissant Story." When Jennifer went into labor, it became clear that all her birthing plans were for naught: she needed a cesarean. The doctor sent Eric into the waiting room. Eventually, Jennifer delivered a healthy baby girl. Afterward, in the recovery room, Eric mentioned to her that he recently ate a croissant.

Three years later, Jennifer's blood still boils when she thinks about that piece of bread. "Eric wasn't actually physically present [in the waiting room] during the whole thing. He went out and got a croissant! When they rolled me into the operating room, Eric walks out of the clinic, goes down the street, goes to the bakery, and buys a couple of croissants. He comes back, eats his croissant!"

This is not what Jennifer had envisioned. "My husband needs to be

sitting there biting his nails, thinking, 'Oh, will it be a boy or a girl?'"
she says. She mentions that there was a vending machine near the waiting room. He could have bought a bag of peanuts.

When Eric tells his own version of the Croissant Story, he gets mad,
too. Yes, there was a vending machine. But "it was very stressful; I
needed some sugar," he says. "I was sure there was a bakery just at the
corner, and the bakery ended up being a bit far away. But they took
her at seven. I knew that they had one hour of preparation and things
like that, and I think she came back at eleven. So in all this time, yes,
I spent at least fifteen minutes going to get some food."

At first, I see the Croissant Story as a classic men-are-from-Mars
tale. But I eventually realize that it's a Franco-American parable. For
Jennifer, Eric's selfish pursuit of the croissant signaled that he wouldn't
sacrifice his own comfort for the sake of his family and the new baby.
She worried that he wasn't sufficiently invested in the project of
parenting.

For Eric, it signaled no such thing. He felt thoroughly invested in
the birth and is an extremely involved father. But at that moment,
he was also calm, detached, and self-interested enough to walk down
the street. He wanted to be a dad, but he also wanted a croissant. "In
the U.S. sometimes I have the feeling that if it's not difficult for you,
you have to feel bad about that," he says.

I'd like to think I'm the sort of wife who wouldn't be bothered by
the croissant, or at least that Simon is the sort of husband who would
hide the crumbs. I do submit a PG-rated birth plan, stating that under
no circumstances should Simon be permitted to cut the umbilical
cord. But since I tend to scream when I get my legs waxed, I don't
think I'm a great candidate for natural childbirth. I suspect I'll have
trouble viewing the pain as a cultural construct.

I'm more concerned about getting to the hospital in time. Following a friend's advice, I've registered to give birth at a hospital all the way across town. If the baby makes a break for it during rush hour, there could be trouble.

And that's if I can get a taxi. The rumor among Paris's Anglophones (who, being here temporarily, tend not to have cars) is that French taxi drivers refuse to pick up women in labor for fear that they'll end up scraping placenta off their seats. A backseat delivery wouldn't be ideal for other reasons. Simon is too spooked to even read the instructions for emergency home deliveries in *What to Expect*.

My contractions begin around eight o'clock at night. That means I can't eat the steaming Thai food we've just picked up. (I will fantasize about pad thai from my hospital bed.) But at least the streets are clear. Simon calls a taxi, and I'm quiet while getting in. Let the driver—a mustachioed man in his fifties—try to pry me out.

I needn't have worried. As soon as we're on the road and he hears my yelps from the backseat, the driver becomes ecstatic. He says he's been waiting his whole career as a chauffeur for this cinematic event.

As we cross Paris in the dark, I open my seatbelt and slide to the floor of the taxi, moaning from the mounting pain. This is no leg wax. I ditch my faux fantasies of a natural childbirth. Simon opens the windows, either to give me some air or to cover the sounds I'm making.

Meanwhile, the driver speeds up. I can see the street lamps zipping past overhead. He begins loudly reciting the story of his own son's birth twenty-five years earlier. "Slower, please!" I plead from the floor, between contractions. Simon is silent and pale, staring straight ahead.

"What are you thinking about?" I ask him.

"Dutch football," he says.

When we arrive at the hospital, the driver pulls up at the emergency entrance, jumps out of the car, and sprints inside. It seems he's expecting to join us for the birth. Moments later he's back, sweaty and panting. "They're expecting you!" he shouts.

I lurch into the building, leaving Simon to pay the fare and persuade

the driver to leave. The moment I see a midwife, I declare in my clear-
est French: "*Je voudrais une péridurale!*" (I would like an epidural). If
I'd had a wad of cash I would have waved it at her.

It turns out that despite the French passion for epidurals, they don't
just perform them on demand. The midwife takes me into an examining
room to check my cervix, then looks up at me with a bemused smile.
I'm barely three centimeters dilated, out of a possible ten. Women
don't usually ask for epidurals this early on, she says. She won't summon the anesthetist from *his* pad thai for this.

She does put on the most soothing music I've ever heard—a sort of
Tibetan lullaby—and rigs me up to a drip that softens the pain. Eventually, exhausted, I fall asleep.

I'll spare you the details of my very medicated, very pleasant birth.
Thanks to the epidural, pushing the baby out has the precision and
intensity of a yoga move, without the discomfort. I'm so focused that
I don't even mind when my obstetrician's teenage daughter, who lives
around the corner, pops in after the delivery to ask her mom for
some cash.

As it happens, the anesthesiologist, midwife, and doctor are all
women. (Simon, stationed far from the business end, is there, too.)
The baby comes out as the sun is rising.

I've read that babies look like their fathers when they're born, to
assure the dads of their paternity and motivate them to go out hunting
(or investment banking) for the family. My first thought when our
daughter comes out is that she doesn't merely resemble Simon; she
has his face.

We cuddle with her for a while. Then they dress her in a chicly
understated French outfit supplied by the hospital, complete with an
ecru-colored beanie on her head. We do give her a proper name. But
thanks to the hat, we mostly just call her Bean.

I stay in the hospital for six days, which is standard French practice.
I see no reason to leave. There is fresh-baked bread with every meal

(no need to leave for a croissant) and a sun-dappled garden where I steal away for walks. The extensive in-room wine list includes champagne. On day three, I can't stop saying to Bean, "You weren't born yesterday!" Simon doesn't even pretend this is funny.

As if to emphasize that there are universal parenting principles in France, babies born here come with instructions. Each newborn is issued a white softcover book called a *carnet de santé*, which follows the child until age eighteen. Doctors record every checkup and vaccination in this book, and plot the child's height, weight, and head size. It also has commonsense basics on what to feed babies, how to bathe them, when to go for checkups, and how to spot medical problems.

The book doesn't prepare me for Bean's transformation. For the first month or so, she continues to look just like Simon, with dark brown eyes and hair. She even has his dimples. If anything's in doubt, it's her maternity. My fair-haired, fair-eyed genes seem to have lost to his swarthy Mediterranean ones in a first-round knockout.

But at about two months old, Bean has a metamorphosis. Her hair turns blond, and her brown eyes morph improbably into blue. Our little Mediterranean baby suddenly looks like a Swede.

Technically, Bean is American. (She can request French citizenship when she's older.) But I suspect that her French will surpass mine within a few months. I'm not sure whether we're going to raise a little American girl or a little French one. We might not have a choice.

Chapter 3

doing her nights

A few weeks after we bring Bean home, neighbors on our little courtyard begin asking, "Is she doing her nights?" (*Elle fait ses nuits?*)

This is the first time I hear the French formulation of "Is she sleeping through the night?" At first I find it comforting. If they're *her* nights, then she'll inevitably claim them. Whereas if they're just *the* nights, she might not.

But I soon find the question irritating. Of course she's not "doing her nights." She's two months old (and then three months, and then four). Everyone knows that tiny babies sleep badly. I know a few Americans who—by sheer luck—have babies that age who go down at nine P.M. and wake up at seven. But most parents I know don't get an uninterrupted night's sleep until their kids are around a year old. Heck, I know four-year-olds who still wander into their parents' rooms at night.

My Anglophone friends and family appreciate this. They tend to ask the more open-ended question, "How is she sleeping?" And even that isn't really a request for information; it's a chance for the exhausted parents to vent.

For us, babies are automatically associated with sleep deprivation. A headline in the British *Daily Mail* declares: "Parents of Newborns Miss Out on SIX MONTHS Worth of Sleep in Their Child's First Two Years," citing a study commissioned by a bed company. The article seems credible to readers. "Sadly this is true," one comments. "Our one year old daughter hasn't slept a single night in twelve months, and if we have four hours sleep it's a good night." A poll by the National Sleep Foundation in the United States found that 46 percent of toddlers wake up during the night, but just 11 percent of parents believed that their child had a sleep problem. A toddler's T-shirt I see in Ft. Lauderdale says simply, "Party tonight at my crib 3 A.M."

My English-speaking friends tend to view their kids as having unique sleep needs, which they just have to accommodate. I'm walking around Paris with a British friend of mine one day when her toddler son climbs into her arms, reaches under her shirt to clutch her breast, then falls asleep. My friend is clearly embarrassed that I've witnessed this ritual, but she whispers that it's the only way he can nap. She carries him around in this position for the next forty-five minutes.

Simon and I had of course chosen a sleep strategy. Ours was premised on the idea that it's critical to keep a baby awake after she feeds. Once Bean is born, we go to enormous effort to do this. As far as I can tell, it has no effect.

Eventually, we ditch this theory and try other ones. We keep Bean in the daylight all day and in the dark at night. We bathe her at the same time each evening and try to stretch out the time between her feeds. For a few days I eat almost nothing but crackers and Brie, after someone tells me that fatty food will thicken my breast milk. A New Yorker who stops by says she read that we should make loud whooshing sounds to mimic the sounds in the womb. We whoosh obediently for hours.

Nothing seems to make a difference. At three months old, Bean still wakes up several times a night. We have a long ritual in which I nurse her back to sleep, then hold her for fifteen more minutes so that she doesn't wake up again when I put her in her bassinet. Simon's forward-looking view of the world suddenly seems like a curse: he's thrown into a nightly depression, convinced that this is going to last forever. Whereas my myopia suddenly looks like a stroke of evolutionary brilliance. I don't think about whether this will last six more months (though it will); I just live night to night.

What's also consoling is that this is all to be expected. Parents of infants aren't supposed to get any sleep. Almost all the American and British parents I know say that their kids began sleeping through the night at eight or nine months, or much later. "It was really early," a friend of Simon's from Vermont says, consulting with his wife about when their son's three A.M. wake-ups stopped. "What was it, at one year old?" Kristin, a British lawyer in Paris, tells me that her sixteen-month-old sleeps through the night, then adds: "Well, when I say 'sleeps through the night,' she gets up twice. But each time, only for five minutes."

I take comfort in hearing about parents who have it worse than we do. They're easy to find. My cousin, who co-sleeps with her ten-month-old, hasn't gone back to her teaching job, in part because she's up feeding the baby much of the night. I frequently phone up to ask, "How's he sleeping?"

The worst story I hear comes from Alison, a friend of a friend in Washington, D.C., whose son is seven months old. Alison tells me that for the first six months of her son's life, she nursed him every two hours *around the clock*. At seven months old, he began sleeping four-hour stretches. Alison—a marketing expert with an Ivy League degree—shrugs off her exhaustion and the fact that her career is on pause. She feels that she has no choice but to cater to her baby's punishing, peculiar sleep schedule.

The alternative to all this night waking is supposedly "sleep training," in which parents leave their babies alone to "cry it out." I read up on this, too. It seems to be for babies who are at least six or seven months old. Alison tells me that she tried this one night, but gave up because it felt cruel. Online discussions about sleep training quickly devolve into brawls, in which opponents claim the practice is at best selfish and at worst abusive. "Sleep training disgusts me," one mother posts on babble.com. Another writes: "If you want to sleep through the night—don't have babies. Adopt a three-year-old or something."

Although sleep training sounds awful, Simon and I are theoretically in favor of it. But we're under the impression that Bean is too young for something so militaristic. Like our Anglophone friends and family, we think Bean wakes up at night because she's hungry or because she needs something from us or just because that's what babies do. She's very small. So we give in to her.

I talk to French parents about sleep, too. They're neighbors, work acquaintances, and friends of friends. They all claim that their own kids began sleeping through the night much earlier. Samia says her daughter, who's now two, started "doing her nights" at six weeks old; she wrote down the exact date. Stephanie, a skinny tax inspector who lives on our courtyard, looks ashamed when I ask when her son, Nino, began "doing his nights."

"Very late, very late!" Stephanie says. "He started doing his nights in November, so it was . . . four months old! For me it was very late."

Some French sleep stories sound too good to be true. Alexandra, who works in a French day-care center and lives in a suburb of Paris, says that both of her daughters began sleeping through the night almost from birth. "Already in the maternity ward, they woke up for their bottles around six A.M.," she says.

Many of these French babies are bottle-fed, or they drink a combination of breast milk and formula. But that doesn't seem to make a crucial difference. The French breast-fed babies I meet do their nights early on, too. Some French moms tell me they quit breastfeeding when they went back to work, at about three months. But by that time their babies were already doing their nights.

At first I figure that I'm just meeting a few lucky French parents. But soon the evidence becomes overwhelming: having a baby who sleeps through the night early on seems to be the norm in France. Just as stories of terrible sleepers are easy to find among Americans, stories of spectacular sleepers are easy to find among the French. My neighbors suddenly seem less obnoxious. They weren't baiting me; they actually believed that a two-month-old might already be "doing her nights."

French parents don't expect their babies to sleep well right after they're born. But by the time these broken nights start to seem unbearable—usually after two or three months—they usually end. Parents talk about night wake-ups as a short-term problem, not a chronic one. Everyone I speak to takes for granted that babies can and probably will do their nights by about six months, and often much sooner. "Certain babies do their night at six weeks, others need four months to find their rhythm," an article in *Maman!* magazine says. *Le sommeil, le rêve et l'enfant* (*Sleep, Dreams and the Child*), a top-selling sleep guide, says that between three and six months, "He's going to sleep complete nights, of eight or nine hours at a minimum. The parents will finally rediscover the pleasure of long uninterrupted nights."

There are exceptions, of course. That's why France has baby sleep books and pediatric sleep specialists. Some babies who do their nights at two months start waking again a few months later. I do hear about French kids who take a year to start doing their nights. But the truth is, over many years in France, I don't meet them. Marion, the mother of a little girl who becomes one of Bean's close friends, says her baby boy did his nights at six months. That's the longest among any of my Parisian friends and acquaintances. Most of them are like Paul, another architect, who says that his three-and-a-half-month-old son sleeps a full twelve hours, from eight P.M. to eight A.M.

What's maddening is that while French parents can tell you exactly when their kids began sleeping through the night, they can't explain how this came about. They don't mention sleep training, "Ferberizing"—a sleep technique developed by Dr. Richard Ferber—or any other branded method. And they claim that they never let their babies cry for long periods. In fact, most French parents look a little queasy when I mention this practice.

Speaking to older parents isn't much help either. A French publicist in her fifties—who goes to work in pencil skirts and stilettos—is shocked to learn that I have any baby sleep issues. "Can't you give her something to sleep? You know, some medicine or something like that?" she asks. At the very least, she says, I should leave the baby with someone and recover at a spa for a week or two.

None of the younger French parents I meet either drug their kids to sleep or hide in a sauna. Most insist that their babies learned to sleep long stretches all by themselves. Stephanie, the tax inspector, claims she didn't have much to do with it. "I think it's the child, he's the one who decides," she said.

I hear this same idea from Fanny, thirty-three, the publisher of a group of financial magazines. Fanny says that at around three months old, her son Antoine spontaneously dropped his three A.M. feedings and slept through the night.

"He decided to sleep," Fanny explains. "I never forced anything. You give him food when he needs food. He just regulated it all by himself."

Fanny's husband, Vincent, who's listening to our conversation, points out that three months is exactly when Fanny went back to work. Like other French parents I speak to, he says this timing isn't a coincidence. He says Antoine understood that his mother needed to wake up early to go to the office. Vincent compares this understanding to the way ants communicate through chemical waves that pass between their antennae.

"We believe a lot in *le* feeling," Vincent says, using the English word. "We guess that children understand things."

French parents do offer a few sleep tips. They almost all say that in the early months, they kept their babies with them in the light during the day, even for naps, and put them to bed in the dark at night. And almost all say that, from birth, they carefully "observed" their babies, and then followed the babies' own "rhythms." French parents talk so much about rhythm, you'd think they were starting rock bands, not raising kids.

"From zero to six months, the best is to respect the rhythms of their sleep," explains Alexandra, the mother whose babies slept through the night practically from birth.

I observe Bean, too, often at three A.M. So why is there no rhythm in our house? If sleeping through the night "just happens," why hasn't it just happened to us?

When I pour out my frustration to Gabrielle, one of my new French acquaintances, she recommends that I look at a book called *L'enfant et son sommeil* (*The Child and His Sleep*). She says the author, Hélène De Leersnyder, is a well-known pediatrician in Paris who specializes in sleep.

The book is baffling. I'm used to the straightforward, self-help style of American baby books. De Leersnyder's book opens with a quotation from Marcel Proust, then launches into an ode to slumber.

"Sleep reveals the child and the life of the family," De Leersnyder writes. "To go to bed and fall asleep, to separate himself from his parents for a few hours, the child must trust his body to keep him alive, even when he's not in control of it. And he must be serene enough to approach the strangeness of *pensée de la nuit* (thoughts that come in the night)."

Sleep, Dreams and the Child also says that a baby can only sleep well once he accepts his own separateness. "The discovery of peaceful, long and serene nights, and an acceptance of solitude, is that not a sign that the child has recovered his inner peace, that he has moved beyond sorrow?"

Even the scientific sections of these books sound existential. What we call "rapid-eye-movement sleep" the French call *sommeil paradoxal* (paradoxical sleep) because the body is still but the mind is extremely active. "To learn to sleep, to learn to live, are these not synonyms?" De Leersnyder asks.

I'm still not sure what I'm supposed to do with this information. I'm not looking for a meta-theory on how to think about Bean's nights. I just want her to sleep. How can I figure out why French babies sleep so well if their own parents can't explain it and their sleep books read like cryptic poetry? What does a mother have to do for a good night's rest?

Oddly enough, my epiphany about the French sleep rules happens while I'm visiting New York. I've come to the United States to visit family and friends, and also to get a hands-on feel for one corner of American parenting. For part of the trip I stay in Tribeca, the neighborhood in lower Manhattan where industrial buildings have been converted into tony loft apartments. I hang out at a local playground, chatting with the other mothers.

I thought I knew my parenting literature. But these women make it clear that I'm just a dilettante. Not only have they read everything, they've also assembled their own parenting styles like eclectic designer outfits, following separate gurus for sleep, discipline, and food. When I naively mention "attachment parenting" to one Tribeca mother, she immediately corrects me.

"I don't like that term, because who's not attached to their child?" she says.

When talk turns to how their kids sleep, I expect these women to cite lots of theories, then to give the usual American complaints about one-year-olds waking up twice per night. But they don't. Instead, they say that lots of babies in Tribeca do their nights à la française at about two months old. One mother, a photographer, mentions that she and many others bring their kids to a local pediatrician named Michel Cohen. She pronounces his first name "me-shell," like the Beatles' song.

"Is he French?" I venture.

"Yeah," she says.

"French from France?" I ask.

"French from France," she says.

I immediately make an appointment to meet Cohen. When I walk into his waiting room, there's no doubt that I'm in Tribeca and not in Paris. There's an Eames lounge chair, retro seventies wallpaper, and a lesbian mother in a fedora. A receptionist in a black tank top is calling out the names of the next patients: "Ella? Benjamin?"

When Cohen comes out, I immediately see why he's such a hit with mothers. He has tousled brown hair, doelike eyes, and a deep tan. He wears his designer shirts untucked, with sandals and Bermuda shorts. Despite two decades in the United States, he has hung onto a charming French accent and parlance ("When I give my advices to parents . . ."). He's done for the day, so he suggests that we sit outside at a local café. I readily agree.

Cohen clearly loves America, in part because America venerates its mavericks and entrepreneurs. In the land of managed care, he's fashioned himself into a neighborhood doctor. (He greets a dozen passersby by name as we sip our beers.) His practice, Tribeca Pediatrics, has expanded to five locations. And he's published a pithy parenting book called *The New Basics* with his picture on the cover.

Cohen is reluctant to credit France for the innovations he's brought to lower Manhattan. He left France in the late 1980s and remembers it as a country where newborn babies were left to cry it out in the hospital. Even now, he says, "You can't go to a park without seeing a kid take a beating." (Perhaps this used to be true. However, in the scores of hours I've clocked in Parisian parks recently, I witnessed a spanking only once.)

But some of Cohen's "advices" are exactly what today's Parisian parents do. Like the French, he starts babies off on vegetables and fruits rather than bland cereals. He's not obsessed with allergies. He talks about "rhythm" and teaching kids to handle frustration. He values calm. And he gives real weight to the parents' own quality of life, not just to the child's welfare.

So how does Cohen get the babies of Tribeca to do their nights?

"My first intervention is to say, when your baby is born, just don't jump on your kid at night," Cohen says. "Give your baby a chance to self-soothe, don't automatically respond, even from birth."

Maybe it's the beer (or Cohen's doe eyes), but I get a little jolt when he says this. I realize that I've seen French mothers and nannies pausing exactly this little bit before tending to their babies during the day. It hadn't occurred to me that this was deliberate or that it was at all significant. In fact, it had bothered me. I didn't think that you were supposed to make babies wait. Could this explain why French babies do their nights so early on, supposedly with few tears?

Cohen's advice to pause a little bit does seem like a natural extension of "observing" a baby. A mother isn't strictly "observing" if she jumps up and holds the baby the moment he cries.

For Cohen, this pause—I'm tempted to call it *La Pause*—is crucial. He says that using it very early on makes a big difference in how babies sleep. "The parents who were a little less responsive to late-night fussing always had kids who were good sleepers, while the jumpy folks had kids who would wake up repeatedly at night until it became unbearable," he writes. Most of the babies Cohen sees are breast-fed. That doesn't seem to make a difference.

One reason for pausing is that young babies make a lot of movements and noise while they're sleeping. This is normal and fine. If parents rush in and pick the baby up every time he makes a peep, they'll sometimes wake him up.

Another reason for pausing is that babies wake up between their sleep cycles, which last about two hours. It's normal for them to cry a bit when they're first learning to connect these cycles. If a parent automatically interprets this cry as a demand for food or a sign of distress and rushes in to soothe the baby, the baby will have a hard time learning to connect the cycles on his own. That is, he'll need an adult to come in and soothe him back to sleep at the end of each cycle.

Newborns typically can't connect sleep cycles on their own. But from about two or three months they usually can, if given a chance to learn how. And according to Cohen, connecting sleep cycles is like riding a bike: if a baby manages to fall back to sleep on his own even once, he'll have an easier time doing it again the next time. (Adults wake up between their sleep cycles, too, but typically don't remember this because they've learned to plunge right into the next one.)

Cohen says that sometimes babies do need to be fed or picked up. But unless we pause and observe them, we can't be sure. "Of course, if [the baby's] requests become more persistent, you'll have to feed her," Cohen writes. "I'm not saying let your baby wail." What he's saying is, just give your baby a chance to learn.

This idea isn't entirely new to me. It sounds familiar from some of my American sleep books. But it's usually mentioned among lots of other advice. I may have tried it once or twice with Bean but never with particular conviction. No one ever pointed it out to me as the one, crucial, most important thing to do and to stick with.

Cohen's singular instruction could solve the mystery of why French parents claim they never let their babies cry for long periods. If parents do "The Pause" in a baby's first two months, the baby can learn to fall back to sleep on his own. So his parents won't need to resort to "crying it out" later on.

The Pause doesn't have the brutal feeling of sleep training. It's more like sleep teaching. But the window for it is pretty small. According to Cohen, it's only until the baby is four months old. After that, bad sleep habits are formed.

Cohen says his sleep methods are an easy sell for the results-oriented parents in his Tribeca practice. But elsewhere, he says, parents often need more coaxing. They're opposed to letting their babies cry even a little. Cohen says he eventually persuades almost all the parents of newborns in his practice to try his methods. "I try to explain the roots of things," he says. That is, he teaches them about sleep.

When I get back to Paris, I immediately ask French mothers whether they do The Pause. Every single one says that, yes, of course they do. They say this is so obvious they hadn't thought to mention it. Most say they started doing The Pause when their babies were a few weeks old.

Alexandra, whose daughters slept through the night while they were still in the hospital, says that of course she didn't rush over to them the second they cried. She sometimes waited five or ten minutes before picking them up. She wanted to see whether they needed to fall back to sleep between sleep cycles or whether something else was bothering them: hunger, a dirty diaper, or just anxiety.

Alexandra—who wears her curly blond hair in a ponytail—looks like a cross between an earth mother and a high school cheerleader. She's extremely warm. She wasn't ignoring her newborn babies. To the contrary, she was carefully *observing* them. She trusted that when they cried, they were telling her something. During The Pause, she watched and listened. (She adds that there's another reason for The Pause: "to teach them patience.")

French parents don't have a name for The Pause; they just consider it common sense. (It's the American in me who needs to brand it.) But they all seem to do it and to remind one another that it's critical. It's such a simple thing. It strikes me that the French genius isn't coming up with a novel, mind-blowing sleep trick. It's clearing out the clutter of competing ideas and focusing on one thing that truly makes a difference.

Now that I'm attuned to The Pause, I start to notice that it's mentioned a lot in France. "Before responding to an interrogation, common sense tells us to listen to the question," says an article on Doctissimo, a popular French Web site. "It's exactly the same thing with a crying baby: the first thing to do is to listen to him."

Once you get past the philosophical sections, the authors of *Sleep, Dreams and the Child* write that intervening between sleep cycles "indisputably" leads to sleep problems, such as a baby who fully wakes up after every ninety-minute or two-hour cycle.

It's suddenly clear to me that Alison, the marketing expert whose son fed every two hours for six months, wasn't handed a baby with weird sleep needs. She unwittingly taught him to need a feed at the end of every two-hour sleep cycle. Alison wasn't just catering to her son's demands. Despite her best intentions, she was creating those demands.

I never hear of a single case like Alison's in France. The French treat The Pause as sleep solution number one, and something to wheel out when the baby is only a few weeks old. An article in *Maman!* magazine points out that in the first six months of a baby's life, 50 percent to 60 percent of his sleep is *sommeil agité* (agitated sleep). In this state, a sleeping baby suddenly yawns, stretches, and even opens and closes his eyes. "The error would be to interpret this as a call, and thus derail our baby's sleep train by picking him up," the article says.

The Pause isn't the only thing that French parents do. But it's a critical ingredient. When I visit Hélène De Leersnyder, the Proust-quoting sleep doctor, she immediately mentions The Pause, without any prompting. "Sometimes when babies sleep their eyes move, they make noise, they suck, they move around a bit. But in reality, they're sleeping. So you mustn't go in all the time and disturb him while he's sleeping. You have to learn how the baby sleeps."

"What if he wakes up?" I ask.

"If he wakes up completely, you pick him up, of course."

When I talk to American parents about sleep, science rarely comes up. Faced with so many different and seemingly valid sleep philosophies, the one they ultimately choose seems like a matter of taste. But once I get French parents talking, they mention sleep cycles, circadian rhythms, and *sommeil paradoxal*. They know that one reason babies cry in the night is that they're in between sleep cycles or they're in *sommeil agité*. When these parents said that they "observed" their babies, they meant that they were training themselves to recognize these stages. When French parents pause, they do it consistently and confidently. They're making informed decisions based on their understanding of how babies sleep.

Behind this is an important philosophical difference. French parents believe it's their job to gently teach babies how to sleep well, the same way they'll later teach them to have good hygiene, eat balanced meals, and ride a bike. They don't view being up half the night with an eight-month-old as a sign of parental commitment. They view it as a sign that the child has a sleep problem and that his family is wildly out of balance. When I describe Alison's case to Frenchwomen, they say it's "impossible"—both for the child and for his mother.

The French believe, as we do, that their children are beautiful and special. But they also realize that some things about them are just biological. Before we assume that our own children sleep like no others, we should probably think about science.

Armed with my revelation about the The Pause, I decide to look at some of the scientific literature on babies and sleep. What I find shocks me: American parents may be fighting the "baby sleep wars," but American sleep researchers aren't. The researchers mostly agree about the best way to get kids to sleep. And their recommendations sound remarkably French.

Sleep researchers, like French parents, believe that beginning very early on parents should play an active role in teaching their babies to sleep well. They say it's possible to begin teaching a healthy baby to sleep through the night when he's just a few weeks old, without the baby ever "crying it out."

A meta-study of dozens of peer-reviewed sleep papers[1] concludes that what's critical is something called "Parent education/prevention." This involves teaching pregnant women and parents of newborns about the science of sleep and giving them a few basic sleep rules. Parents are supposed to start following these rules from birth or when their babies are just a few weeks old.

What are these rules? The authors of the meta-study point to a paper that tracked pregnant women who planned to breastfeed.[2] Researchers gave some of the women a two-page handout with instructions. One rule on the handout was that parents should not hold, rock, or nurse a baby to sleep in the evenings, in order to help him learn the difference between day and night. Another instruction for week-old babies was that if they cried between midnight and five A.M., parents should re-swaddle, pat, rediaper, or walk the baby around, but that the mother should offer the breast only if the baby continued crying after that.

An additional instruction was that, from the child's birth, the mothers should distinguish between when their babies were crying and when they were just whimpering in their sleep. In other words, before picking up a noisy baby, the mother should pause to make sure he's awake.

The researchers explained the scientific basis for these instructions. A "control group" of breastfeeding mothers had gotten no instructions. The results were remarkable: from birth to three weeks old, babies in the treatment and control groups had nearly identical sleep patterns.

But at four weeks old, 38 percent of the treatment-group babies were sleeping through the night, versus 7 percent of the control-group babies. At eight weeks, all of the treatment babies were sleeping through the night, compared with 23 percent of the control babies. The authors' conclusion is resounding: "The results of this study show that breast-feeding need not be associated with night waking."

The Pause isn't just some French folk wisdom. Neither is the belief that sleeping well, early on, is better for everyone. "In general, night wakings fall within the diagnostic category of behavioral insomnia of childhood," the meta-study explains.

The study says there's growing evidence that young children who don't sleep enough, or who have disturbed sleep, can suffer from irritability, aggressiveness, hyperactivity, and poor impulse control, and can have trouble learning and remembering things. They are more prone to accidents, their metabolic and immune functions are weakened, and their overall quality of life diminishes. And sleep problems that begin in infancy can persist for many years. In the study of breast-feeding mothers, the treatment-group infants were afterward rated more secure, more predictable, and less fussy.

The studies I read point out that when children sleep badly there's spillover to the rest of the family, including maternal depression and lower overall family functioning. Conversely, when babies slept better, their parents reported that their marriages improved and that they became better and less-stressed parents.

Of course, some French babies miss the four-month window for sleep teaching. When this happens, French experts usually recommend some version of crying it out.

Sleep researchers aren't ambivalent about this either. The meta-study found that letting kids cry it out, either by going cold turkey (known by the unfortunate scientific term "extinction") or in stages ("graduated extinction"), works extremely well and usually succeeds in just a few days. "The biggest obstacle associated with extinction is lack of parental consistency," the study says.

Michel Cohen, the French doctor in Tribeca, recommends a rather extreme version of this for parents who miss the four-month window. He says they should make the baby feel cozy with his usual nighttime bath and songs. Then they should put him in bed at a reasonable hour, preferably while he's still awake, and come back at seven A.M.

In Paris, crying it out has a French twist. I start to realize this when I meet Laurence, a nanny from Normandy who's working for a French family in Montparnasse. Laurence has been looking after babies for two decades. She tells me that before letting a baby cry it out, it's crucial to explain to him what you're about to do.

Laurence walks me through this: "In the evening, you speak to him. You tell him that, if he wakes up once, you're going to give him his pacifier once. But after that, you're not going to get up. It's time to sleep. You're not far away, and you're going to come in and reassure him once. But not all night long."

Laurence adds that a crucial part of getting a baby to do his nights, at any age, is to truly believe that he's going to do it. "If you don't believe it, it's not going to work," she says. "Me, I always think that the child is going to sleep better the next night. I always have hope, even if he wakes up three hours later. You have to believe."

It does seem possible that French babies rise to meet their parents' and caregivers' expectations. Perhaps we all get the sleepers we expect, and the simple fact of believing that babies have a rhythm helps us to find it.

To believe in The Pause, or in letting an older baby cry it out, you also have to believe that a baby is a person who's capable of learning things (in this case, how to sleep) and coping with some frustration. Michel Cohen spends a lot of time converting parents to this French idea. To the common worry that a four-month-old is hungry at night, he writes: "She is hungry. But she does not need to eat. You're hungry in the middle of the night too; it's just that you learn not to eat because it's good for your belly to take a rest. Well, it's good for hers, too."

The French don't believe that babies should withstand biblical-sized trials. But they also don't think that a bit of frustration will crush kids. To the contrary, they believe it will make children more secure. According to *Sleep, Dreams and the Child*, "to always respond to his demands, and never tell him 'no,' is dangerous for the construction of his personality. Because the child won't have any barrier to push up against, to know what's expected of him."

For the French, teaching a small baby to sleep isn't a self-serving strategy for lazy parents. It's a crucial first lesson for children in self-reliance and enjoying one's own company. A psychologist quoted in *Maman!* magazine says that babies who learn to play by themselves during the day—even in the first few months—are less worried when they're put into their beds alone at night.

De Leersnyder writes that even babies need some privacy. "The little baby learns in his cradle that he can be alone from time to time, without being hungry, without being thirsty, without sleeping, just being calmly awake. At a very young age, he needs time alone, and he needs to go to sleep and wake up without being immediately watched by his mother."

De Leersnyder even devotes a portion of her book to what a mother should do while her baby sleeps. "She forgets about her baby, to think about herself. She now takes her own shower, gets dressed, puts on makeup, becomes beautiful for her own pleasure, that of her husband and of others. Evening comes, and she prepares herself for the night, for love."

As an American parent, this film noir scene—with its suggestion of kohl eyeliner and silk stockings—is hard to imagine in anything but the movies. Simon and I just assumed that, for quite a while, we'd rearrange our lives around Bean's whims.

The French don't think that's good for anyone. They view learning to sleep as part of learning to be part of the family, and adapting to what other members of the family need, too. De Leersnyder tells me, "If he wakes up ten times at night, [the mother] can't go to work the next day. So that makes the baby understand that—*voilà*—he can't wake up ten times a night."

"The baby understands that?" I ask.

"Of course he understands that," she says.

"How can he understand that?"

"Because babies understand everything."

French parents think The Pause is essential. But they don't hold it up as a panacea. Instead, they have a bundle of beliefs and habits that, when applied patiently and lovingly, put babies in the mood to sleep well. The Pause works in part because parents believe that tiny babies aren't helpless blobs. They can learn things. This learning, done gently and at a baby's own pace, isn't damaging. To the contrary, parents believe it gives the babies confidence and serenity, and makes them aware of other people. And it sets the tone for the respectful relationship between parents and children that I see later on.

If only I had known all this when Bean was born.

We definitely miss the four-month window for painlessly teaching her to sleep through the night. At nine months old, she still wakes up every night at around two A.M. So we brace ourselves to let her cry it out. On the first night, she cries for twelve minutes. (I clutch Simon and cry, too.) Then she goes back to sleep. The next night she cries for five minutes.

On the third night, Simon and I both wake up to silence at two A.M. "I think she was waking up for us," Simon says. "She thought that we needed her to do it." Then we go back to sleep. Bean has been doing her nights ever since.

Chapter 4

wait!

I'm getting more used to living in France. After a march around the local parks one morning, I announce to Simon that we've finally joined the global elite.

"We're global, but we're not elite," he replies.

Though I've made some inroads in France, I miss the United States. I miss grocery shopping in sweatpants, smiling at strangers, and being able to banter. Mostly, I miss my parents. I can't believe I'm raising a child while they're 4,500 miles away.

Neither can my mother. My meeting and marrying a handsome foreigner was the thing she most dreaded when I was growing up. She discussed this fear so extensively that it's probably what planted the idea. On one visit to Paris, she takes me and Simon out to dinner and breaks down in tears at the table. "What do they have here that they don't have in America?" she demands to know. (Had she been eating escargot, I could have pointed at her plate. Unfortunately, she had ordered the chicken.)

Although living in France has gotten easier, I haven't really assimilated. To the contrary, having a baby—and speaking better French—makes me realize just how foreign I am. Soon after Bean begins sleeping through the night, we arrive for her first day at France's state-run day-care center, called the crèche. During the intake interview, we sail through questions about her pacifier use and favorite sleeping positions. We're ready with her inoculation records and emergency-contact numbers. But one question stumps us: What time does she have her milk?

On the matter of when to feed babies, American parents are once again in sparring camps. You could call it a food fight: One camp believes in feeding babies at fixed times. Another says to feed them whenever they seem hungry. The American Web site BabyCenter gives eight different sample schedules for five- and six-month-olds, including one in which the baby eats ten times a day.

We've drifted into a hybrid. Bean always has milk when she wakes up and again before bedtime. In between, we feed her whenever she seems hungry. Simon thinks there isn't a problem that a bottle or a boob can't solve. We'll both do anything to keep her from yowling.

When I finish explaining our feeding system to the crèche lady, she looks at me like I've just said that we let our baby drive the family car. We don't know when our child eats? This is a problem she will soon solve. Her look says that while we're living in Paris, we're raising a child who eats and sleeps—and yes, probably poops—like an American.

The crèche lady's look also reveals that on this, too, there are no sparring camps in France. Parents don't anguish about how often their children should eat. From the age of about four months, most French babies eat at regular times. As with sleep techniques, French parents see this as common sense, not as part of a parenting philosophy.

What's even stranger is that these French babies all eat at roughly the same times. With slight variations, mothers tell me that their babies eat at about eight A.M., twelve P.M., four P.M., and eight P.M. *Votre Enfant* (*Your Child*), a respected French parenting guide, has just one sample menu for four- or five-month-olds. It's this same sequence of feeds.

In French these aren't even called "feeds," which after all sounds like you're pitching hay to cows. They're called "meals." And their sequence resembles a schedule I'm quite familiar with: breakfast, lunch, and dinner, plus an afternoon snack. In other words, by about four months old, French babies are already on the same eating schedule that they'll be on for the rest of their lives (grown-ups usually drop the snack).

You'd think the existence of this national baby meal plan would be obvious. Instead, it feels like a state secret. If you merely ask French parents if their babies eat on a schedule, they almost always say no. As with sleep, they insist that they're merely following their babies' "rhythms." When I point out that French babies all seem to eat at roughly the same times, parents shrug this off as a coincidence.

The deeper mystery to me is how all these French babies are capable of waiting four hours from one meal to the next. Bean gets anxious if she has to wait even a few minutes for a feed. We get anxious, too. But I'm beginning to sense that there's a lot of waiting going on all around me in France. First there was The Pause, in which French parents wait after their baby wakes up. Now there's the baby meal plan, in which they wait long stretches from one feeding to the next. And of course there are all those toddlers waiting contentedly in restaurants until their food arrives.

The French seem collectively to have achieved the miracle of getting babies and toddlers not just to wait, but to do so happily. Could this ability explain the difference between French and American kids?

To get my head around these questions, I e-mail Walter Mischel, the world's expert on how children delay gratification. He's eighty years old and a chaired professor of psychology at Columbia University. I've read all about him, and read some of his many published papers on the topic. I explain that I'm in Paris researching French parenting and ask if he might have time to speak with me on the phone.

Mischel replies a few hours later. To my surprise, he says that he's in Paris, too. Would I like to come by for a coffee? Two days later we're at the kitchen table in his girlfriend's apartment in the Latin Quarter, just down the hill from the Panthéon.

Mischel hardly looks seventy, and certainly not eighty. He has a shaved head and the coiled energy of a boxer, but with a sweet, almost childlike face. It's not hard to envision him as the eight-year-old boy from Vienna who fled Austria with his family after the Nazis annexed the country.

The family eventually landed in Brooklyn. When Walter entered public school at age nine, he was assigned to kindergarten to learn English and remembers "trying to walk on my knees to not stick out from the five-year-olds when our class marched through the corridors." Mischel's parents—who were cultured and comfortably middle class in Vienna—opened a struggling five-and-dime. His mother, who'd been a minor depressive in Vienna, was energized by America. But his father never recovered from his fall in status.

This early experience gave Mischel a permanent outsider's perspective and helped frame the questions that he has spent his career answering. In his thirties, he upended the science of personality by arguing that people's traits aren't fixed; they depend on context. Despite marrying an American and raising their three daughters in California, Mischel began making annual pilgrimages to Paris. "I always felt myself to be European and felt Paris was the capital of Europe," he tells me. (Mischel, who divorced in 1996, has lived with a Frenchwoman for the last decade. They divide their time between New York and Paris.)

Mischel is most famous for devising the "marshmallow test" in the late 1960s, when he was at Stanford. In it, an experimenter leads a four- or five-year-old into a room where there's a marshmallow on a table. The experimenter tells the child he's going to leave the room for a little while. If the child manages not to eat the marshmallow until he comes back, he'll be rewarded with two marshmallows. If he eats the marshmallow, he'll get only that one.

It's a very hard test. Of the 653 kids who took it back in the sixties and seventies, only one in three managed to resist eating the marshmallow for the full fifteen minutes that the experimenter was away. Some ate it as soon as they were alone. Most could wait only about thirty seconds.[1]

In the mid-1980s, Mischel revisited the kids from the original experiment, to see if there was a difference between how good and bad delayers were faring as teenagers. He and his colleagues found a remarkable correlation: the longer the children had resisted eating the marshmallow as four-year-olds, the higher Mischel and his colleagues assessed them in all sorts of other categories later on. Among other skills, the good delayers were better at concentrating and reasoning. And according to a report that Mischel and his colleagues published in 1988, they "do not tend to go to pieces under stress."

Could it be that making children delay gratification—as middle-class French parents do—actually makes them calmer and more resilient? Whereas middle-class American kids, who are in general more used to getting what they want right away, go to pieces under stress? Are French parents once again doing—by tradition and instinct— exactly what scientists like Mischel recommend?

Bean, who usually gets what she wants almost immediately, can go from calm to hysterical in seconds. And whenever I go back to America, I realize that miserable, screaming toddlers demanding to get out of their strollers or pitching themselves onto the sidewalk are part of the scenery of daily life.

I rarely see such scenes in Paris. French babies and toddlers, who are used to waiting longer, seem oddly calm about not getting what they want right away. When I visit French families and hang out with their kids, there's a conspicuous lack of whining and complaining. Often—or at least much more often than in my house—everyone's calm and absorbed in what they're doing.

In France I regularly see what amounts to a minor miracle: adults in the company of small children at home, having entire cups of coffee and full-length adult conversations. Waiting is even part of the parenting vernacular. Instead of saying "quiet" or "stop" to rowdy kids, French parents often just issue a sharp *attend*, which means "wait."

Mischel hasn't performed the marshmallow test on any French children. (He'd probably have to do a version with *pain au chocolat*.) But as a longtime observer of France, he says he's struck by the difference between French and American kids.

In America, he says, "certainly the impression one has is that self-control has gotten increasingly difficult for kids." That's sometimes true even with his own grandchildren. "I don't like it when I call a daughter, if she tells me that she can't talk now because a child is pulling on her and she can't say, 'Hold on, I'm talking to Papa.' "[2]

Having kids who can wait makes family life more pleasant. Children in France "seem much more disciplined and more raised the way I was," Mischel says. "With French friends coming over with small children, you can still have a French dinner . . . the expectation with French kids is that they'll behave themselves in an appropriate, quiet way and enjoy the dinner."

"Enjoy" is an important word here. For the most part, French parents don't expect their kids to be mute, joyless, and compliant. Parents just don't see how their kids can enjoy themselves if they can't control themselves.

I often hear French parents telling their kids to be *sage*. (In French, *sage* rhymes with the "Taj" in "Taj Mahal.") Saying *"sois sage"* is a bit like saying "be good." But it implies more than that. When I tell Bean to be good before we walk into someone's house, it's as if she's a wild animal who must act tame for an hour but who could turn wild again at any moment. It implies that being good goes contrary to her true nature.

When I tell Bean to be *sage*, I'm also telling her to behave appropriately. But I'm asking her to use good judgment and to be aware and respectful of other people. I'm implying that she has a certain wisdom about the situation and that she's in command of herself. And I'm suggesting that I trust her.

Being *sage* doesn't mean being dull. The French kids I know have a lot of fun. On weekends, Bean and her friends run shouting and laughing through the park for hours. Recess at her day care, and later at her school, are free-for-alls. There's also a lot of organized fun in Paris, like children's film festivals, theaters, and cooking classes, which require patience and attention. The French parents I know want their kids to have rich experiences and to be exposed to art and music.

Parents just don't see how kids can fully absorb these experiences if they don't have patience. In the French view, having the self-control to be calmly present, rather than anxious, irritable, and demanding, is what allows kids to have fun.

French parents and caregivers don't think that kids have infinite patience. They don't expect toddlers to sit through symphonies or formal banquets. They usually talk about waiting in terms of minutes or seconds.

But even these small delays seem to make a big difference. I'm now convinced that the secret of why French kids rarely whine or collapse into tantrums—or at least do so less than American kids—is that they've developed the internal resources to cope with frustration. They don't expect to get what they want instantly. When French parents talk about the "education" of their children, they are talking, in large part, about teaching them how not to eat the marshmallow.

. . . .

So how exactly do the French turn ordinary children into expert delayers? And can we teach Bean how to wait, too?

Walter Mischel watched videotapes of hundreds of squirming four-year-olds taking the marshmallow test. He eventually figured out that the bad delayers focused on the marshmallow, whereas the good delayers distracted themselves. "The kids who manage to wait very easily are the ones who learn during the wait to sing little songs to themselves, or pick their ears in an interesting way, or play with their toes and make a game of it," he tells me. The ones who didn't know how to distract themselves and just fixated on the marshmallow ended up eating it.[3]

Mischel concludes that having the willpower to wait isn't about being stoic. It's about learning techniques that make waiting less frustrating. "There are many many ways of doing that, of which the most direct and the simplest . . . is to self-distract," he says.

Parents don't have to specifically teach their kids "distraction strategies." Mischel says kids learn this skill on their own, if parents just allow them to practice waiting. "I think what's often underestimated in parenting is how extraordinary . . . the cognitive facilities of very young kids are, if you engage them," he says.

This is exactly what I've been seeing French parents doing. They don't explicitly teach their kids distraction techniques. Mostly, they just seem to give them lots of opportunities to practice waiting.

On a gray Saturday afternoon, I take a commuter train to Fontenay-sous-Bois, a suburb just east of Paris. A friend has arranged for me to visit a family that lives there. Martine, the mother, is a pretty labor lawyer in her midthirties. She lives with her husband, an emergency-room doctor, and their two kids, in a modern low-rise building set amid a patch of trees.

I'm immediately struck by how much Martine's apartment resembles my own. Toys line the perimeter of the living room, which is attached to an open kitchen (known in French as a *cuisine americaine*). We have the same stainless-steel appliances.

But the similarities end there. Despite having two young kids, Martine's house has a calm that we could only wish for. When I arrive, her husband is working on his laptop in the living room, while one-year-old Auguste naps nearby. Paulette, their three-year-old with a pixie haircut, is sitting at the kitchen table plopping cupcake batter into little wrappers. When each wrapper is full, she tops it with colored sprinkles and fresh red gooseberries.

Martine and I sit down to chat at the other end of the table. But I'm transfixed by little Paulette and her cupcakes. Paulette is completely absorbed in her task. She somehow resists the temptation to eat the batter. When she's done she asks her mother if she can lick the spoon.

"No, but you can have some sprinkles," Martine says, prompting Paulette to shake out several tablespoons of sprinkles onto the table.

My daughter Bean is the same age as Paulette, but it wouldn't have occurred to me to let her do a complicated task like this all on her own. I'd be supervising, and she'd be resisting my supervision. There would be much stress and whining (mine and hers). Bean would probably grab batter, berries, and sprinkles each time I turned around. I certainly wouldn't be chatting calmly with a visitor.

The whole scene wouldn't be something I'd want to repeat a week later. Yet baking seems to be a weekly ritual in France. Practically every time I visit a French family on a weekend, they're either making a cake or serving the one they made earlier that day.

At first I think this must be because I'm visiting. But I soon realize that it has nothing to do with me. There's a national bake-off in Paris every weekend. Practically from the time kids can sit up, their moms begin leading them in weekly or biweekly baking projects. These kids don't just spill some flour and mash a few bananas. They crack eggs, pour in cups of sugar, and mix with preternatural confidence. They actually make the whole cake themselves.

The first cake that most French kids learn to bake is *gâteau au yaourt* (yogurt cake), in which they use empty yogurt containers to measure out the other ingredients. It's a light, not-too-sweet cake to which berries, chocolate chips, lemon, or a tablespoon of rum can be added. It's pretty hard to screw up.

All this baking doesn't just yield lots of cakes. It also teaches kids how to control themselves. With its orderly measuring and sequencing of ingredients, baking is a perfect lesson in patience. So is the fact that French families don't devour the cake as soon as it comes out of the oven, as I would. They typically bake in the morning or early afternoon, then wait and eat the cake or muffins as a *goûter* (pronounced gew-tay)—the French afternoon snack.

It's hard for me to imagine a world in which moms don't walk around with baggies of Goldfish and Cheerios in their purses to patch over the inevitable moments of angst. Jennifer, a mother and a reporter for *The New York Times*, complains that every activity her daughter attends, no matter how brief or at what time of day, now includes snacks.[4] "Apparently we have collectively decided as a culture that it is impossible for children to take part in any activity without simultaneously shoving something into their pie holes," she writes.

In France the *goûter* is the official, and only, snack time. It's usually at about four thirty P.M., when kids get out of school. It has the same fixed status as other mealtimes and is universally observed for kids.

The *goûter* helps explain why those French kids I saw at the restaurant were eating so well. They were actually hungry, because they hadn't been snacking all day. (Adults might have a coffee, but rarely a snack. A friend of mine who was visiting France complained that he had a hard time finding any adult snack food.)

Martine, the mother in the suburbs, says she never set out specifically to teach her kids patience. But her family's daily rituals—which

I see reenacted in many other middle-class French homes—are an on-going apprenticeship in how to delay gratification.

Martine says she often buys Paulette candy. (Bonbons are on display in most bakeries.) But Paulette isn't allowed to eat the candy until that day's *goûter*, even if that means waiting many hours. Paulette is used to this. Martine sometimes has to remind her of the rule, but Paulette doesn't protest.

Even the *goûter* isn't a free-for-all. "The great thing is that there was cake to eat," recalls Clotilde Dusoulier, a French food writer. "But the flip side of the coin was that my mom would say, 'that's enough.' It was also teaching kids restraint." Clotilde, who's now in her early thirties, says that as a kid she baked with her mother "pretty much every weekend."

It's not just what and when French families eat that make their meals little capsules of patience training. It's also how they eat, and with whom. From a very young age, French kids get used to eating meals in courses, with—at a minimum—a starter, a main course, and a dessert. They also get used to eating with their parents, which has to be better for learning patience. According to UNICEF, 90 percent of French fifteen-year-olds eat the main meal of the day with their parents several times per week. In the United States and the United Kingdom, it's about 67 percent.

These meals aren't rushed affairs. In that study of women in Rennes, France, and in Ohio, the Frenchwomen spent more than twice as much time eating each day. They surely pass on this pace to their kids.

Fortunately it's *goûter* time when the cupcakes come out of the oven at Martine's. Paulette happily eats two of them. But Martine doesn't even taste one. She seems to have tricked herself into thinking of cupcakes as child's food in order not to eat them. (Sadly, I think she assumes I'm doing the same trick and doesn't offer me one.)

This is yet another way that French parents teach their kids to wait.

They model waiting themselves. Little girls who grow up in homes where the mother doesn't eat the cupcake surely grow up to be women who don't eat the cupcake either. (My own mother has many wonderful qualities, but she always eats the cupcake.)

It strikes me that Martine doesn't expect her daughter to be perfectly patient. She assumes that Paulette will sometimes grab stuff and make mistakes. But Martine doesn't overreact to these mistakes, the way that I tend to. She understands that all this baking and waiting is practice in building a skill.

In other words, Martine is even patient about teaching patience.

When Paulette tries to interrupt our conversation, Martine says, "Just wait two minutes, my little one. I'm in the middle of talking." It's both very polite and very firm. I'm struck both by how sweetly Martine says it and by how certain she seems that Paulette will obey her.

Martine has been teaching her children patience since they were tiny. When Paulette was a baby, Martine usually waited five minutes before picking her up when she cried (and, of course, Paulette did her nights at two and a half months).

Martine also teaches her kids a related skill: learning to play by themselves. "The most important thing is that he learns to be happy by himself," she says of her son, Auguste.

A child who can play by himself can draw upon this skill when his mother is on the phone. And it's a skill that French mothers explicitly try to cultivate in their kids more than American mothers do. In another study, of college-educated mothers in the United States and France, the American moms said that encouraging one's child to play alone was of average importance. But the French moms said it was very important.[5]

Parents who value this ability are probably more apt to leave a child alone when he's playing well by himself. When French mothers say that it's important to take cues from a child's own rhythm, part of what they mean is that when the child is busy playing, they leave him alone.

This seems to be another example of French mothers and caregivers intuitively following the best science. Walter Mischel says the worst-case scenario for a kid from eighteen to twenty-four months of age is "the child is busy and the child is happy, and the mother comes along with a fork full of spinach. . . .

"The mothers who really foul it up are the ones who are coming in when the child is busy and doesn't want or need them, and are not there when the child is eager to have them. So becoming alert to that is absolutely critical."

Indeed, an enormous U.S. government study of the effects of child care[6] found that what's especially crucial is the mother's or caregiver's "sensitivity"—how attuned she is to her child's experience of the world. "The sensitive mother is aware of the child's needs, moods, interests, and capabilities," a backgrounder explains. "She allows this awareness to guide her interactions with her child." Conversely, having a depressed mother is very bad, because the depression stops the mother from tuning in to her child.

Mischel's conviction about the importance of sensitivity doesn't just come from research. He says that his own mother was alternately smothering and absent. Mischel still can't ride a bike, because she was too afraid of head injuries to let him learn. But neither of his parents came to hear him give the valedictory address at his high school graduation.

Of course American parents want their kids to be patient. We believe that "patience is a virtue." We encourage our kids to share, to wait their turns, to set the table, and to practice the piano. But patience isn't a skill that we hone quite as assiduously as French parents do. As with sleep, we tend to view whether kids are good at waiting as a matter of temperament. In our view, parents either luck out and get a child who waits well or they don't.

French parents and caregivers can't believe that we're so laissez-faire about this crucial ability. For them, having kids who need instant gratification would make life unbearable. When I mention the topic of this book at a dinner party in Paris, my host—a French journalist—launches into a story about the year he lived in Southern California. He and his wife, a judge, had befriended an American couple and decided to spend a weekend away with them in Santa Barbara. It was the first time they'd met one another's kids, who ranged in age from about seven to fifteen.

From my hosts' perspective, the weekend quickly became maddening. Years later, they still remember how the American kids frequently interrupted the adults midsentence. And there were no fixed mealtimes; the American kids just went to the refrigerator and took food whenever they wanted.

To the French couple, it seemed like the American kids were in charge. "What struck us, and bothered us, was that the parents never said 'no,'" the journalist said. "They did *n'importe quoi*," his wife added. This was apparently contagious. "The worst part is, our kids started doing *n'importe quoi*, too," she says.

After a while, I realize that most French descriptions of American kids include this phrase *n'importe quoi*, meaning "whatever" or "anything they like." It suggests that the American kids don't have firm boundaries, that their parents lack authority, and that anything goes. It's the antithesis of the French ideal of the *cadre*, or frame, that French parents talk about. *Cadre* means that kids have very firm limits—that's the frame—and that the parents strictly enforce those limits. But within those limits, the kids have a lot of freedom.

American parents impose limits, too, of course. But often they're different from the French ones. In fact, French people often find these

American limits shocking. Laurence, the nanny from Normandy, tells me she won't work for American families anymore, and that several of her nanny friends won't either. She says she quit her last job with Americans after just a few months, mostly over the issue of limits.

"It was difficult because it was *n'importe quoi*; the child does what he wants, when he wants," Laurence says.

Laurence is tall and has short hair and a gentle, no-nonsense manner. She's reluctant to offend me. But she says that compared with the French families she's worked for, in the American homes there was much more crying and whining. (This is the first time that I hear the onomatopoeic French verb *chouiner*—to whine.)

The last American family she worked for had three kids, ages eight, five, and eighteen months. For the five-year-old girl, whining "was her national sport. She whined all the time, with tears that could fall at a moment's notice." Laurence believed that it was best to ignore the girl, so as not to reinforce the whining. But the girl's mother—who was often home, in another room—usually rushed in and capitulated to whatever the girl was asking for.

Laurence says the eight-year-old son was worse. "He always wanted a little bit more, and a little bit more." She says that when his escalating demands weren't met, he became hysterical.

Laurence's conclusion is that, in such a situation, "the child is less happy. He's a little bit lost. . . . In the families where there is more structure, not a rigid family but a bit more *cadre*, everything goes much more smoothly."

Laurence's breaking point came when the mother of the American family insisted that Laurence put the two older kids on a diet. Laurence refused, and said she would simply feed them balanced meals. Then she discovered that after she put the kids to bed and left, at about eight thirty P.M., the mother would feed them cookies and cake.

"They were stout," Laurence says of the three children.

"Stout?" I ask.

"I say 'stout' so I don't say 'fat,'" she says.

I'd like to write off this story as a stereotype. Obviously not all American kids behave this way. And French kids do plenty of *n'importe quoi*, too. (Bean will later say sternly to her eight-month-old brother, in imitation of her own teachers, *"Tu ne peux pas faire n'importe quoi"*— you can't do whatever.)

But the truth is, in my own home, I've witnessed American kids doing quite a lot of *n'importe quoi*.[7] When American families come over, the grown-ups spend much of the time chasing after or otherwise tending to their kids. "Maybe in about five years we'll be able to have a conversation," jokes a friend from California who's visiting Paris with her husband and two daughters, ages seven and four. We've been trying for an hour just to finish our cups of tea.

She and her family arrived at our house after spending the day touring Paris, during which the younger daughter, Rachel, threw a series of spectacular tantrums. When the dinner I'm preparing isn't ready, both parents come into the kitchen and say that their girls probably can't wait much longer. When we finally sit down, they let Rachel crawl under the table while the rest of us (Bean included) eat dinner. The parents explain that Rachel is tired, so she can't control herself. Then they wax about her prodigious reading skills and her possible admission to a gifted kindergarten.

During the meal, I feel something stroking my foot.

"Rachel is tickling me," I tell her parents, nervously. A moment later, I yelp. The gifted child has bitten me.

Setting limits for kids isn't a French invention, of course. Plenty of American parents and experts also think limits are very important. But in the United States, this runs up against the competing idea that kids need to express themselves. I sometimes feel that the things Bean wants—to have apple juice instead of water, to wear a princess dress to the park, to be carried instead of pushed in a stroller—are immutable and primordial. I don't concede to everything. But repeatedly blocking her urges feels wrong and possibly even damaging.

It's also just hard for me to conceive of Bean as someone who can sit through a four-course meal or play quietly when I'm on the phone. I'm not even sure I want her to do those things. Will it crush her spirit? Would I be stifling her self-expression and her possibility of starting the next Facebook? With all these doubts, I often capitulate.

I'm not the only one. At Bean's fourth birthday party, one of her English-speaking friends walks in carrying a wrapped present for Bean and another one for himself. His mother says he got upset at the shop because he wasn't getting a present, too. My friend Nancy tells me about a new parenting philosophy that's meant to eliminate this battle of wills: you never let your child hear the word "no," so that he can't say it back to you.

In France, there's no such ambivalence about "*non*." "You must teach your child frustration" is a French parenting maxim. In my favorite series of French kids' books, Princesse Parfaite (Perfect Princess), the heroine, Zoé, is pictured pulling her mother toward a crêpe stand. The text explains, "While walking past the *crêperie*, Zoé made a scene. She wanted a crêpe with blackberry jam. Her mother refused, because it was just after lunch."

On the next page, Zoé is back in the bakery, dressed as the Perfect Princess of the title. This time she's covering her eyes so she won't see the piles of fresh brioche. She's being *sage*. "As [Zoé] knows, to avoid being tempted, she turns her head to the other side," the text says.

It's worth noting that in the first scene, where Zoé isn't getting what she wants, she's crying. But in the second one, where she's distracting herself, she's smiling. The message is that children will always have the impulse to give in to their vices. But they're happier when they're *sage* and in command of themselves. (It's also worth noting that Parisian parents don't let their little girls go shopping in princess outfits. Those are strictly for parties, and for dressing up at home.)

In the book *Un enfant heureux* (*A Happy Child*) French psychologist Didier Pleux argues that the best way to make a child happy is to frustrate him. "That doesn't mean that you prevent him from playing, or that you avoid hugging him," Pleux says. "One must of course respect his tastes, his rhythms and his individuality. It's simply that the child must learn, from a very young age, that he's not alone in the world, and that there's a time for everything."

I'm struck by how different the French expectations are when—on that same seaside holiday when I witnessed all the French kids happily eating in restaurants—I take Bean into a shop filled with perfectly aligned stacks of striped "mariner" T-shirts in bright colors. Bean immediately begins pulling them down. She barely pauses when I scold her.

To me, Bean's bad behavior seems predictable for a toddler. So I'm surprised when the saleswoman says, without malice, "I've never seen a child do that before." I apologize and head for the door.

Walter Mischel says that capitulating to kids starts a dangerous cycle: "If kids have the experience that when they're told to wait, that if they scream, Mommy will come and the wait will be over, they will very quickly learn not to wait. Non-waiting and screaming and carrying on and whining are being rewarded."

French parents delight in the fact that each child has his own temperament. But they take for granted that any healthy child is capable of not whining, not collapsing after he's told "no," and generally not nagging or grabbing stuff.

French parents are more inclined to view a child's somewhat random demands as *caprices*—impulsive fancies or whims. They have no problem saying no to these demands. "I think [Frenchwomen] understand earlier than American women that kids can have demands and those demands are unrealistic," a pediatrician who treats French and American children tells me.

A French psychologist writes[8] that when a child has a *caprice*—for instance, his mother is in a shop with him and he suddenly demands a toy—the mother should remain extremely calm and gently explain that buying the toy isn't in the day's plan. Then she should try to bypass the *caprice* by redirecting the child's attention, for example by telling a story about her own life. "Stories about parents are always interesting to children," the psychologist says. (After reading this, in every crisis I shout to Simon: "Tell a story about your life!")

The psychologist says that throughout this the mother should stay in close communication with the child, by embracing him or looking him in the eye. But she must also make him understand that "he can't have everything right away. It's essential not to leave him thinking that he is all-powerful, and that he can do everything and have everything."

French parents don't worry that they're going to damage their kids by frustrating them. To the contrary, they think their kids will be damaged if they can't cope with frustration. They also treat coping with frustration as a core life skill. Their kids simply have to learn it. The parents would be remiss if they didn't teach it.

Laurence, the nanny, says that if a child wants her to pick him up while she's cooking, "It's enough to explain to him, 'I can't pick you up right now,' and then tell him why."

Laurence says her charges don't always take this well. But she stays firm and lets the child express his disappointment. "I don't let him cry eight hours, but I let him cry," she says. "I explain to him that I can't do otherwise."

This happens a lot when she's watching several children at once. "If you are busy with one child and another child wants you, if you can pick him up obviously you do. But if not, I let him cry."

The French expectation that even little kids should be able to wait comes in part from the darker days of French parenting, when children were expected to be quiet and obedient. But it also comes from the belief that even babies are rational people who can learn things. According to this view, when we rush to feed Bean whenever she whimpers, we're treating her like an addict. Whereas expecting her to have patience would be a way of respecting her.

As with teaching kids to sleep, French experts view learning to cope with "no" as a crucial step in a child's evolution. It forces them to understand that there are other people in the world, with needs as powerful as their own. A French child psychiatrist writes that this *éducation* should begin when a baby is three to six months old. "His mother begins to make him wait a bit sometimes, thus introducing a temporal dimension into his spirit. It's thanks to these little frustrations that his parents impose on him day after day, along with their love, that lets him withstand, and allows him to renounce, between ages two and four, his all-powerfulness, in order to humanize him. This renunciation is not always loud, but it's an obligatory passage."[9]

In the French view, I'm doing Bean no service by catering to her whims. French experts and parents believe that hearing "no" rescues children from the tyranny of their own desires. "As small children you have needs and desires that basically have no ending. This is a very basic thing. The parents are there—that's why you have frustration—to stop that [process]," says Caroline Thompson, a family psychologist who runs a bilingual practice in Paris.

Thompson, who has a French mother and an English father, points out that kids often get very angry at their parents when parents block them. She says English-speaking parents often interpret this anger as a sign that the parents are doing something wrong. But she warns that parents shouldn't mistake angering a child for bad parenting.

To the contrary, "If the parent can't stand the fact of being hated, then he won't frustrate the child, and then the child will be in a situation where he will be the object of his own tyranny, where basically he has to deal with his own greed and his own need for things. If the parent isn't there to stop him, then he's the one who's going to have to stop himself or not stop himself, and that's much more anxiety-provoking."

Thompson's view reflects what seems to be the consensus in France: making kids face up to limitations and deal with frustration turns them into happier, more resilient people. And one of the main ways to gently induce frustration, on a daily basis, is to make children wait a bit. As with The Pause as a sleep strategy, French parents have homed in on this one thing. They treat waiting not just as one important skill among many but as a cornerstone of raising kids.

I'm still mystified by France's national baby-feeding schedule. How do French babies all end up eating at the same times, if their mothers don't make them do it? When I point this out, mothers continue to wax about rhythms and flexibility, and about how each child is different.

But after a while, I realize that they also take a few principles for granted, even if they don't always mention them. The first is that, after the first few months, a baby should eat at roughly the same times each day. The second is that babies should have a few big feeds rather than a lot of small ones. And the third is that the baby should fit into the rhythm of the family.

So while it's true that mothers don't force their babies onto a schedule, they do nudge them toward it by observing these three principles. The parenting book *Votre Enfant* says the ideal is to breastfeed on demand for the first few months and then bring the baby "progressively and flexibly, to regular hours that are more compatible with daily life."

If parents follow these principles and the baby wakes up at seven or eight, and they think he should wait about four hours between meals, he is going to be routed onto the national meal plan. He'll eat in the morning. He'll eat again around noon. He'll have an afternoon feed around four. And then he'll eat again at about eight P.M., before going to bed. When the baby cries at ten thirty A.M., his parents are going to assume that what's best for him is to wait until lunchtime and have a big feed then. It might take a while for him to ease into this rhythm. Parents ease babies on to this schedule gradually, not abruptly. But eventually the baby gets used to it, the same way that grown-ups do. His parents get used to it, too. And it allows the whole family to eat together.

Martine says that for the first few months she nursed Paulette on demand. Around the third month, to get her to wait three hours between feeds, she took her for walks or put her in a sling, where Paulette would usually quickly stop crying. Martine then did the same thing when she wanted to space the feeding times out to four hours. She says she never let either of her kids cry for very long. Gradually they just fell into the rhythm of eating four times a day. "I was really flexible, I'm just like that," she says.

The critical assumption is that while the baby has his own rhythm, the family and the parents have rhythms, too. The ideal, in France, is finding a balance between these two. *Votre Enfant* explains, "You and your baby each have your rights, and every decision is a compromise."

Bean's regular pediatrician never mentioned this four-meal-a-day plan to me. But he's away at Bean's next appointment. His replacement is a young Frenchwoman who has a daughter about Bean's age. When I ask her about the schedule, she says that—*bien sûr*—Bean should only be eating four times a day. Then the doctor grabs some Post-its and scribbles down The Schedule. It's the same one again: morning, noon, four P.M., and eight P.M. When I later ask Bean's regular doctor why he never mentioned this, he says he prefers not to suggest schedules to American parents, because they tend to become too doctrinaire about them.

It takes a few weeks, but we gradually nudge Bean onto this schedule. It turns out that she can take the wait. She just needed a bit of practice.

gâteau au yaourt
(Yogurt Cake)

2 six-ounce containers plain whole-milk (not reduced-
  fat) yogurt. Use the empty containers to measure the
  other ingredients
2 eggs
2 containers sugar (or just one, depending on how
  sweet you like it)
1 teaspoon vanilla
Just under 1 container vegetable oil
4 containers flour
1 ½ teaspoons baking powder
Crème fraîche (optional)

Preheat oven to 375°F.

Use vegetable oil to grease a 9-inch round cake pan or a
loaf pan.

Gently combine the yogurt, eggs, sugar, vanilla, and oil. In
a separate bowl, mix the flour and baking powder. Add the
dry ingredients to the wet ingredients; mix gently until ingredients are just combined (don't overmix). You can add
2 containers frozen berries, a container of chocolate chips,
or any flavoring you like. Bake for 35 minutes, then five
minutes more if the cake doesn't pass the knife test. It
should be almost crispy on the outside, but springy on the
inside. Let it cool. The cake is delicious served with tea and
a dollop of crème fraîche.

Chapter 5

tiny little humans

When Bean is a year and a half, we register her at the Center for the Adaptation of the Young Child to the Aquatic Milieu, also known as Babies in the Water. It's a weekly paid swimming class organized by our local town hall and held every Saturday at one of the public pools in our neighborhood.

A month before the first class, the organizers summon parents to an informational meeting. The other parents seem a lot like us: college-educated and willing to push strollers into the cold on Saturday mornings in order to teach their kids to swim. Each family is assigned a forty-five-minute swimming slot and reminded that—as in all public pools in Paris—men must wear Speedos, not trunks. (This is supposedly for hygiene. Men could wear swim trunks elsewhere and thus carry dirt into the pool.)

The three of us arrive at the pool, get undressed, and put on our swimsuits as discreetly as possible in the co-ed changing room. Then we slip into the pool alongside the other kids and their parents. Bean throws around some plastic balls, goes down the slide, and jumps off the rafts. At one point an instructor paddles up to us and introduces himself, then swims away. Before we know it, our time is up and the next shift of parents and kids is climbing into the pool.

I figure that this must be an introductory class, and that the lessons will begin the following week. But at the next class it's the same thing: lots of splashing around but no one teaching anyone how to kick, blow bubbles, or otherwise begin to swim. In fact, there's no organized instruction at all. Every so often the same instructor paddles by and makes sure we're happy.

This time, I corner him in the pool: When is he going to start teaching my daughter how to swim? He smiles indulgently at me. "Children don't learn how to swim in Babies in the Water," he says, as if this is completely obvious. (I later learn that Parisian kids typically don't learn to swim until they're six.)

So what are we all doing here? He says the point of these sessions is for children to *discover* the water, and to *awaken* to the sensations of being in it.

Huh? Bean has already "discovered" water in the bathtub. I want her to swim! And I want her to swim as early as possible, preferably by age two. That's what I thought I'd paid for, and why I dragged my family out of bed on a frigid Saturday morning.

I suddenly look around and realize that all those parents at the informational meeting knew that they were signing up for their kid to merely "discover" and "awaken" to the water, not to learn how to swim. Do their kids "discover" the piano, too, instead of learning how to play it?

It strikes me that French parents aren't just doing a few things differently. They have a whole different view of how kids learn and of who they are. I don't just have a swimming-class problem; I seem to have a philosophical problem, too.

In the 1960s, the Swiss psychologist Jean Piaget came to America to share his theories on the stages of children's development. After each talk, someone in the audience typically asked him what he began calling the American Question. It was: How can we speed these stages up?

Piaget's answer was: Why would you want to do that? He didn't think that pushing kids to acquire skills ahead of schedule was either possible or desirable. He believed that children reach these milestones at their own speeds, driven by their own inner motors.

The American Question sums up an essential difference between French and American parents. We Americans assign ourselves the job of pushing, stimulating, and carrying our kids from one developmental stage to the next. The better we are at parenting, we think, the faster our kids will develop. In my Anglophone playgroup in Paris, some of the mothers flaunt the fact that their kids take music classes or that they go to a separate Portuguese-speaking playgroup. But often these same mothers are cagey about revealing any details of the activities, so that no one else can sign up their kids. These mothers would never admit that they're being competitive, but the feeling is palpable.

French parents just don't seem so anxious for their kids to get head starts. They don't push them to read, swim, or do math ahead of schedule. They aren't trying to prod them into becoming prodigies. I don't get the feeling that—surreptitiously or otherwise—we're all in a race for some unnamed prize. They do sign their kids up for tennis, fencing, and English lessons. But they don't parade these activities as proof of what good parents they are. Nor are they guarded when talking about the classes, like they're some sort of secret weapon. In France, the point of enrolling a child in Saturday-morning music class isn't to activate some neural network. It's to have fun. Like that swimming instructor, French parents believe in "awakening" and "discovery."

In fact, French parents have a different view of the nature of a child. When I start to read about what this view is, I keep coming across two people who lived two hundred years apart: the philosopher Jean-Jacques Rousseau, and a Frenchwoman I had never previously heard of named Françoise Dolto. They're the two great influences on French parenting. And their spirits are very much alive in France today.

The modern French idea of how to parent starts with Rousseau. The philosopher wasn't himself much of a parent (or, like Piaget, even a native Frenchman). He was born in Geneva in 1712 and didn't have an ideal childhood. His mother died ten days after he was born. His only sibling, an older brother, ran away from home. Later his father, a watchmaker, fled Geneva because of a business dispute, leaving Jean-Jacques behind with an uncle. Rousseau eventually moved to Paris, where he abandoned his own children to orphanages soon after they were born. He said this was to protect the honor of their mother, a former seamstress whom he'd hired as a servant.

None of this stopped Rousseau from publishing *Émile, or On Education*, in 1762. It describes the education of a fictional boy named Émile (who will, after puberty, meet the lovely and equally fictional Sophie). The German philosopher Immanuel Kant later compared the book's significance to that of the French Revolution. French friends tell me they read it in high school. Émile's impact is so enduring that passages and catchphrases from it are modern-day parenting clichés, like the importance of "awakening." And French parents still take many of its precepts for granted.

Émile was published during a dire time for French parenting. A Parisian police official estimated that of the 21,000 babies born in Paris in 1780, 19,000 were sent to live with wet nurses as far away as Normandy or Burgundy.[1] Some of these newborns died en route, bouncing around in the back of cold wagons. Many others died in the care of the poorly paid, overburdened wet nurses, who took on too many babies and often kept them tightly swaddled for long periods, supposedly to keep them from hurting themselves.

For working-class parents, wet nurses were an economic choice; it was cheaper to pay a nurse than to hire someone to replace the mother in the family store.[2] For upper-class mothers, however, it was a lifestyle choice. There was social pressure to be free to enjoy a sophisticated social life. The child "interferes not just in his mother's married life, but also in her pleasures," writes a French social historian.[3] "Taking care of a child was neither amusing, nor *chic.*"

Rousseau tried to upend all of this with *Émile.* He urged mothers to breastfeed their own babies. He decried swaddling, "padded bonnets," and "leading strings," the child-safety devices of his day. "Far from being attentive to protecting Émile from injury, I would be most distressed if he were never hurt and grew up without knowing pain," Rousseau wrote. "If he grabs a knife he will hardly tighten his grip and will not cut himself very deeply."

Rousseau thought children should be given space to let their development unfold naturally. He said Émile should be "taken daily to the middle of a field; there let him run and frisk about; let him fall a hundred times a day." He imagined a child who is free to explore and discover the world and let his senses gradually "awaken." "In the morning let Émile run barefoot in all seasons," he wrote. He allows the fictional Émile to read just a single book: *Robinson Crusoe.*

Until I read *Émile,* I was mystified by all the talk among French parents and educators about letting children "awaken" and "discover." One of the teachers at Bean's day care gushed at a parents' meeting that the kids go to a local gymnasium on Thursday mornings, not to exercise but to "discover" their bodies. The day care's mission statement says that kids should "discover the world, in pleasure and gaiety . . ." Another center nearby is simply called Enfance et Découverte (Childhood and Discovery). The highest compliment anyone seems to pay a baby in France is that she is *éveillée* (alert and awakened). Unlike in America, this isn't a euphemism for "ugly."

Awakening is about introducing a child to sensory experiences, including tastes. It doesn't always require the parent's active involvement. It can come from staring at the sky, smelling dinner as it's being prepared, or playing alone on a blanket. It's a way of sharpening the child's senses and preparing him to distinguish between different experiences. It's the first step toward teaching him to be a cultivated adult who knows how to enjoy himself. Awakening is a kind of training for children in how to *profiter*—to soak up the pleasure and richness of the moment.

I'm in favor of all this awakening, of course. Who wouldn't be? I'm just puzzled by the emphasis. We American parents—as Piaget discovered—tend to be more interested in having kids acquire concrete skills and reach developmental milestones.

And we tend to think that how well and how quickly kids advance depends on what their parents do. That means that parents' choices and the quality of their intervention are extremely important. In this light, baby sign language, prereading strategies, and picking the right preschool understandably seem crucial. So does the never-ending American search for parenting experts and advice.

I see this cultural difference in my little Parisian courtyard. Bean's room is filled with black-and-white flash cards, baby blocks with the ABCs printed on them, and the (now discredited) Baby Einstein DVDs that we've gladly received as gifts from American friends and family. We play Mozart constantly, to stimulate her cognitive development.

But my French neighbor Anne, the architect, had never heard of Baby Einstein. She wasn't interested when I told her about it. Anne likes to let her little girl sit and play with old toys bought at yard sales or meander around our shared courtyard.

I later mention to Anne that there is an opening at our local preschool. Bean, who is among the oldest kids in her day care, could start a year early. This would mean taking her out of day care, where I fear she isn't being sufficiently challenged.

"Why would you want to do that?" Anne asks. "There are so few years to just be a child."

A University of Texas study found that with all this awakening,

French mothers aren't trying to help their kids' cognitive development or make them advance in school. Rather, they believe that awakening will help their kids forge "inner psychological qualities such as self-assurance and tolerance of difference." Others believe in exposing children to a variety of tastes, colors, and sights, simply because doing so gives the children pleasure.[4]

This pleasure is "the motivation for life," one of the mothers says. "If we didn't have pleasure, we wouldn't have any reason to live."

In the twenty-first-century Paris of parents and children that I inhabit, Rousseau's legacy takes two apparently contradictory forms. On the one hand, there's the frolicking in the fields (or the pool). But on the other hand, there's quite strict discipline. Rousseau says that a child's freedom should be bound by firm limits and strong parental authority.

"Do you know the surest means of making your child miserable?" he writes. "It is to accustom him to getting everything. Since his desires grow constantly due to the ease of satisfying them, sooner or later powerlessness will force you, in spite of yourself, to end up with a refusal. And this unaccustomed refusal will give him more torment than being deprived of what he desires."

Rousseau says the biggest parenting trap is to think that because a child can argue well, his argument deserves the same weight as your own. "The worst education is to leave him floating between his will and yours and to dispute endlessly between you and him as to which of the two will be the master."

For Rousseau, the only possible master is the parent. He often seems to be describing the *cadre*—or frame—that is the model for today's French parents. The ideal of the *cadre* is that parents are very strict about certain things but very relaxed about most everything else.

Fanny, the publisher with two young children, tells me that before she even had kids, she heard a well-known French actor on the radio talking about being a parent. He put her ideas about the *cadre*—and the way she herself was raised—into words.

"He said, 'Education is a firm *cadre*, and inside is liberty.' I really like that. I think the kid is reassured. He knows he can do what he wants, but some limits will always be there."

Almost all the French parents I meet describe themselves as "strict." This doesn't mean that they're constantly ogres. It means that, like Fanny, they are very strict about a few key things. These form the backbone of the *cadre*.

"I tend to be severe all of the time, a little bit," Fanny says. "There are some rules I found that if you let go, you tend to take two steps backward. I rarely let these go."

For Fanny, these areas are eating, sleeping, and watching TV. "For all the rest she can do what she wants," she tells me about her daughter, Lucie. Even within these key areas, Fanny tries to give Lucie some freedom and choices. "With the TV, it's no TV, just DVDs. But she chooses which DVD. I just try to do that for everything. . . . Dressing up in the morning, I tell her, 'At home, you can dress however you want. If you want to wear a summer shirt in wintertime, okay. But when we go out, we decide.' It works for the moment. We'll see what happens when she's thirteen."

The point of the *cadre* isn't to hem in the child; it's to create a world that's predictable and coherent to her. "You need that *cadre* or I think you get lost," Fanny says. "It gives you confidence. You have confidence in your kid, and your kid feels it."

The *cadre* feels enlightened and empowering for kids. But Rousseau's legacy has a darker side, too. When I bring Bean to get her first inoculations, I cradle her in my arms and apologize to her for the pain she's about to experience. The French pediatrician scolds me.

"You don't say 'I'm sorry,'" he says. "Getting shots is part of life. There's no reason to apologize for that." He seems to be channeling Rousseau, who said, "If by too much care you spare them every kind of discomfort, you are preparing great miseries for them." (I'm not sure what Rousseau thought about suppositories.)

Rousseau wasn't sentimental about children. He wanted to make good citizens out of impressionable lumps of clay. Many thinkers continued to view babies as tabulae rasae—blank slates—for hundreds of years. Near the end of the nineteenth century, the American psychologist and philosopher William James said that to an infant, the world is "one great blooming, buzzing confusion." Well into the twentieth century, it was taken for granted that children only slowly begin understanding the world and the fact of their own presence in it.

In France, the idea that kids are second-class beings who only gradually gain status persisted into the 1960s. I've met Frenchmen now in their forties who, as children, weren't allowed to speak at the dinner table unless they were first addressed by an adult. Children were often expected to be "*sage comme une image*" (quiet as a picture), the equivalent of the old English dictum that children should be seen but not heard.

This conception of children began changing in France in the late 1960s. In March 1968, a student protest at the University of Paris, Nanterre, snowballed into a series of student and worker revolts across the country. Two months later, 11 million French workers were on strike, and President Charles de Gaulle dissolved the National Assembly.

Although the protesters had some specific financial demands, what many of them really wanted was a whole different way of life. France's religious, socially conservative, male-dominated society, in place for centuries, suddenly seemed dated. The protesters envisioned a kind of personal liberation that included different life options for women, a less rigid class hierarchy, and a daily existence that wasn't just about "*métro, boulot, dodo*" (commute, work, sleep). Eventually the French government broke up the protests, sometimes violently. But the revolt had a profound impact on French society. (France is now, for example, one of the least religious countries in Europe.)

. The authoritarian model of parenting was a casualty of 1968, too. If everyone was equal, why couldn't children speak at dinner? The pure Rousseauian model—children as blank slates—didn't suit France's newly emancipated society. And the French were fascinated by psychoanalysis. It suddenly seemed that by shutting kids up, parents might be screwing them up, too.

French kids were still expected to be well behaved and to control themselves, but gradually after 1968 they were encouraged to express themselves, too. The young French parents I know often use *sage* to mean self-controlled but also happily absorbed in an activity. "Before it was '*sage* like a picture.' Now it's '*sage* and awakened,'" explained the French psychologist and writer Maryse Vaillant, herself a member of the famous "Generation of '68."

Into this generational upheaval walked Françoise Dolto, the other titan of French parenting. French people I speak to—even those without kids—can't believe that Americans haven't heard of Françoise Dolto, or that only one of her books has ever been translated into English (it is long out of print).

In France, Dolto is a household name, a bit like Dr. Benjamin Spock used to be in the United States. The centenary of her birth was celebrated in 2008 with a flood of articles, tributes, and even a made-for-TV movie about her life. UNESCO convened a three-day conference on Dolto in Paris. Her books are for sale in practically every French bookshop.

In the mid-1970s, Dolto was in her late sixties and was already the most famous psychoanalyst and pediatrician in France. In 1976, a French radio station began broadcasting daily twelve-minute programs in which Dolto responded to listeners' letters about parenting. "Nobody imagined the immediate and lasting success" of the program, recalled Jacques Pradel, then its twenty-seven-year-old host. He describes her responses to readers' questions as "brilliance bordering on premonition." "I don't know where she got her answers," he says.[5]

When I watch film clips of Dolto from that period, I can see why she appealed to anxious parents. With her thick glasses and matronly outfits, she had the bearing of a wise grandmother. (The famous person she most resembles is Golda Meir.) And like her American counterpart, Dr. Spock, Dolto had the gift of making everything she said—even her more outrageous claims—sound like common sense.

Dolto may have looked like everyone's *grand-mère*, but her message about how to treat kids was deliciously radical and fitting for the new times. In a sort of emancipation of babies, she claimed that even infants are rational, and indeed that they understand language as soon as they're born. It's an intuitive, almost mystical message. And it's a message that ordinary French people still embrace, even if they don't all articulate it exactly. Once I read Dolto, I realize that so many of the most curious claims that I've heard French parents make, like the one that you're supposed to talk to babies about their sleep troubles, come straight from her.

Dolto's radio broadcasts made her into an almost mythic figure in France. Well into the 1980s, books containing transcripts of the broadcasts, and other conversations, were stacked like produce in French supermarkets. A whole cohort of children were known as "*Génération Dolto.*" A psychoanalyst quoted in a special Dolto-themed edition of *Télérama* magazine in 2008 recalled riding in a taxi whose driver said he never missed the radio show. "He was dumbfounded. He said, 'She talks to children like they are human beings!'"

Dolto's core message isn't a "parenting philosophy." It doesn't come with a lot of specific instructions. But if you accept that children are rational as a first principle—as French society does—then many things begin to shift. If babies understand what you're saying to them, then you can teach them quite a lot, even while they're very young. That includes, for example, how to eat in a restaurant.

The future Françoise Dolto was born Françoise Marette in 1908, into a large, well-off Catholic family in Paris. On the surface she had a charmed life: violin lessons, a cook in the kitchen, and peacocks prancing around the backyard. She was groomed to marry well.

But Françoise wasn't the discreet and obedient daughter that her parents expected. She wasn't *sage comme une image*. She was willful, outspoken, and passionately curious about the people around her. In her early letters, the young Dolto seems preternaturally aware of the troubling gap of understanding between herself and her parents. At age eight she resolved to become a "doctor of education" who intermediates between adults and children. It was a job that didn't yet exist, but that she later created.[6]

Having a profession was suddenly becoming possible for Frenchwomen. Like Simone de Beauvoir, who was also born in 1908, Françoise was part of the first generation of girls allowed to take the French *baccalauréat*, an exam at the end of high school that makes you eligible for university.

After passing *le bac*, Dolto succumbed to her parents' pressure and settled for a nursing degree. It was only when her younger brother Philippe prepared to enter medical school that her parents allowed her to begin her medical studies, too, chaperoned by him. She also entered psychoanalysis, which was then still quite unusual. Her family seemed to think this would purge Dolto of her unfeminine ambitions. In a letter to her written in 1934,[7] Dolto's father said he hoped that psychoanalysis would "help you to transform your nature, and that you will be as you say, a real woman, which will add charm to your other qualities . . ."

But it was psychoanalysis—under René Laforgue, who founded

France's first psychoanalytic institute—that instead liberated Dolto to finally become a "doctor of education." She studied both psychoanalysis and pediatrics, and trained in hospitals around France.

Unusually for a parenting expert, Dolto was apparently an excellent parent to her own three children. Her daughter Catherine writes of her parents: "They never made us do our homework, for example. However we did get bawled out, like everyone, when we had bad grades. I got detention every Thursday for bad behavior. Mom said to me, 'It's too bad for you, it's you who has detention. When you get tired of it, you'll be able to hold your tongue.'"

Dolto always maintained an unusually lucid memory of how she had seen the world as a child. She rejected the prevailing view that children should be treated as a collection of physical symptoms. (At the time, bed wetters were still attached to "peepee-stops" that released electric shocks.) Instead, she spoke to children about their lives and assumed that many of their physical symptoms had psychological origins. "And you, what do you think?" she would ask her young patients.[8]

Dolto famously insisted that older children "pay" her at the end of each session, with an object, like a stone, to emphasize their independence and accountability. This respect for children resonated strongly with Dolto's students. "She changed everything, and we, the students, wanted things to change," the psychoanalyst Myriam Szejer recalls.

Dolto's respect extended even to babies. A former student described her dealing with an upset infant who was several months old: "All of her senses on alert, totally receptive to the emotions that the baby aroused in her. It was not to console [the baby], but to understand what the baby was telling her. Or more precisely, what the baby saw." There are legendary stories about Dolto approaching previously inconsolable infants in the hospital and simply explaining to them why they were there and where their parents were. According to legend, the babies suddenly calmed down.

This isn't American-style talking to babies, where you believe that babies recognize the mother's voice or are soothed by a calming sound. Nor is it a method to teach a child to speak or to prime him to become the next Jonathan Franzen.

Rather, Dolto insisted that the content of what you say to a baby matters tremendously. She said it was crucial that parents tell their babies the truth in order to gently affirm what the babies already know.

In fact, she thought that babies begin eavesdropping on adult conversations—and intuiting the problems and conflicts swirling around them—from the womb. She envisioned (in the presonogram days) a conversation between a mother and her minutes-old baby going something like this: "You see, we were waiting for you. You're a little boy. Maybe you heard us saying that we wanted a little girl. But we're very happy that you're a little boy."

Dolto wrote that a child should be included in conversations about his parents' divorce from the age of six months. When a grandparent dies, she said that even a young child should briefly attend the funeral. "Someone in the family goes with him to say, 'Voilà, it's the burial of your grandfather.' It's something that happens in a society." For Dolto, "the child's best interest is not always what will make him or her happy, but rational understanding," wrote MIT sociologist Sherry Turkle in an introduction to Dolto's When Parents Separate. Turkle writes that what a child most needs, according to Dolto, is "a structured inner life able to support autonomy and further growth."

Dolto was criticized by some foreign psychoanalysts for relying too much on her own intuition. But inside France, parents seemed to take both an intellectual and an aesthetic pleasure in her imaginative leaps.

If Dolto's ideas ever reached English-speaking parents, they probably just sounded strange. American parents were under the sway of Dr. Spock, who was born five years before Dolto and also trained as a psychoanalyst. Spock wrote that a child can understand that he's about to have a baby brother or sister only from the age of about eighteen months. His forte was listening carefully to parents, not to babies. "Trust yourself. You know more than you think you do," is the famous opening salvo of his parenting guide *Baby and Child Care*.

For Dolto, it was children who knew more than anyone thought. Even into old age, when she was hooked to an oxygen tank, Dolto would get down on the floor with her young patients to see the world as they did. Her view from there was appealingly blunt.

"If there's no jealousy when the baby comes . . . it's a very bad sign. The older child *should* show signs of jealousy, because for him it *is* a problem, the first time that he sees everyone admiring someone younger than him," she said.

Dolto insisted that children have rational motives, even when they misbehave, and she said that it's the job of parents to listen and grasp these motives. "The child who has an unusual reaction always has a reason for having it. . . . Our task is to *understand* what has happened," she says.

Dolto gives the example of a small child who suddenly refuses to continue walking down the street. To the parent, it just seems like sudden stubbornness. But to the child, there's a reason. "We should try to understand him, and say, 'There's a reason. I don't understand, but let's think about it.' Above all, don't suddenly make a drama out of it."

In one of the centennial tributes to Dolto, a French psychoanalyst summed up Dolto's teachings this way: "Human beings speak to other human beings. Some of them are big, some of them are small. But they communicate."[9]

Spock's giant tome *Baby and Child Care* seems like it's straining to contain every possible scenario involving children, from obstructed tear ducts to (in posthumous editions) gay parenting. But Dolto's books are pocket-sized. Instead of giving lots of specific instructions, she keeps returning to a few basic principles and seems to expect that parents will think things through on their own.

Dolto agreed to do the radio broadcasts on the condition that she could answer letters from parents rather than phone calls. She thought that parents would begin to see solutions simply by writing out their problems. Pradel, the radio host, remembers: "She told me, 'you'll see, one day we'll get a letter from a person who's going to say to us, "I'm sending you these pages, but I think I already understand."'" And we received one, exactly like she predicted."

Like Spock in the United States, Dolto has been blamed in France for unleashing a wave of overly permissive parenting, especially in the 1970s and '80s. It's easy to see how her advice could be interpreted this way. Some parents surely thought that if they listened to what a child said, they then had to do what he said.

This wasn't what Dolto advocated. She thought that parents should listen carefully to their kids and explain the world to them. But she thought that this world would of course include many limits, and that the child, being rational, could absorb and handle these limits. She didn't want to upend Rousseau's *cadre* model. She wanted to preserve it. She just added a huge measure of empathy and respect for the child—something that may have been lacking in France pre-1968.

The parents I see in Paris today really do seem to have found a balance between listening to their kids and being clear that it's the parents who are in charge (even if they sometimes have to remind themselves of this). French parents listen to their kids all the time. But if little Agathe says she wants *pain au chocolat* for lunch, she isn't going to get it.

French parents have made Dolto (standing on the shoulders of Rousseau) part of their parenting firmament. When a baby has a nightmare, "You always reassure him by speaking to him," says Alexandra, who works in the Parisian day care. "I'm very much in favor of speech and language with children, even the smallest ones. They understand. For me, they understand."

The French magazine *Parents* says that if a baby is scared of strangers, his mother should warn him that a visitor will be coming over soon. Then, when the doorbell rings, "Tell him that the guest is here, take a few seconds before opening the door . . . if he doesn't cry when he sees the stranger, don't forget to congratulate him."

I hear of several cases where, upon bringing a baby home from the maternity hospital, French parents give the baby a tour of the house.[10] French parents often just tell babies what they're doing to them: I'm picking you up; I'm changing your diaper; I'm getting ready to give you a bath. This isn't just to make soothing sounds; it's to convey information. And since the baby is a person, like any other, parents are often quite polite to him. (Plus it's apparently never too early to start instilling good manners.)

The practical implications of believing that a baby or toddler understands what you say and can act on it are considerable. It means you can teach him to sleep through the night early on, to not barge into your room every morning, to sit properly at the table, to eat only at mealtimes, and to not interrupt his parents. You can expect him to accommodate—at least a little bit—what his parents need, too.

I get a strong taste of this when Bean is about ten months old. She begins pulling herself up in front of a bookcase in our living room and pulling down all the books she can reach.

This is irritating, of course. But I don't think I can stop her. Often I just pick up the books and put them back. But one morning, Simon's French friend Lara is visiting. When Lara sees Bean pulling the books down, she immediately kneels next to her and explains, patiently but firmly, "We don't do that." Then she shows Bean how to put the books back on the shelf and tells her to leave them there. Lara keeps using the French word *doucement*—gently. (After this, I start to notice that French parents say *doucement* all the time.) I'm shocked when Bean listens to Lara and obeys.

This incident revealed the enormous cultural gap between Lara and me, as parents. I had assumed that Bean was a very cute, very wild creature with a lot of potential but almost no self-control. If she occasionally behaved well, it was because of a kind of animalistic training, or just luck. After all, she couldn't talk, and didn't even have hair yet.

But Lara (who at the time was childless, but now has two well-behaved daughters) assumed that, even at ten months old, Bean could understand language and learn to control herself. She believed that Bean could do things *doucement* if she wanted to. And as a result, Bean did.

Dolto died in 1988. Some of her intuitions about babies are now being confirmed by scientific experiments. Scientists have figured out that you can tell what babies know by measuring how long they look at one thing versus another. Like adults, babies look longer at things that surprise them. Beginning in the early 1990s, research using this method has shown that "babies can do rudimentary math with objects" and that "babies have an actual understanding of mental life: they have some grasp of how people think and why they act as they do," writes Yale psychologist Paul Bloom.[11] A study at the University of British Columbia found that eight-month-olds understand probabilities.[12]

There's also evidence that babies have a moral sense. Bloom and other researchers showed six- and ten-month-old babies a sort of puppet show in which a circle was trying to roll up a hill. A "helper" character helped the circle go up, while a "hinderer" pushed it down. After the show, the babies were offered the helper and the hinderer on a tray. Almost all of them reached for the helper. "Babies are drawn to the nice guy and repelled by the mean guy," Paul Bloom explains.

Of course, these experiments don't prove that—as Dolto claims—babies understand speech. But they do seem to prove her point that, from a very young age, babies are rational. Their minds aren't a "blooming, buzzing confusion." At the very least, we should watch what we say to them.

Chapter 6

day care?

When I call my mother to tell her that Bean has been accepted into a day-care center run by the city of Paris, there's a long pause on her end of the line.

"Day care?" she asks, finally.

Friends back home are skeptical, too.

"It's just not a situation I want," sniffs a friend whose son is nine months old, about the same age Bean will be when she starts day care. "I want him to have a little more individual attention."

But when I tell my French neighbors that Bean has been accepted to the crèche, as the full-time day cares are known here, they congratulate me and practically crack open the champagne.

It's the sharpest difference between the countries I've seen so far. Middle-class mothers in the United States generally aren't fans of day care. The very words "day care" conjure images of pedophiles and howling babies in dirty, dimly lit rooms. "I want him to have a little more individual attention" is a euphemism for, "Unlike you, I actually love my child and don't want to institutionalize him." American parents who can afford it tend to hire full-time nannies, then start easing their kids into preschool when they're two or three. Those who must send their kids to day care do so warily and often full of guilt.

But middle-class French parents—architects, doctors, fellow journalists—are clawing past one another to get a spot in their neighborhood crèche, which is open five days a week, usually from eight to six. Mothers apply when they're pregnant, then harangue, cajole, and beg. Crèches are subsidized by the state, and parents are charged sliding fees based on their incomes.

"I felt that it was a perfect system, absolutely perfect," gushes my friend Esther, a French lawyer, whose daughter started at the crèche when she was nine months old. Even friends of mine who don't work try to enroll their kids in the crèche. As a distant second choice, they consider part-time day care or nannies, which are subsidized, too. (Government Web sites give all the options.)

All this gives me a kind of cultural vertigo. Will day care make my child aggressive, neglected, and insecurely attached, as the scary American headlines say? Or will she be socialized, "awakened," and skillfully looked after, as French parents assure me?

For the first time, I worry that we're taking our little intercultural experiment too far. It's one thing to start holding a fork in my left hand, and giving blank looks to strangers. It's quite another to subject my child to a potentially weird and damaging experience for the bulk of her toddlerhood. Are we going a bit too native? Bean can try foie gras, but should she try the crèche?

I decide to read up on this day care with a funny name. Why is it even called a crèche? I thought that was the name for a Nativity scene.

It turns out that the story of the French crèche began in the 1840s. Jean-Baptiste-Firmin Marbeau, an ambitious young lawyer in search of a cause to champion, was deputy mayor of Paris's first district. It was the middle of the Industrial Revolution, and cities like Paris were

teeming with women who'd arrived from the provinces to work as
seamstresses and in factories. Marbeau was charged with writing a
study of the *salles d'asile*, free nursery schools for kids aged two to six.

He was impressed. "How carefully, I said to myself, society watches
over the children of the poor!" he wrote.

But Marbeau wondered who looked after poor children between
birth and age two, while their mothers worked. He consulted the district's "poor list" and set off to visit several mothers. "At the far end
of a filthy backyard, I call out for Madame Gérard, a washerwoman.
She comes down, not wanting me to enter her home, *too dirty to be seen*
(those are her words). She holds a new-born baby on her arm, and a
child of eighteen months by the hand."

Marbeau discovered that when Madame Gérard went off to wash
laundry, she left her children with a babysitter. This cost her seventy
centimes a day, about a third of her daily wages. And the babysitter
was an equally poor woman who, when Marbeau visited, was "at her
post, watching over three young children on the floor in a shabby
room."

That wasn't bad child care by the day's standards for the poor.
Some mothers locked kids alone in apartments or tied them to bedposts for the day. Slightly older kids were often left to watch their
siblings while their mothers worked. Many very young babies still
lived at the homes of wet nurses, where conditions could be life-
threatening.

Marbeau was seized with an idea: the crèche! (The name was meant
to invoke the cozy manger in the Christmas story.) It would be all-day
care for poor children from birth to age two. Funding would come
from donations by wealthy patrons, some of whom would also help
oversee crèches. Marbeau envisioned a spartan but spotless building,
where women called nurses looked after babies and counseled mothers on hygiene and morals. Mothers would pay just fifty cents a day.
Those with unweaned infants would return twice a day to breastfeed.

Marbeau's idea struck a chord. There was soon a crèche commission to study the matter, and he set off to woo potential donors. Like
any good fund-raiser, he appealed to both their sense of charity and
to their economic self-interest.

"These children are your fellow citizens, your brothers. They are
poor, unhappy and weak: you should rescue them," he wrote in a
crèche manual published in 1845. Then he added, "If you can save the
lives of 10,000 children, make haste: 20,000 extra arms a year are not
to be disdained. Arms are work and work creates wealth." The crèche
was also supposed to give a mother peace of mind, so she could "devote herself to her work with an easy conscience."

In his manual, Marbeau instructs crèches to open from five thirty
A.M. to eight thirty P.M., to cover the typical workday for laborers. The
life Marbeau describes for mothers isn't too different from that of a
lot of working mothers I know today: "She gets up before 5 o'clock,
dresses her child, does some housework, runs to the Crèche, runs to
work . . . at 8 o'clock she hastens back, fetches her child with the day's
dirty linen, rushes home to put the poor little creature to bed, and to
wash his linen so it will be dry the next day, and every day the whole
process is repeated! . . . how on earth does she manage!"

Evidently Marbeau was quite persuasive. The first crèche opened
in a donated building on the rue de Chaillot in Paris. Two years later
there were thirteen crèches. The number continued to grow, especially
in Paris.

After World War II, the French government put crèches under the
control of the newly formed Mother and Infant Protection service
(PMI) and created an official degree program for the job of *puéricultrice*, a person who specialized in caring for babies and young children.

By the beginning of the 1960s, the French poor were less desperate,
and there were fewer of them. However, more middle-class mothers
were working, so the crèche began attracting middle-class families, too.
The number of spots nearly doubled in ten years, reaching 32,000 in

1971. Suddenly, middle-class mothers got sulky if they couldn't get a place in a crèche. It was starting to seem like an entitlement for working mothers.

All kinds of variants on the crèche opened, too. There were part-time day cares, "family" crèches where parents pitched in, and "company" crèches for employees. Guided by Françoise Dolto's insistence that babies are people, too, there was a new interest in child care that didn't merely keep kids from getting sick or treat them like potential delinquents. Soon crèches were spouting middle-class values like "socialization" and "awakening."

I first hear about the crèche when I'm pregnant, from my friend Dietlind. She's a Chicagoan who's lived in Europe since she graduated from college. (In Paris there's a whole caste of semester-abroad expatriates, who married their junior-year boyfriends or just never got around to leaving.) Dietlind is warm, speaks effortless French, and still charmingly refers to herself as a "feminist." She's one of the few people I know who's actually striving to make the world a better place. About the only thing wrong with Dietlind is that she can't cook. Her family subsists almost entirely on food from Picard, the French frozen-food chain. She once tried to serve me defrosted sushi, rice and all.

Despite this, Dietlind is a model mother. So when she tells me that her two sons, ages five and eight, attended the crèche around the corner from me, I take note. She says the crèche was excellent. Years later, she still stops by to greet the *directrice* and her sons' old teachers. The boys still talk about their crèche days with joyful nostalgia. Their favorite caregiver used to give them haircuts.

What's more, Dietlind offers to put in a good word with the *directrice*. She keeps repeating to me that the crèche isn't *fancy*. I'm not sure what this means. Does she think that I require Philippe Starck playpens? Is "not fancy" code for "dirty"?

Though I've put up a brave multicultural front for my mother, the truth is that I share some of her doubts. The fact that the crèche is run by the city of Paris seems kind of creepy. It feels like I'll be dropping off my baby at the post office, or the department of motor vehicles. I have visions of faceless bureaucrats rushing past Bean's bassinet, as she weeps. Maybe I do want "fancy," whatever that means. Or maybe I just want to look after Bean myself.

Unfortunately, I can't. I'm midway through writing the book that I was supposed to hand in before Bean was born. I took a few months off after her birth. But now my (already once extended) deadline looms. We've hired a lovely nanny, Adelyn, from the Philippines, who shows up in the morning and looks after Bean all day. The problem is, I work from home in a little alcove office. The temptation to micromanage them both—to the irritation of everyone—is irresistible.

Bean does seem to be developing a decent passive understanding of Tagalog, the main language of the Philippines. But I suspect that Adelyn often ends up speaking Tagalog to her at our local McDonald's, since each time we pass by it, Bean points and shouts. Perhaps the nonfancy crèche is a better option.

I'm also amazed that, thanks to Dietlind, we have an "in" somewhere. I'm used to being out of sync with the rest of the country. Sometimes I don't know it's a national holiday until I walk outside and find that all the shops are closed. Having Bean in a crèche would connect us more to France.

The crèche is also tantalizingly convenient. There's one across the street from our house. Dietlind's is a five-minute walk. Like those nineteenth-century washerwomen, I could pop in to breastfeed Bean and wipe her snot.

Mostly, though, it's hard to resist all this French adult peer pressure. (I'm glad they're not trying to get me to smoke.) Anne and the other French mothers in our courtyard chime in about the wonders of the crèche, too. Simon and I figure that even with our "in," our odds of actually getting in are small. So we go to our local town hall and apply for a spot.

Why are middle-class Americans so skeptical of day care? The answer has its roots in the nineteenth century, too. By the middle of the 1800s, news of Marbeau's crèches reached America, which had its own horror stories about poor kids being tied to bedposts. Curious philanthropists and social activists traveled to Paris. They were impressed. Over the following decades, charity-financed crèches opened in Boston, New York, Philadelphia, and Buffalo for the children of poor, working mothers. A few used the French name, but most were called "day nurseries." By the 1890s there were ninety American day nurseries. Many cared for the children of recent immigrants. They were supposed to keep these kids off the streets and turn them into "Americans."[1]

At the beginning of the twentieth century, there was a separate "nursery school movement" in America to create private preschools and kindergartens for children aged around two to six. These grew out of new ideas about the importance of early learning and of stimulating kids' social and emotional development. From the start, they appealed to middle- and upper-middle-class American parents.

The separate origins of day care and preschool explain why, more than a hundred years later, "day care" still has a working-class connotation in America, while middle-class parents battle to get their two-year-olds into preschool. It also explains why today's American preschools often last just a few hours a day; it's presumed that mothers of the students don't have to work, or can afford nannies.[2]

One segment of American society that isn't ambivalent about day care is the U.S. military. The Department of Defense runs America's largest day-care system, with about eight hundred child development centers—or CDCs—on military installations around the world. The centers accept kids from the age of six weeks and are typically open from six A.M. to six thirty P.M.[3]

The American military's day-care system looks remarkably like the French crèche. Operating hours wrap around the workday. Fees are scaled according to parents' combined income. The government subsidizes about half the cost. And like the French crèche, the military's day-care centers are so popular they usually have long waiting lists.

But outside the military, middle-class American parents remain ambivalent about day care.[4] This is partly an issue of nomenclature. "If you call it 'early childhood education, zero through five,' they think it's worthwhile," says Sheila Kamerman, a professor at Columbia University who's been tracking day care for decades. These days it's often simply called "child care."

Americans remain consumed by the question of how even normal day care affects a child's fragile psyche. There are headlines on whether day care causes learning delays, makes kids more aggressive, or leaves them insecurely attached to their mothers. I know American moms who quit their jobs rather than subject their kids to day care.

They are often right to worry, since the quality of American day care is extremely uneven. There are no national regulations. Some states don't require caregivers to have any training. The U.S. Department of Labor says child-care workers earn less than janitors, and that "dissatisfaction with benefits, pay, and stressful working conditions cause many to leave the industry." Annual turnover rates of 35 percent are common.

There are some good day-care centers, of course. But these can be extremely expensive, or limited to employees of certain companies. And bad centers are amply in evidence, with poor kids getting especially bad care. Other centers—usually the expensive ones—treat babyhood like a college-prep course. Perhaps to calm nervous parents, a Colorado-based company boasts that, in its centers, children under the age of one are taught "literacy."

....

French mothers are convinced that the crèche is good for their kids. In Paris, about a third of kids under the age of three go to the crèche, and half are in some kind of collective care. (There are still fewer crèches outside Paris.) French mothers do worry about pedophiles, but not at the crèche. They think kids are safer in settings with lots of trained adults looking after them, rather than being "alone with a stranger," according to a report by a national group that advocates for parents. "If she's going to be tête-à-tête with someone, I want it to be me," the mother of an eighteen-month-old at Bean's crèche tells me. The mother says if she hadn't gotten a spot in the crèche, she would have quit her job.

French mothers do worry about the anguish they'll feel when they drop off their children at a crèche for the first time. But they view this as their own separation issue. "In France parents are not afraid of sending their children to the crèche," explains Marie Wierink, a sociologist with France's Ministry of Labor. "*Au contraire*, they fear that if they cannot find a place in the crèche their child will be missing out on something."

Kids don't learn to read in a crèche. They don't learn letters or other preliteracy skills. What they do is socialize with other kids. In America, some parents mention this to me as a benefit of day care. In France, all parents do. "I knew that it was very good, it was an opening to social life," says my friend Esther, the lawyer, whose daughter entered a crèche at nine months old.

French parents take for granted that crèches are of universally high quality and that the members of their staffs are caring and highly skilled. In French parenting chat rooms, the most serious complaint I can find about a crèche is from a mother whose child was served ravioli along with moussaka, a similarly heavy dish. "I sent a letter to the crèche, and they responded to me, saying their regular chef was not there," she explains. She adds, darkly: "Let's see what happens the rest of the week."

This certainty that the crèche is good for kids erases a lot of maternal guilt and doubt. My friend Hélène, an engineer, didn't work during the first few years after her youngest daughter was born. But she was never remotely apologetic about sending the little girl to the crèche five days a week. This was in part so that Hélène could have time to herself, but also because she didn't want her daughter to miss out on the communal experience.

The main question people in France ask about day care is how to get more kids into it. Thanks to France's current baby boom, you can't run for public office in France—on the right or the left—without promising to build more crèches or expand existing ones. I read about a program to turn disused baggage areas in train stations into crèches for the children of commuters (much of the construction cost would go toward soundproofing).

Competition for the existing spots in a crèche is—as the French say—énergique. A committee of bureaucrats and crèche directors in each of Paris's twenty arrondissements convenes to dole out their available spots. In the well-heeled 16th arrondissement there are four thousand applicants for five hundred spots. In our less rarefied area in eastern Paris the odds of getting a spot are one in three.

Scrambling for a spot in a crèche is one of the initiation rituals of new parenting. In Paris, women can officially begin petitioning the town hall when they're six months pregnant. But magazines urge women to schedule a meeting with the director of their preferred crèche as soon as they have a positive pregnancy test.

Priority goes to single parents, multiple births, adoptees, households with three or more kids, or families with "particular difficulties." How to fit into this last, ambiguous category is the topic of furious speculation in online forums. One mother advises writing to town hall officials about your urgent need to return to work and your epic but ultimately failed efforts to find any other form of child care. She suggests copying this letter to the regional governor and the president of France, then requesting a private audience with the district mayor. "You go there with the baby in your arms, looking desperate, and you retell the same story as in the letter," she says. "I can assure you that this will work."

Simon and I decide to work our only angle: being foreign. In a letter attached to our crèche application, we extol Bean's budding multilingualism (she doesn't actually speak yet) and describe how her Anglo-Americanism will enrich the crèche. As promised, Dietlind talks us up to the director of the crèche that her sons went to. I meet with this woman and try to project a mix of desperation and charm. I call the town hall once a month (for some reason, as with French couples, most of the crèche courting falls to me) to remind them of our "enormous interest and need for a spot." Since I'm not French and can't vote here, I decide not to bother the president.

Amazingly, these attempts to massage the process actually work. A congratulatory letter arrives from our town hall explaining that Bean has been assigned a spot in a crèche for mid-September, when she'll be nine months old. I call Simon, triumphant: we foreigners have beaten the natives at their own game! We're amazed and giddy from the victory. But we also have the feeling that we've won a prize that we don't quite deserve and aren't even sure we want.

I still have my doubts when we take Bean to her first day of crèche. It's at the end of a dead-end street, in a three-story concrete building with a little Astroturf courtyard out front. It looks like a public school in America but with everything in miniature. I recognize some of the kids' furniture from the IKEA catalog. It's not fancy, but it's cheerful and clean.

The kids are divided by age into sections called small, medium, and large. Bean's class is in a sunlit room with play kitchens, tiny furniture, and cubbyholes full of age-appropriate toys. Attached to the room is a glassed-in sleeping area where each child has his own crib, stocked with his pacifier and stuffed-animal companion, called a *doudou*.

Anne-Marie, who'll be Bean's main caregiver, greets us. (She's the same lady who gave haircuts to Dietlind's sons.) Anne-Marie is a grandmother in her sixties, with short blond hair and a rotating collection of printed T-shirts from places her charges have traveled to. (We'll eventually bring her one attesting to her love of Brooklyn.) Employees have worked at the crèche for an average of thirteen years. Anne-Marie has been there much longer. She and most of the other caregivers are trained as *auxiliaires de puériculture*, which has no exact American equivalent.

A pediatrician and a psychologist each visit the crèche once a week. The caregivers chart Bean's daily naps and poops, and report to me about how she's eaten. They feed the kids Bean's age one at a time, with the child either on someone's lap or in a bouncy seat. They put the kids down to sleep at roughly the same time each day and claim not to wake them up. For this initial adaptation period, Anne-Marie asks me to bring in a shirt that I've worn so that Bean can sleep with it. This feels a bit canine, but I do it.

I'm struck by the confidence that Anne-Marie and the other caregivers have. They're quite certain about what children of each age need, and they're equally confident in their abilities to provide this. They convey this without being smug or impatient. My one gripe is that Anne-Marie insists on calling me "mother of Bean" rather than Pamela; she says it's too difficult to learn the names of all the parents.

Given our doubts about day care, we've compromised by enrolling Bean just four days a week, from about nine thirty to three thirty. Plenty of her classmates will be there five days a week, for much longer each day. (The crèche is open from seven thirty to six.)

As in Marbeau's day, Bean is supposed to arrive with a clean diaper. This becomes an almost Talmudic point of discussion between Simon and me. What constitutes "arrival"? If Bean poops on her way in the door, or while we're saying good-bye, who changes the offending diaper? Is it us, or the *auxiliaires*?

The first two weeks are an adaptation period, in which she stays for increasingly long periods at the crèche, with and without us. She cries a bit each time I leave, but Anne-Marie assures me that she quiets down soon after I go. Often one of the caregivers holds her up at the window facing the street so I can wave when I get outside.

If the crèche is damaging Bean, we can't tell. Pretty soon she's cheerful when we drop her off and happy when we pick her up. Once Bean has been at the crèche for a while, I begin to notice that the place is a microcosm of French parenting. That includes the bad stuff. Anne-Marie and the other caregivers are mystified that I'm still nursing Bean when she's nine months old and especially when I nurse her on the premises. They're not thrilled with my short-lived plan to drop off pumped breast milk before lunch each day, though they don't try to stop me.

But all the big, positive French parenting ideas are in evidence, too. Since there's so much agreement anyway on the best way to do things, French parents don't have to worry that the caregivers aren't following their personal parenting philosophy. For the most part, the caregivers reinforce the same schedule and habits as parents.

For example, the caregivers talk to even very young children all the time at the crèche, with what seems like perfect conviction that the children understand.[5] And there's a lot of talk about the *cadre*. At a parents' meeting, one of the teachers speaks almost poetically about it: "Everything is very *encadré*—built into a framework—the hour that they arrive and leave, for example. But inside this framework we try to introduce flexibility, fluidity and spontaneity, for the children and also for the [teaching] team."

Bean spends a lot of the day just ambling around the room, playing with whatever she wants. I'm concerned about this. Where are the

music circles and organized activities? I soon realize that all this freedom is by design. It's the French *cadre* model yet again: kids get firm
boundaries, but lots of freedom within those boundaries. And they're
supposed to learn to cope with boredom and to play by themselves.
"When the child plays, he constructs himself," Sylvie, another of
Bean's caregivers, tells me.

A mayor's report on Parisian crèches calls for a spirit of "energetic
discovery," in which the children are "left to exercise their appetite for
experimentation of their five senses, of using their muscles, of sensations, and of physical space." As kids get older they do have some
organized activities, but no one is obliged to participate.

"We propose, we don't force," another of Bean's teachers explains.
There's soothing background music to launch the kids into their naps
and a pile of books that they can read in bed. The kids gradually wake
up to their *goûter*, the afternoon snack. The crèche isn't the department of motor vehicles. It's more like Canyon Ranch.

In the playground there are few rules, also by design. The idea is to
give kids as much freedom as possible. "When they're outside, we
intervene very little," says Mehrie, another one of Bean's caregivers.
"If we intervene all the time, they go a little nuts."

The crèche also teaches kids patience. I watch as a two-year-old
demands that Mehrie pick her up. But Mehrie is cleaning up the table
where the children have just had lunch. "For the moment I'm not
free. You wait two seconds," Mehrie says gently to the little girl. Then
she turns to me and explains: "We try to teach them to wait, it's very
important. They can't have everything right away."

The caregivers speak calmly and respectfully to the kids, using the
language of rights: you have the right to do this; you don't have the
right to do that. They say this with that same utter conviction that
I've heard in the voices of French parents. Everyone believes that for
the *cadre* to seem immutable, it has to be consistent. "The prohibitions

are always consistent, and we always give a reason for them," Sylvie tells me.

I know the crèche is strict about certain things because, after a while, Bean repeats phrases she's learned. We know they're "crèche" phrases because the teachers there are her only source of French. It's like she's been wearing a wire all day, and now we get to listen to the tape. Most of what Bean repeats is in the command form, like *"on va pas crier!"* (we're not going to scream). My rhyming favorites, which I immediately begin using at home, are *"couche-toi!"* (go to sleep) and *"mouche-toi!"* (blow your nose), said when you're holding a tissue up to a child's face.

For a while Bean speaks French *only* in the command form or in these declarations of what's permissible and what isn't. When she plays "teacher" at home, she stands on a chair, wags her finger, and shouts instructions to imaginary children, or occasionally to our surprised lunch guests.

Soon, in addition to commands, Bean is coming home with songs. She often sings one that we know only as *"tomola tomola, vatovi!"* in which she sings more and more loudly with each line, while making a spinning motion with her arms. It's only later that I learn this is one of the most popular French children's songs (which actually goes *"ton moulin, ton moulin va trop vite"*), about a windmill that's going too fast.

What really wins us over about the crèche is the food, or, more specifically, the dining experience. Each Monday, the crèche posts its menu for the week on a giant whiteboard near the entrance.

I sometimes photograph these menus and e-mail them to my mother. They read like the chalkboard menus at Parisian brasseries. Lunch is served in four courses: a cold vegetable starter, a main dish with a side of grains or cooked vegetables, a different cheese each day, and a dessert of fresh fruit or fruit puree. There's a slightly modified version for each age group; the youngest kids mostly have the same foods, but pureed.

A typical menu starts with hearts of palm and tomato salad. This is followed by sliced turkey *au basilic* accompanied by rice in a Provençal cream sauce. The third course is a slice of St. Nectaire cheese with a slice of fresh baguette. Dessert is fresh kiwi.

An in-house cook at each crèche prepares lunch from scratch each day. A truck arrives several times a week with seasonal, fresh, sometimes even organic ingredients. Aside from the occasional can of tomato paste, nothing is processed or precooked. A few vegetables are frozen, but never precooked.

I have trouble imagining two-year-olds sitting through a meal like this, so the crèche lets me sit in on lunch one Wednesday, when Bean is home with a babysitter. I'm stunned when I realize how my daughter eats lunch most days. I sit quietly with my reporter's notebook while her classmates assemble in groups of four at square-toddler-sized tables. One of her teachers wheels up a cart filled with covered serving plates and bread wrapped in plastic to keep it fresh. There's a teacher at each table.

First, the teacher uncovers and displays each dish. The starter is a bright-red tomato salad in vinaigrette. "This is followed by *le poisson*," she says, to approving glances, as she displays a flaky white fish in a light butter sauce and a side dish of peas, carrots, and onions. Next she previews the cheese course: "Today it's *le bleu*," she says, showing the kids a crumbly blue cheese. Then she shows them dessert: whole apples, which she'll slice at the table.

The food looks simple, fresh, and appetizing. Except for the melamine plates, the bite-sized pieces, and the fact that some of the diners have to be prodded to say *"merci,"* I might be in a high-end restaurant.

....

Just who are the people taking care of Bean? To find out, I show up one windy fall morning at the annual entrance examination for ABC Puériculture, one of the schools that train crèche workers. There are hundreds of nervous women (and a few men) in their twenties, who are looking shyly at one another or doing last-minute practice questions in thick workbooks.

They're understandably anxious. Of the more than five hundred people who sit for this test, just thirty will be admitted to the training school. Applicants are grilled on reasoning, reading comprehension, math, and human biology. Those who advance to the second round face a psychological exam, an oral presentation, and interrogation by a panel of experts.

The thirty winners then do a year of coursework and internships, following a curriculum set by the government. They learn the basics of child nutrition, sleep, and hygiene, and practice mixing baby formula and changing diapers. They'll do additional weeklong trainings throughout their careers.

In France, working in day care is a career. There are schools all over the country with similarly rigorous entrance standards, creating an army of skilled workers to staff the crèches. Just half of caregivers at a crèche must be *auxiliaires* or have a similar degree. A quarter must have degrees related to health, leisure, or social work. A quarter are exempt from any qualifications but must be trained in-house.[6] At Bean's crèche, thirteen of the sixteen caregivers are *auxiliaires* or similar.

I start to see Anne-Marie and other caregivers at Bean's crèche as the Rhodes Scholars of baby care. And I understand their confidence. They've mastered a field and earned the respect of parents. And I'm indebted to them. During nearly three years that Bean is at the crèche, they potty-train her, teach her table manners, and give her a French immersion course.

By Bean's third year at the crèche, I suspect that the days are starting to feel long and that perhaps she's not being stimulated enough. I'm ready for her to move on to preschool. But Bean still seems to like the crèche. She chatters all the time about Maky and Lila (pronounced Lee-lah), her two best friends. (Interestingly, she's gravitated to other children of foreigners: Lila's parents are Moroccan and Japanese. Maky's dad is from Senegal.) She has definitely been socialized. When Simon and I take Bean to Barcelona for a long weekend, she keeps asking where the other children are.

The kids in Bean's section spend a lot of time running around and shouting in the Astroturf courtyard, which is stocked with little scooters and carts. Bean is usually out there when I pick her up. As soon as she spots me, she bolts over and bursts happily into my arms, shouting the news of the day.

On Bean's last day at the crèche, after the good-bye party and the clearing-out of her locker, Bean gives a big hug and kiss good-bye to Sylvie, who's been her main caregiver. Sylvie has been the model of professionalism all year. But when Bean embraces her, Sylvie begins to cry. I cry, too.

By the end of crèche, Simon and I feel that Bean has had a good experience. But we did often feel guilty dropping her off each day. And we can't help but notice the drip of alarming headlines in the American press about how day care affects kids.

Continental Europeans aren't really asking about that anymore. Sheila Kamerman at Columbia says that Europeans pretty much take for granted that high-quality day care, with small groups and warm, well-trained caregivers who have made the job a career, are good for kids. And conversely, they assume that bad day care is bad for kids.

Americans have too many misgivings about day care to take this for granted. So the U.S. government has funded the largest-ever study of how early child-care arrangements correlate with the way kids develop and behave later in life.[7]

Many of the headlines on day care in America come out of data from this giant study. One of its principal findings is that early child-care arrangements just aren't very significant. "Parenting quality is a much more important predictor of child development than type, quantity or quality of child care," explains a backgrounder. Children fared better when their parents were more educated and wealthier, when they had books and play materials at home, and when they had "enhancing experiences" like going to the library. This was the same whether the child went to day care for thirty or more hours a week, or had a stay-at-home mother.

And as I mentioned earlier, the study found that what's especially crucial is the mother's "sensitivity"—how attuned she is to her child's experience of the world. This is also true at day care. One of the study's researchers[8] writes that kids get "high-quality" day care when the caregiver is "attentive to [the child's] needs, responsive to her verbal and non-verbal signals and cues, stimulating of his curiosity and desire to learn about the world, and emotionally warm, supportive and caring."

Kids fared better with a caregiver who was sensitive, whether it was a nanny, a grandparent, or a day-care worker. "It would not be possible to go into a classroom and with no additional information, pick out which children had been in center care," the researcher writes.

I realize that what we Americans should be fretting about isn't just whether bad day care has bad outcomes (of course it does), but how unpleasant it is for kids to be in bad day care. We're so concerned about cognitive development that we're forgetting to ask whether children in day care are happy and whether it's a positive experience for them while it's happening. That's what French parents are talking about.

• • • • • • • • •

Even my mother gets used to the crèche. She starts calling it "the crèche," instead of "day care," which probably helps. The crèche certainly has benefits for us. We feel more like we're part of France, or at least part of our neighborhood. Thankfully, we put our ongoing "to stay or not to stay in Paris" conversation on pause. We can't really imagine moving someplace where we'd struggle to find decent, affordable child care. And we can see the next excuse for staying in France coming down the pike: the *école maternelle*, free public preschool, with spots for just about everyone.

Mostly, we like the French crèche because Bean likes it. She eats blue cheese, shares her toys, and plays "*tomate, ketchup*" (a French version of "duck, duck, goose"). Also, she has mastered the command form of French. She is a bit too aggressive: she likes to kick me in the shins. But I suspect that her anger comes from her father, anyway. I don't think I can blame day care for any of her faults.

Maky and Lila are still Bean's dear friends. Occasionally we even take Bean back to the crèche to stare through the gates at the children who are now playing in the courtyard. And every once in a while, out of nowhere, Bean turns to me and says, "Sylvie cried." This was a place where she mattered.

bébé au lait

Warming up to the crèche turned out to be easy. Warming up to the other mothers there wasn't. I'm aware that American-style instant bonding between women doesn't happen in France. I've heard that female friendships here start out slowly and can take years to ramp up. (Though once you're finally "in" with a Frenchwoman, you're supposedly stuck with her for life. American insta-friends can drop you anytime.)

I have managed to befriend a few Frenchwomen in the time I've now lived in Paris. But most either don't have kids or live across town. I'd just assumed that I'd also meet some other moms in my neighborhood with kids the same age as Bean. In my fantasy, we'd swap recipes, organize picnics, and complain about our husbands. That's how it happens in America. My own mother is still close with women she met in the playground when I was small.

So I'm unprepared when the French mothers at the crèche—who all live in my neighborhood and have age-appropriate kids—are practically indifferent to me. They barely say *bonjour* when we plop our toddlers down next to one another in the morning. I eventually learn the names of most of the kids in Bean's classes. But even after a year or so, I don't think any of the mothers know Bean's name. They certainly don't know mine.

This initial stage, if that's what it is, doesn't feel like a ramp up to friendship. Mothers I see several days a week at the crèche seem not to recognize me when we pass one another in the supermarket. Perhaps, as the cross-cultural books claim, they're giving me privacy; to speak would be to forge a relationship and thus create obligations. Or perhaps they're just stuck up.

It's the same at the playground. The Canadian and Australian mothers I occasionally meet there treat the playground like I do: as a place to mingle, and perhaps make friends for life. Within minutes of spotting one another, we've each revealed our hometown, marital status, and views on bilingual schooling. Soon we're mirroring like nobody's business: "You trek to Concorde to buy Grape-Nuts cereal? Me too!"

But usually it's just me and the French mothers. And they don't do "me-toos." In fact, they barely exchange glances with me, even when our kids are sparring over sandbox toys. When I try icebreakers like "How old is he?" they usually mutter a number, then eye me like I'm a stalker. They rarely ask any questions back. When they do, they turn out to be Italian.

Granted, I'm in the middle of Paris, surely one of the world's least friendly places. The sneer was probably invented here. Even people from the rest of France tell me that they find Parisians cold and distant.

I should probably just ignore these women. But I can't help it: they intrigue me. For starters, many of them look so much better than we Americans do. I drop Bean off at the crèche in the morning wearing a ponytail and whatever was on the floor next to my bed. They arrive fully coiffed and perfumed. I don't even gawk anymore when French mothers prance into the park dressed in high-heeled boots and skinny jeans, while pushing strollers with tiny newborns in them. (Moms do get a bit fatter as you get farther from central Paris.)

These mothers aren't just chic; they're also strangely collected. They don't shout the names of their children across the park or rush out with a howling toddler. They have good posture. They don't radiate that famous combination of fatigue, worry, and on-the-vergeness that's bursting out of most American moms I know (myself included). Except for the actual child, you wouldn't know that they're mothers.

Part of me just wants to force-feed these women some spoonfuls of fatty pâté. But another part of me is dying to know their secrets. Having kids who sleep well, wait, and don't whine surely helps them stay so calm. But there must be more to it. Are they secretly struggling with anything? Where's their belly fat? Are French mothers really perfect? And if so, are they happy?

After the baby is born, the first obvious difference between French and American moms is breastfeeding. For us Anglophone mothers, the length of time that we breastfeed—like the size of a Wall Street bonus—is a measure of performance. One former businesswoman in my Anglophone playgroup regularly sidles up to me and asks, faux innocently, "Oh, are you still nursing?"

It's faux because we all know that our breastfeeding "number" is a concrete way to compete with one another. A mother's score is reduced if she mixes in formula, relies too heavily on a breast-milk pump, or actually breastfeeds for too long (at which point she starts to seem like a crazed hippie).

In middle-class circles in the United States, many mothers treat infant formula as practically a form of child abuse. The fact that breastfeeding requires endurance, inconvenience, and in some cases physical suffering only increases its status.

You get bonus points from American moms for nursing in France, where breastfeeding isn't encouraged and many people find the sight of it disturbing. "The breastfeeding mother is regarded, if not as an interesting oddity, then as someone who is performing above and beyond the call of duty," explains the parenting guide published by Message, the organization for Anglophone mothers in Paris.

We expatriates exchange horror stories about French doctors who—when confronted with the occasional cracked nipple or blocked duct—blithely tell mothers to switch to formula. To combat this, Message has its own army of volunteer "breastfeeding supporters." Before I delivered Bean, one of them warned me never to hand over my baby to the hospital staff while I slept, lest they defy my instructions and give her a bottle when she cried. This woman made "nipple confusion" sound scarier than autism.

All this adversity makes Anglophone mothers in Paris feel like lactating superheroes, battling the evil doctors and strangers who would like to steal antibodies from our babies. In chat rooms, expatriate mothers list the strangest places they've nursed in Paris: inside Sacré-Coeur cathedral, on a tomb at Père Lachaise cemetery, and at a cocktail party at the Four Seasons Hotel George V. One mother says she breastfed her baby "while standing and complaining at the easyJet counter in Charles de Gaulle Airport. I sort of laid him on the counter." I pity the poor clerk.

Given our zeal, we can't fathom why French mothers barely breastfeed. About 63 percent of French mothers do some breastfeeding.[1] A bit more than half are still nursing when they leave the maternity hospital, and most abandon it altogether soon after that. Long-term nursing is extremely rare. In the United States, 74 percent of mothers do at least some breastfeeding, and a third are still nursing exclusively at four months.[2]

It's harder still for us Anglophones to understand why even a certain type of middle-class French mother—the ones who steam and puree organic leeks for their seven-month-olds and send their three-year-olds to the same African drumming classes that we do—don't breastfeed much either.

"Don't they have the same medical information we have?" one incredulous American mother asks me. Among Anglophone mothers, the reigning theories about why Frenchwomen don't nurse include: they can't be bothered; they care more about their boobs than about their babies (though apparently it's pregnancy, not breastfeeding, that stretches out breasts); and they just don't know how important it is.

Locals tell me that breastfeeding still has a peasant image, from the days when babies were farmed out to rural wet nurses. Others say that artificial-milk companies pay off hospitals, give away free samples in maternity wards, and advertise mercilessly. Olivier, who's married to my journalist friend Christine, theorizes that nursing demystifies the female breast, turning it into something utilitarian and animalistic. Just as French fathers strategically avoid a woman's "business end" during the birth, they avoid viewing the female breast when it's used for unsexy purposes.

There are small pockets of breastfeeding enthusiasts in France, and, increasingly, there's some pressure to nurse for a bit. But mostly there's little peer pressure to nurse for a long time. When my British friend Alison, who teaches English in Paris, told her doctor that she was still nursing her thirteen-month-old, she says the doctor asked, "What does your husband say? And your shrink?" *Enfant Magazine*, one of the main French glossies, says that "breastfeeding after three months is always viewed badly by one's entourage."

Alexandra, the mother of two girls who works in a crèche, tells me that she didn't give a drop of breast milk to either of her daughters. She says this without apology or guilt. She says she was thrilled that her husband, who's a fireman, wanted to help care for the girls, and that bottle-feeding them was a great way for him to pitch in. She points out that both girls are now perfectly healthy.

Alexandra adds, "It was good practice for the father to give a bottle at night. And I could sleep, and drink wine in restaurants. It wasn't so bad for *maman*."

Pierre Bitoun, a French pediatrician and longtime proponent of breastfeeding in France, says many Frenchwomen think they just don't have enough milk. Dr. Bitoun says the real problem is that French maternity hospitals often don't encourage mothers to feed their newborns every few hours. That's critical in the beginning to stimulate mothers to produce enough milk. Otherwise, a recourse to formula starts to seem inevitable. "By day three the kid has lost two hundred grams, and they say, 'Oh, you don't have enough milk, let's give him some formula, the kid is starving.' That's what happens. It's crazy."

Dr. Bitoun speaks often at French hospitals to explain the science and the benefits of breastfeeding. But "the culture is stronger than the science," he says. "Three quarters of the people I work with in hospitals don't believe that breast milk is healthier than formula. They think there's no difference. They think artificial milk is fine, or at least that's what they say to mothers to avoid making them feel guilty."

In fact, even though French children consume enormous amounts of formula, they beat American kids on nearly all measures of health. France ranks about six points *above* the developed-country average in UNICEF's overall health-and-safety ranking, which includes infant mortality, immunization rates until age two, and deaths from accidents and injury up to age nineteen. The United States ranks about eighteen points *below* the average.

French parents see no reason to believe that artificial milk is terrible or to treat breastfeeding as a holy rite. They assume that breast milk is far more critical for a baby born to a poor mother in sub-Saharan Africa than it is for one born to middle-class Parisians. "We look around and see that all the babies who drink formula are fine," says Christine, the journalist, who has two young kids. "We all drank formula, too."

I'm not so calm about it. In fact, I'm so panicked by my conversation with the breastfeeding consultant that, when I'm in the maternity hospital after Bean is born, I insist that she stay in the room with me around the clock. I wake up each time she whimpers and barely get any rest.

This suffering and self-sacrifice just seems like the natural order to me. But after a few days, I realize I'm probably the only mother in the maternity ward who's subjecting herself to this torture. The others, even the ones who are breastfeeding, hand their babies over to the nursery down the hall at night. They feel entitled to a few hours sleep.

I finally feel shattered enough to give this a try, too, even though it feels enormously indulgent. I'm immediately won over by the system, and Bean doesn't seem any worse for it. Contrary to the rumors, the nurses and *puéricultrices* who work in the nursery are more than happy to wheel her to my room whenever she needs to nurse and then take her away again.

France is probably never going to be ground zero for breastfeeding. But it does have the Protection maternelle et infantile (Mother and Infant Protection service), the same agency that oversees the crèche. This government health service has offices all over Paris that give free checkups and injections to all children until age six, even those who are in France illegally. Middle-class parents rarely use the PMI because the government insurance plan covers much of the cost of their visits to private pediatricians. (The French government is the main insurer, but most French doctors are in private practice.)

I'm reluctant to use a public clinic. Will it be impersonal? Will it be clean? One crucial fact convinces me: it will be completely free. Our local PMI office is a ten-minute walk from our house. It turns out that we can see the same doctor each time we go. There's a giant indoor playground in the immaculate waiting area. The PMI will send a *puéricultrice* to your house to check in on you and your baby when you get back from the hospital. If you get the baby blues, they've got an in-house shrink. All of this is free, too: there's not even a bill. It's worth weighing that against an ounce of breast milk.

I'm not taking any chances about breastfeeding. The American

Academy of Pediatrics says I should nurse for twelve months, so I do, practically to the day. I give Bean a final, valedictory feed on her first birthday. Sometimes I do enjoy nursing. But often I find it irritating to interrupt whatever I'm doing to rush back home for feeds or—increasingly—for a date with my electric breast pump. Mostly I forge on because of everything I've read about the health benefits and because I want to stick it to that lady in my playgroup.

All the American peer pressure to breastfeed does serve a public-health purpose: it gets breast milk into our babies' mouths. But it also makes us a little crazy. Frenchwomen can see that steamroller of anxiety and guilt coming from a few kilometers away, and they're at least trying to resist it.

Dr. Bitoun says that in his years of campaigning for breastfeeding, he's found that French mothers generally aren't won over by the health arguments involving IQ points and secretory IgA. What does persuade them to nurse, he says, is the claim that both they and the baby will enjoy it. "We know that the pleasure argument is the best—the mother's pleasure and the baby's pleasure," he says.

Many French mothers would surely like to breastfeed longer than they do. But they don't want to do it under moral duress or flaunt it at two-year-olds' birthdays. Powdered milk may be worse for babies, but it no doubt makes the early months of motherhood a lot more relaxing for French moms.

French mothers may be relaxed about not breastfeeding, but they aren't relaxed about getting back in shape after they give birth. I'm shocked when I find out that the skinny waitress at the café where I go to write most days has a six-year-old. I had taken her for a twenty-three-year-old hipster.

When I tell her about the expression "MILF" ("Mom I'd Like to Fuck"), she thinks it's hilarious. There's no French-language equivalent. In France, there's no a priori reason why a woman wouldn't be sexy just because she happens to have children. It's not uncommon to hear a Frenchman say that being a mother gives a woman an appealing air of *plenitude* (happiness and fullness of spirit).

Of course some American moms quickly shed their baby weight, too. But it's easy to find role models urging women in the other direction. A "New-Mom Makeover" fashion spread in *American Baby* magazine shows three embarrassed, still slightly chubby women smiling uncomfortably in loose-fitting dresses. They've strategically positioned their toddlers in front of their hips. The text is unapologetic: "Giving birth changes your body, and becoming a mom changes your life," it says, before singing the praises of drawstring pants.

For some American moms, there's something morally righteous about committing to motherhood at the expense of their bodies. It's like giving yourself over to a higher cause. A sports-marketing consultant from Connecticut, who has a six-month-old, tells me that a Frenchwoman showed up at her local playgroup recently and immediately asked the group, in what I imagine to be a charming Gallic accent, "Okay, *zo* how *eez* everyone losing *ze* weight?" According to the consultant, she and the other American mothers fell silent. This wasn't something they usually discussed. Sure, they would have loved to snap their fingers and knock off twenty pounds. But none of them were losing much weight. It seemed selfish to take time away from their babies to tend to their fat or even to talk too much about it.

You won't silence any rooms in Paris by asking how new mothers lose their baby weight. Just as there's enormous social pressure for women not to gain too much weight while they're pregnant, there's similar pressure to shed the weight soon after they give birth.

The sister of the sports-marketing consultant is my American friend Nancy, who lives in Paris and has a son with her French boyfriend. The two sisters, who even look alike, are a kind of social experiment. Just by virtue of where they live and who their partners are, they're facing opposite social pressures. Nancy, the sister in Paris, tells me that a few months after she gave birth, her French boyfriend began needling her to stop wearing sweatpants and to shed her spare tire. As an incentive, he offered to take her shopping for new clothes.

Nancy says she was both surprised and offended. Like her sister in Connecticut, she had imagined herself to be in a protected "mom zone," where she got a pass on her appearance for a while so she could devote herself to looking after the baby. But Nancy's French boyfriend was working from a different script. He still viewed her fully as a woman and felt entitled to the aesthetic benefits that go with that. He was equally surprised and bothered that she was willing to just give that up.

In Paris, three months seems to be the magic number: women of all ages keep telling me they "got back their *ligne*" (figure) by three months postpartum. Audrey, a French journalist, tells me over coffee that she got her figure back right away after both of her pregnancies—one of which was with twins. "Of course. It was natural," she says. "You too, no?" (I was already sitting down when she arrived at the café.)

As a foreigner who's not married to a Frenchman, I've excused myself from the three-month rule. I'm not sure I even heard about it until Bean was six months old. My body has charmingly decided to store its extra bulk around my belly and hips, giving the impression that I might be holding on to at least the placenta.

I'd surely be skinnier if I had French in-laws to needle me. It seems that just as obesity spreads through social networks, so does thinness. If everyone around you assumes that they're going to drop the extra pounds, you're more likely to actually do it. (It's also easier to lose weight if you haven't gained too much.)

To lose their baby weight, Frenchwomen seem to do a slightly more intensified version of what they do the rest of the time.

"I pay a lot of attention," is how my friend Virginie, a svelte mother of three, explains it to me over lunch one day, as I gorge on a giant bowl of Cambodian noodle soup. (Any country that France has occupied or colonized is overrepresented in cheap, delicious ethnic restaurants in Paris.)

Virginie says she never goes on a diet, known in French as a *régime*. She just pays a lot of attention, some of the time.

"What do you mean?" I ask Virginie between slurps.

"No bread," she says, firmly.

"No bread?" I repeat, incredulous.

"No bread," Virginie says, with steely, calm conviction.

Virginie doesn't mean no bread ever. She means no bread during the week, from Monday to Friday. On the weekends, and on the occasional night out during the week, she says she eats whatever she wants.

"You mean 'whatever you want' in moderation, right?" I ask.

"No, I eat whatever I want," she says, with that conviction again.

This is similar to what Mireille Guiliano prescribes in *French Women Don't Get Fat*. (Guiliano suggests taking just one day "off," and even then not overdoing it too much.) It's inspiring to see someone who's actually implementing this, evidently with great success.

Paying attention may be another example of Frenchwomen intuitively following the best science. Researchers have found that the best way to lose weight and keep it off is to carefully monitor yourself—for instance, by keeping a food diary and weighing yourself daily.[3] They have also discovered that people have more willpower when they don't rule out ever eating certain foods but rather tell themselves that they will eat those foods later[4] (such as, presumably, during the weekend).

I also like the neutral, pragmatic French formulation "paying attention" over the value-laden American one, "being good" (and its guilt-ridden, demoralizing opposites: "cheating" and "being bad"). If you've merely stopped paying attention and had some cake, it seems easier to forgive yourself and to eat mindfully again at the next meal.

Virginie says this way of eating is an open secret among women in Paris. "Everyone you see who is thin"—she draws a kind of imaginary line down her small frame—"pays very close attention." When Virginie feels like she's put on a few pounds, she pays closer attention still. (My friend Christine, the French journalist, later sums up this system very succinctly for me: "Women in Paris don't eat very much.")

Over lunch, Virginie looks me up and down, and evidently decides that I have not been paying attention.

"You drink *café crème*, don't you?" she says. *Café crème* is what Parisians call café au lait. It's a cup of steaming milk poured onto a shot of espresso, without the foam that would make it a cappuccino.

"Yes, but I use fat-free milk," I say, weakly. I do this when I'm at home. Virginie says that even fat-free milk is hard to digest. She drinks *café allongé*—lengthened coffee—which is espresso diluted with boiling water. (Filtered American coffee or tea is fine, too.) I scribble down Virginie's suggestions—Drink more water! Climb the stairs! Go for walks!—as if I'm receiving revelation.

I'm not obese. Like my friend Nancy, I'm just sort of motherly. There's no risk of Bean's getting jabbed by a hip bone when I bounce her on my lap. I have skinny aspirations, though. I've promised myself that I won't think of getting pregnant again until I finish my book and reach my target number of kilograms. (After years in France, I still don't know whether to wear a sweater when I hear the temperature in Celsius or how tall someone is when they give their height in centimeters. But I immediately know whether my weight in kilograms means I'll fit into my jeans or not.)

Of course, French mothers aren't just different because they're thin. Not all of them are, anyway. And I meet American women who fit back into their pre-pregnancy jeans by the three-month mark, too. But

I can spot these American mothers from a distance in the park just by their body language. Like me, they're hunched over their kids, setting out toys on the grass while scanning the ground for choking hazards. They're transparently given over to the service of their children.

What's different about French moms is that they get back their pre-baby identities, too. For starters, they seem more physically separate from their children. I've never seen a French mother climb a jungle gym, go down a slide with her child, or sit on a seesaw—all regular sights back in the United States and among Americans visiting France. For the most part, except when toddlers are just learning to walk, French parents park themselves on the perimeter of the playground or the sandbox and chat with one another (though not with me).

In American homes, every room in the house is liable to be overrun with toys. In one home I visited, the parents had taken all the books off the shelves in their living room and replaced them with stacks of kids' toys and games.

Some French parents store toys in the living room. But plenty don't. The children in these families have loads of playthings, but these don't engulf the common spaces. At a minimum, the toys are put away at night. Parents see doing this as a healthy separation and a chance to clear their minds when the kids go to bed. Samia, my neighbor who during the day is the extremely doting mother of a two-year-old, tells me that when her daughter goes to bed, "I don't want to see any toys. . . . Her universe is in her room."

It's not just the physical space that's different in France. I'm also struck by the nearly universal assumption that even good mothers aren't at the constant service of their children, and that there's no reason to feel bad about that.[5]

American parenting books typically tack on reminders for mothers to have lives of their own. But I frequently hear American stay-at-home mothers say they never use babysitters because they consider all child care to be *their* job.

In Paris, even mothers who don't work take for granted that they'll enroll their toddlers in part-time child care in order to have some time alone. They grant themselves guilt-free windows to go to yoga class and to get their highlights retouched. As a result, even the most harried stay-at-home moms don't show up at the park looking frazzled and disheveled, as if they're part of a separate tribe.

French women don't just permit themselves physical time off; they also allow themselves to mentally detach from their kids. In Hollywood films, you know instantly if a female character has kids. That's often what the film is about. But in the French romantic dramas and comedies I occasionally sneak out to watch, the fact that the protagonist has kids is often irrelevant to the plot. In one typical French film, *Les Regrets*, a small-town schoolteacher rekindles a love affair with her former boyfriend, who comes back to town when his mother becomes ill. During the film, we're vaguely aware that the schoolteacher has a daughter. But the little girl appears only briefly. Mostly, the movie is a love story, complete with steamy sex scenes. The protagonist isn't supposed to be a bad mother; it's just that being a mother isn't part of the story.

In France, the dominant social message is that while being a parent is very important, it shouldn't subsume one's other roles. Women I know in Paris express this by saying that mothers shouldn't become "enslaved" to their children. When Bean is born, one of the main television channels runs a talk show most mornings called *Les Maternelles*, in which experts and parents dissect all aspects of parenting. Right afterward there's another program, *We're Not Just Parents*, which covers work, sex, hobbies, and relationships.

Of course some middle-class Frenchwomen lose themselves in motherhood, just as some American mothers manage not to. But the ideals in each place are very different. I'm struck by a fashion spread in a French mothers' magazine,[6] featuring the French actress Géraldine

Pailhas. Pailhas, thirty-nine, is a real-life mother of two who's posing as different types of moms. In one photograph she's smoking a cigarette, pushing a stroller, and gazing into the distance. In another she's wearing a blond wig and reading a biography of Yves Saint Laurent. In a third, she's wearing a black evening gown and impossibly high feathered stilettos, while pushing an old-fashioned pram.

The text describes Pailhas as an ideal of French motherhood: "She is at her base the most simple expression of female liberty: happy in her role as mother, avid and curious about new experiences, perfect in 'crisis situations,' and always attentive to her children, but not chained to the concept of perfect mother, which, she assures us, 'does not exist.'"

There's something in this text, and in Pailhas's bearing, that reminds me of those French mothers who snub me in the park. In real life, they mostly aren't prancing around in Christian Louboutin heels. But like Pailhas, they signal that while they are devoted mothers, they also think about stuff that has nothing to do with their kids and enjoy moments of guilt-free *liberté*.

Pailhas of course shed her baby weight the instant her kids came out. But that inner life, which we glimpse in the photos, and which I see in those French moms at the crèche and in the park, is also required to keep her looking and feeling seductive.[7] Pailhas doesn't look like a cartoonish MILF. She just looks like a sexy, relaxed woman. I can't imagine her telling me that she's only as happy as her least-happy child.

I consult my friend Sharon, who's a Francophone Belgian literary agent married to a handsome Frenchman. She's lived all over the world with him and their two kids. Sharon immediately homes in on another thing I'm seeing in the Pailhas pictures and in the mothers all around me in Paris.

"For American women, the role of mom is very segmented, very absolute," Sharon says. "When they wear the mom 'hat,' they wear the mom clothes. When they're sexy, they're totally sexy. And the kids can see only the 'mom' part."

In France (and apparently in Belgium, too) the "mom" and "woman" roles ideally are fused. At any given time, you can see both.

the perfect mother
doesn't exist

Here's something you might not know: spending twelve hours a day at the computer, stress-eating chocolate M&Ms, does not promote weight loss.

It does, however, enable me to finish my book. And the mere presence of this book on Amazon.com jolts awake the "woman" in me. So does the book tour. I travel to New York, *sans* husband and child, to talk about the book to anyone who'll listen, and stare lovingly at it in bookstores. (One salesman has seen this behavior before. He approaches me and asks, "Are you the author?")

My real transformation happens when the book comes out in French. After years of having a semidetached presence in Paris, I'm suddenly thrust into the national conversation. The book is a journalistic study of how different cultures treat infidelity. (This was as far as I could get from financial writing, and it seemed like a salient topic to research from France.) Americans treated the book as a serious moral inquiry. The French assume that the book is meant to be amusing.

A talk show called *Le Grand Journal* invites me to come on and discuss it, live and in French. I'd vaguely noticed *Le Grand Journal*, which is broadcast five nights a week at 7:05 P.M. My French publisher—a

wizened woman in her fifties with a solid-gold Rolodex—explains that
the show is a French institution. It's a cross between *The Tonight Show*
and *Meet the Press*. Host Michel Denisot is a legendary journalist. He
and a panel of interviewers grill each guest. Everyone is witty but a bit
savage. It's like a posh French dinner party but broadcast on live TV.

My publisher is thrilled for the publicity, but she's panicked about
my French. She arranges for me to spend hours fielding practice questions in French from a businessman she knows. He seems nervous, too.
He keeps reminding me that *"affaire"* in French doesn't mean anything
extramarital; for that I need to say *aventure* or *liaison*.

By the night of the show, I'm feeling immersed and ready. I have
three cups of espresso and sit for hair and makeup. Then suddenly
I'm standing behind two giant curtains. Michel Denisot says my name,
and the curtains open. I descend the glossy white steps, Miss America–
style, then walk to a large table where Denisot and the three-person
panel are waiting for me.

I'm concentrating so hard on understanding the questions that I'm
not even nervous. Fortunately, they're mostly the questions I've practiced. How did I get the idea for the book? How does France compare
with the United States? When one of the interviewers asks me if I was
unfaithful myself while writing the book, I bat my eyes coquettishly
and say that I'm a journalist, so of course I was *très professionnelle*. The
interviewers—and the studio audience—love this.

On this high note, Denisot starts to wrap up the interview. He seems
to be making a summary statement. I stop paying close attention. My
brother, who watches a replay on the Internet, says at this point I look
visibly relieved.

Then, suddenly, I hear my name again. Denisot is formulating another question for me. He can't let it rest. It's something about
Moïse—French for Moses—and a blog. Moses had a blog? My brother
says that when the camera cuts back to me, I look petrified. I have no
idea what he's asking me.

All at once I get it: Denisot isn't saying "blog"; he's saying "*blague*," the French word for joke. He wants me to retell a joke from my book. It's the one where Moses comes down from the mount and says, "I have good news and bad news. The good news is that I got him down to ten commandments. The bad news is, adultery is still in there."

This isn't one of the questions I had practiced. On the spot, I can't think of exactly how the joke goes, and certainly not how it goes in French. How do you say "mount"? How do you say "commandment"? All I manage to say is, "Adultery's still in there!" The audience, gratefully, is still in a good enough mood to laugh. And Denisot wisely moves on to the next guest.

Despite this incident, I'm grateful to be in the working world again. It puts me in sync with French society. That's because, after boldly not breastfeeding, then reconditioning their minds and bodies, French mothers go back to work. College-educated mothers rarely ditch their careers, temporarily or permanently, after having kids. When I tell Americans that I have a child, they usually ask, "Are you working?" Whereas French people just ask, "What do you do?"

Back in the United States, I know lots of women who've stopped working to raise their kids. In France, I know exactly one. I have a vision of what my life as a stay-at-home mom would have been in France, when I ditch work one morning and take Bean to the park. Our local park was built in the nineteenth century on the site of the former palace of the Knights Templar (take that, Central Park). This may sound like *The Da Vinci Code*, but really it's quite bourgeois. You're more likely to dig up an abandoned pacifier there than a medieval relic. There's a little lake, a forged-iron gazebo, and a playground that fills up as soon as school lets out.

Bean and I are in the gazebo when I'm jolted by the sound of American English, coming from a woman with two little kids. She and I are soon exchanging life stories. She tells me that she quit her job as a fact-checker to accompany her husband on his yearlong sabbatical in

Paris. They agreed that he would do his research, while she soaked up the city and looked after the kids.

Nine months into the sabbatical, she doesn't look like someone who's been relishing the City of Light. She looks like someone who's been schlepping two toddlers back and forth to the park. She stumbles over her words a bit, then apologizes, explaining that she doesn't often speak to adults. She's heard about the playgroups organized by English-speaking moms, but says she didn't want to spend her precious time in France with other Americans. (I try not to take this personally.) She speaks excellent French, and had assumed that she'd meet some French moms and buddy around with them.

"Where are all the mothers?" she asks.

The answer, of course, is that they're at work. French mothers go back to work, in part, because they can. The high-quality crèches, subsidized shared nannies, and other child-care options all make the transition logistically possible. It's no accident that Frenchwomen are supposed to get their figures back in three months. That's roughly when they go back to the office.

French mothers also go back to work because they want to. In a 2010 survey by the Pew Research Center, 91 percent of French adults said the most satisfying kind of marriage is one in which both husband and wife have jobs. (Just 71 percent of Americans and Britons said this.)[1]

Some college-educated women I know do "four-fifths," in which they stay home with their kids on Wednesday, when there's no preschool or primary school. But the mothers I meet say they hardly know any women who opt to stay home full-time. "I know one, and she is about to divorce," says my friend Esther, the lawyer. Esther recounts this woman's story as a cautionary tale: She quit her job as a saleswoman to look after the kids. But then she was financially dependent on her husband and thus less entitled to voice her opinions.

"She was withholding her feelings and complaints, and therefore after a while the misunderstandings got worse and worse," Esther explains. She goes on to say that there are circumstances when mothers can't really work, such as when a third child arrives. But she says any break from work should be for a limited time, say until the youngest is two.

French professional women tell me that quitting work for even a few years is a precarious choice. "If tomorrow your husband is unemployed, what will you do?" asks my friend Danièle. Hélène, the engineer with three kids, says that she'd really prefer not to work and to rely on her husband's salary. But she won't quit. "Husbands can disappear," she explains.

Frenchwomen work not just for financial security but also for status. Stay-at-home moms don't have much, at least not in Paris. There's a recurring French image of a housewife sitting sullenly at a dinner party because no one wants to talk to her. "I have two friends who don't work. I feel like nobody is interested in them," Danièle tells me. She's a journalist in her early fifties with a teenage daughter. "When the kids are grown up, what is your social usefulness?"

Frenchwomen also openly question what their own quality of life would be if they looked after children all day. The French media has no problem describing this experience with cold-eyed ambivalence. One article I read says that for mothers "without a professional activity . . . the principal advantage is to see their kids grow up. But the fact of being an at-home mother brings inconveniences, notably isolation and solitude."

Since there aren't many middle-class stay-at-home moms in Paris, there also aren't many weekday playgroups, story-telling hours, or mommy-and-me classes. The ones that do exist are mostly by and for Anglophones. There's one fully French kid in our neighborhood playgroup, but he comes with his nanny. His mother, a lawyer, apparently wants the boy to be exposed to English. (I don't hear him actually speak it.) The mother shows up once, when it's her turn to host.

She has raced back from the office, wearing high heels and a business suit. She looks at us Anglophone mothers, with our sneakers and bulging diaper bags, like we're a bunch of exotic animals.

American-style parenting and its accoutrements—the baby flash cards and competitive preschools—are by now clichés. There's been both a backlash and a backlash to the backlash. So I'm stunned by what I see at a playground in New York City. It's a special toddler area with a low-rise slide and some bouncy animals, separated from the rest of the park by a high metal gate. The playground is designed for toddlers to safely climb around and fall. A few nannies are sitting French-style on benches around the perimeter, chatting and watching their charges play.

Then a white, upper-middle-class mother walks in with her toddler. She follows him around the miniature equipment, while keeping up a nonstop monologue. "Do you want to go on the froggy, Caleb? Do you want to go on the swing?"

Caleb ignores these questions. He evidently plans to just bumble around. But his mother tracks him, continuing to narrate his every move. "You're stepping, Caleb!" she says at one point.

I assume that Caleb just landed a particularly zealous mother. But then the next upper-middle-class woman walks through the gate, pushing a blond toddler in a black T-shirt. She immediately begins narrating all of her child's actions, too. When the boy wanders over to the gate to stare out at the lawn, the mother evidently decides this isn't stimulating enough. She rushes over and holds him upside down.

"You're upside down!" she shouts. Moments later, she lifts up her shirt to offer the boy a nip of milk. "We came to the park! We came to the park!" she chirps while he's drinking.

This scene keeps repeating itself with other moms and their kids.

After about an hour I can predict with total accuracy whether a mother is going to do this "narrated play" simply by the price of her handbag. What's most surprising to me is that these mothers aren't ashamed of how batty they sound. They're not whispering their commentaries; they're broadcasting them.

When I describe this scene to Michel Cohen, the French pediatrician in New York, he knows immediately what I'm talking about. He says these mothers are speaking loudly to flaunt what good parents they are. The practice of narrated play is so common that Cohen included a section in his parenting book called Stimulation, which essentially tells mothers to cut it out. "Periods of playing and laughing should alternate naturally with periods of peace and quiet," Cohen writes. "You don't have to talk, sing, or entertain constantly."

Whatever your view on whether this intensive supervision is good for kids, it seems to make child care less pleasant for mothers.[2] Just watching it is exhausting. And it continues off the playground. "We might not stay up nights worried about how to keep our whites whiter, but you can bet we're losing sleep over why little Jasper isn't yet out of diapers," Katie Allison Granju writes on babble.com. She describes a mother she knows with an MA in biology who spent the previous week—the *whole* week—teaching her child to use a spoon.

That biologist surely questioned her own sanity, too. We American mothers know that parenting this intensively has its costs. But like the parents who asked Piaget the American Question—how can we speed up the stages of a child's development?—we believe that the pace at which our kids advance hinges on the choices we make and on how actively we engage with them. So the cost of not spoon training or narrating a trip down the slide seems unacceptably high, especially when others are doing it.

The standard for how much middle-class mothers should engage with their kids seems to have risen. Narrated play and intensive spoon training are expressions of the "concerted cultivation" that the sociologist Annette Lareau observed among white and African American middle-class parents.[3]

These parents "see their children as a project," Lareau explains. "They seek to develop their talents and skills through a series of organized activities, through an intensive process of reasoning and language development, and through close supervision of their experiences in school."

My decision to live in France is arguably one giant act of concerted cultivation. My project is to make my kids bilingual, international, and lovers of fine cheese. But at least in France, I have other role models, and there are no gifted kindergartens. In America, doing "concerted cultivation" doesn't feel like a choice. To the contrary, the demands seem to have crept upward. A friend of mine, who works full-time, complained to me that she's not just expected to go to her daughter's soccer games; she's also supposed to attend *the practices*.[4]

Elisabeth, a French mother living in Brooklyn, was surprised that American parents were so invested in their children's success at sports. She writes that she had to repeatedly change the date and time of her ten-year-old's birthday party to accommodate the match schedules of his American friends. Each American mother described her own child's presence at the match as "indispensable," and claimed that without him or her, "they might lose!"[5]

The American push to excel often begins before kids can walk. I hear about a mother in New York whose one-year-old had at-home tutors in French, Spanish, and Mandarin Chinese. When her child was two, the mother dropped the French but added lessons in art, music, swimming, and some sort of math. Meanwhile the mother, who'd quit her job as a management consultant, was spending most of her time applying to two dozen preschools.

Such stories aren't just the province of a few extreme New Yorkers.

On a trip to Miami I have lunch with a particularly sane American mother I know, named Danielle. I had thought that if anyone could resist the lure of the frenetic family, she could. She's levelheaded, warm, and—in a city where people tend to closely follow trends in jewelry—decidedly nonmaterialistic. She spent part of her childhood in Italy, speaks three languages, and is generally comfortable in her own skin. She also has an MBA and a résumé full of high-powered marketing jobs.

Danielle dislikes overzealous parenting. She's horrified by a mother in her neighborhood whose four-year-old son already takes tennis, soccer, French, and piano lessons. Danielle says this mother is extreme, but simply having her around makes everyone anxious.

"You start thinking: This kid's doing all that stuff. How is my kid going to compete? And then you have to check yourself and say: That's not the point. We don't want him competing with someone like that."

Nevertheless, Danielle has found herself sliding into a practically nonstop schedule with her own four kids (the youngest are twins). In a typical week her seven-year-old, Juliana, has soccer on Tuesday and Thursday afternoons, Communion class on Wednesday, Brownies every other Thursday (after soccer), and a playdate on Fridays. Once Juliana gets home, she has two hours of homework.

"Last night she had to write a folk tale, she had to write a mini-essay on how Martin Luther King changed America, and she had to study for a Spanish test," Danielle says.

Recently Juliana said she wanted to take an after-school ceramics class, too. "And me, feeling guilty because there's no art at the school, said 'okay, let's do ceramics.' The only day she had free was Monday." Juliana's whole week is now booked. And Danielle has three other kids.

"The logistics of making sure everyone gets to where they need to be at the correct time has been the best use of the skills I acquired in Operations Management class in business school," she says.

Danielle acknowledges that she could simply cut out all these activities, except for soccer (her husband is the coach). But what would her kids do at home? She says there'd be no other children around in the neighborhood, since they're all out doing activities, too.

The net result is that Danielle hasn't gone back to work. "I always thought that when my kids got to elementary school I could get a full-time job again," she says. Then she apologizes and rushes off to her car.

The fact that the French state provides and subsidizes child care certainly makes life easier for French mothers. But when I get back to France, I'm struck by how French mothers make their own lives a lot easier, too. The French equivalent of a playdate is that I drop off Bean at her friend's house, then I leave. (My Anglophone friends assume I'll stay the whole time.) French parents aren't curt; they're practical. They correctly assume that I have other stuff to do. I sometimes stay for a cup of coffee when I return for the pickup.

It's the same at birthday parties. American and British mothers expect me to stick around and socialize, often for several hours. No one ever says it, but I think part of why we're there is to make sure our kids are comforted and okay.

But by the time a child is three, French birthday parties are drop-offs. We're supposed to trust that our kids will be okay without us. Parents are usually invited to come back at the end for a glass of champagne and some hobnobbing with the other moms and dads. Simon and I are thrilled whenever we get invitations: it's free babysitting, followed by a cocktail party.

In France, there's an expression for mothers who spend all their free time schlepping their kids around: *maman-taxi*. This isn't a compliment. Nathalie, a Parisian architect, tells me that she hires a babysitter to bring her three kids to all their activities on Saturday mornings. She and her husband go out to lunch. "When I'm there I give them 100 percent, but when I'm off, I'm off," Nathalie tells me.

Virginie, my diet guru, gets together most mornings with a group of moms from her son's elementary school. I join the group one morning and mention extracurricular activities. The temperature at the table immediately rises. Virginie sits up and speaks for the group. "You have to leave kids alone, they need to be a bit bored at home, they must have time to play," she says.

Virginie and her friends aren't slackers. They have college degrees and nice résumés. They're devoted mothers. Their homes are full of books. Their kids take lessons in fencing, guitar, tennis, piano, and wrestling. But most just choose one activity per school term.

One of the moms at the café, a pretty, zaftig publicist (like me, she's trying to "pay more attention"), says she stopped sending her kids to tennis lessons, or anything else, because she found the lessons "constraining."

"Constraining for whom?" I ask.

"Constraining for me," she says.

She explains: "You bring them and you wait for an hour, then you have to go back and pick them up. For music you have to make them practice at night. . . . It's a waste of time for me. And the children don't need it. They have a lot of homework, they have the house, they have other games at the house, and there are two of them so they can't get bored. They're together. And we go away every weekend."

I'm struck by how these small decisions and assumptions make daily life different for French mothers. When they have moments to spare, French mothers pride themselves on being able to detach and relax. At the hairdresser, I tear out an article from an issue of French *Elle* in which a mother says that she loves taking her two boys to the old-fashioned merry-go-round near the Eiffel Tower.

"While Oscar and Léon try to catch the wooden rings . . . I spend thirty minutes in pure relaxation. I usually turn off my cell phone and I just space out while I'm waiting for them . . . it's like a deluxe baby-sitter!" I know that merry-go-round well. I usually spend my half hour there waiting to wave at Bean each time she comes around.

It's no coincidence that so many French mothers seem to parent this way. The let-them-be principle comes straight from Françoise Dolto, the patron saint of French parenting. Dolto very clearly argued for leaving a child alone, safely, to muddle about and figure things out for herself.

"Why does a mother do everything for her child?" Dolto asks in *The Major Stages of Childhood*, a collection of her remarks. "He's so content to deal with things himself, to pass the morning getting dressed by himself, to put on his shoes, so happy to put on his sweater backwards, to get tangled up in his pants, to play, to rummage around in his corner. So he doesn't go to the market with his mother? Well, too bad, or even better!"

On Bastille Day, I take Bean to the grassy field in our neighborhood park. It's filled with parents and their young kids. I'm not narrating Bean's play, but I don't really expect to have a chance to read the three-week-old magazine that I've brought along for myself, along with a giant sack of books and toys for her. I spend a lot of the day helping her play with the toys and reading to her.

On the next blanket over is a French mother. She's a thin, auburn-haired woman who's chatting with a girlfriend while her year-old daughter plays with, well, not much of anything. The mother seems to have brought just one ball to amuse her daughter for the entire afternoon. They have lunch, and then the little girl plays with the grass, rolls around a bit, and checks out the scene. Meanwhile, her mother has a full adult conversation with her friend.

It's the same sun and the same grass. But I'm having an American picnic and—*voilà*—she's having a French one. Not unlike those mothers back in New York, I'm trying to cheer Bean on to the next stage of development. And I'm willing to sacrifice my own pleasure to do that. The French mom—who looks as though she could buy a fancy handbag if she wanted to—seems content to let her daughter "awaken" all by herself. And her little girl evidently doesn't mind at all.

All this goes a long way toward explaining the mysteriously calm air of French mothers I see all around me. But it still doesn't tell the whole story. There's a crucial missing piece. That ghost in the French mothering machine is, I think, how Frenchwomen cope with guilt.

Today's American mothers spend much more time on child care than parents did in 1965.[6] To do so, they have cut back on housework, relaxing, and sleeping. Nevertheless, today's parents believe they should be spending even more time with their kids.

The result is enormous guilt. I see this when I visit Emily, who lives in Atlanta with her husband and their eighteen-month-old daughter. After I've been with Emily for a few hours, it dawns on me that she has said "I'm a bad mother" a half-dozen times. She says it when she caves in to her daughter's demand for extra milk or when she doesn't have time to read her more than two books. She says it again when she's trying to make the little girl sleep on a schedule and to explain why she occasionally lets her cry a bit at night.

I hear other American moms say "I'm a bad mother," too. The phrase has become a kind of verbal tic. Emily says "I'm a bad mother" so often that, though it sounds negative, I realize that she must find the phrase soothing.

For American mothers, guilt is an emotional tax we pay for going to work, not buying organic vegetables, or plopping our kids in front of the television so we can surf the Internet or make dinner. If we feel guilty, then it's easier to do these things. We're not just selfish. We've "paid" for our lapses.

Here, too, the French are different. French mothers absolutely recognize the temptation to feel guilty. They feel as overstretched and inadequate as we Americans do. After all, they're working while bringing up small children. And like us, they often aren't living up to their own standards as either workers or parents.

The difference is that French mothers don't valorize this guilt. To the contrary, they consider it unhealthy and unpleasant, and they try to banish it. "Guilt is a trap," says my friend Sharon, the literary agent. When she and her Francophone girlfriends meet for drinks, they remind one another that "the perfect mother doesn't exist . . . we say this to reassure each other."

The standards are certainly high for French moms. They're supposed to be sexy, successful, and have a home-cooked meal on the table each night. But they try not to add guilt to their burden. My friend Danièle, the French journalist, coauthored a book called *The Perfect Mother Is You* (*La mère parfaite, c'est vous*).

Danièle still remembers dropping off her daughter at her crèche at five months old. "I felt sick to leave her, but I would have felt sick to stay with her and not work," she explains. She forced herself to face down this guilt and then let it go. "Let's just feel guilty and go on living," she told herself. Anyway, she adds, reassuring both of us, "The perfect mother doesn't exist."

What really fortifies Frenchwomen against guilt is their conviction that it's unhealthy for mothers and children to spend all their time together. They believe there's a risk of smothering kids with attention and anxiety, or of developing the dreaded *relation fusionnelle*, where a mother's and a child's needs are too intertwined. Children—even babies and toddlers—get to cultivate their inner lives without a mother's constant interference.

"If your child is your only goal in life, it's not good for the child," Danièle says. "What happens to the child if he's the only hope for his mother? I think this is the opinion of all psychoanalysts."

This separation can go too far. When French Justice Minister Rachida Dati went back to work five days after giving birth to her daughter, Zohra, there was a collective gasp from the French press. In a survey by the French edition of *Elle* magazine, 42 percent of respondents described Dati as "too careerist." (There was less controversy about the fact that Dati was a forty-three-year-old single mother, and that she wouldn't name the father.)

When we Americans talk about work-life balance, we're describing a kind of juggling, where we're trying to keep all parts of our lives in motion without screwing up any of them too badly.

The French also talk about *l'équilibre*. But they mean it differently. For them, it's about not letting any one part of life—including parenting—overwhelm the rest. It's more like a balanced meal, where there's a good mix of proteins, carbohydrates, fruits, vegetables, and sweets. In that sense, the "careerist" Rachida Dati had the same problem as stay-at-home moms: a life too heavily weighted toward one element.

Of course, for some French mothers, *l'équilibre* is just an ideal. But at least it's a calming ideal. When I ask my Parisian friend Esther, who works full time as a lawyer, to assess herself as a mother, she says something that I find breathtaking in its simplicity and lack of neurotic tension. "In general I don't doubt whether I'm good enough, because I really think I am."

Inès de la Fressange isn't an ordinary Frenchwoman. In the 1980s she was Karl Lagerfeld's muse and main model at Chanel. Then de la

Fressange was asked to be the new face of Marianne, the symbol of the French Republic, who appears on stamps and on busts in town halls. Past Mariannes have included Brigitte Bardot and Catherine Deneuve. De la Fressange and Lagerfeld parted ways after she accepted. He allegedly said he didn't want to "dress a monument."

Now in her early fifties, de la Fressange is still a doe-eyed, languid brunette whose long legs don't seem to fit under café tables. She's had her own eponymous fashion label and occasionally still walks the runway. In 2009, readers of *Madame Figaro* voted her the best embodiment of the Parisian woman.

De la Fressange is also a mother. Her two equally leggy and photogenic daughters have already launched their own fashion and modeling careers. De la Fressange used to make light of her own charms by calling herself the "swarthy asparagus." She says she's an imperfect mother, too. "I forget about morning yoga, and I always put on lip gloss and mascara in the car mirror. What's important is to rid yourself of guilt over not being perfect."

Obviously, de la Fressange isn't typical. But she incarnates a certain French ideal about striking a balance. In an interview with *Paris Match*, she describes how, three years after her husband died, she met a man at a ski resort in the French Alps, where she was vacationing with her daughters. The man just happened to be the head of one of France's most important magazines and a recipient of the French Legion of Honor. (De la Fressange wasn't Lagerfeld's muse for nothing.)

She put off her suitor for a few months, explaining that she wasn't ready. But as she tells *Paris Match*, "Finally, it was me who called him to say, 'Okay, I'm a mother and a working girl, but also a woman.' For the girls, I thought it was good to have a mother in love."

Chapter 9

caca boudin

When Bean is about three, she starts using an expression I've never heard before. At first I think it's *caca buddha*, which sounds like it could be vaguely offensive to my Buddhist friends (as in English, *caca* is a French kid's term for poop). But after a while I realize she's saying *caca boudin* (pronounced caca booh-dah). *Boudin* means sausage. My daughter is going around shouting—if you'll pardon my French—"poop sausage."

Like all good curse words, *caca boudin* is versatile. Bean shouts it gleefully when she's running through the house with her friends. She also uses it to mean "whatever," "leave me alone," and "none of your business." It's an all-purpose retort.

Me: What did you do at school today?

Bean: *Caca boudin.* (snortle)

Me: Would you like some more broccoli?

Bean: *Caca boudin!* (hysterical laughter)

Simon and I aren't sure what to make of *caca boudin*. Is it rude or cute? Should we be angry or amused? We don't understand the social context, and we have no childhood experience of our own in France to draw on. To be safe, we tell her to stop saying it. She compromises by continuing to say it, but then adding, "We don't say *caca boudin*. It's a bad word."

Bean's budding French does have perks. When we go back to America for Christmas, my mother's friends keep asking her to pronounce the name of her hairdresser, Jean-Pierre, with her Parisian accent. (Jean-Pierre has given her a pixie haircut that they coo is oh-so-French, too.) Bean is happy to sing, on demand, some of the dozens of French songs she's learned in school. I'm amazed the first time she opens a present and says, spontaneously, *oh la la!*

But it's becoming clear that being bilingual is more than just a party trick or a neutral skill. As Bean's French improves, she's starting to bring home not just unfamiliar expressions but also new ideas and rules. Her new language is making her into not just a French speaker but into a French person. And I'm not sure I'm comfortable with that. I'm not even sure what a "French person" is.

The main way that France enters our house is through school. Bean has started *école maternelle*, France's free public preschool. It's all day, four days a week, except for Wednesdays. Maternelle isn't compulsory, and kids can go part-time. But pretty much every three-year-old in France goes to maternelle full time and has a similar experience there. It's France's way of turning toddlers into French people.

The maternelle has lofty goals. It is, in effect, a national project to turn the nation's solipsistic three-year-olds into civilized, empathetic people. A booklet for parents from the education ministry explains that in maternelle kids "discover the richness and the constraints of the group that they're part of. They feel the pleasure of being welcomed and recognized, and they progressively participate in welcoming their fellow students."

Charlotte, who's been a teacher at maternelle for thirty years (and still charmingly has the kids call her *maîtresse*—teacher or, literally, mistress), tells me that in the first year the kids are very egotistical. "They don't realize that the teacher is there for everyone," she says. Conversely, the pupils only gradually understand that when the teacher speaks to the group, what she's saying is also intended for each of them individually. Kids typically do activities of their choosing in groups of three or four, at separate tables or parts of the classroom.

To me, maternelle seems like art school for short people. During Bean's first year the walls of her classroom are quickly covered in the students' drawings and paintings. Being able to "perceive, feel, imagine, and create" are goals of maternelle, too. The children learn to raise their hands *à la française*, with one finger pointed up in the air.

I was worried about enrolling Bean. The crèche was a big romper room. Maternelle is a bit more like school. The classes are big. And I've been warned that parents get very little information on what goes on. One American mom tells me she stopped asking her daughter's teacher for feedback after the teacher eventually explained, "If I don't say anything, that means she's fine." Bean's first-year teacher is a glum woman whose only comment about Bean, the entire year, is that she's "very calm." (Bean adores this teacher and loves her classmates.)

And despite all the painting and drawing, there's a lot of emphasis on learning to follow instructions. Bean's first year, I'm jarred to see that the whole class usually paints exactly the same thing. One morning there are twenty-five identical yellow stick figures with green eyes hanging up in the classroom. As someone who can't write anything without a deadline (or two), I recognize the need for some constraints. But seeing all those nearly identical pictures is unsettling. (Bean's second-year artwork is more free-form.)

It takes me a while to realize that in Bean's classroom the first year, there isn't even an alphabet on the wall alongside all the artwork. At a meeting for parents, no one mentions reading. There's more fuss about feeding lettuce to the classroom's tank of escargots (tiny ones, not to be eaten).

In fact, as I'll discover, kids aren't taught to read in maternelle, which lasts until the year they turn six. They just learn letters, sounds, and how to write their own names. I'm told that some kids pick up reading on their own, though I couldn't say which ones, since their parents don't mention it. Learning to read isn't part of the French curriculum until the equivalent of first grade, the year that kids turn seven.

This relaxed attitude goes against my most basic American belief that earlier is better. But even the most upwardly mobile parents of Bean's school friends aren't in any rush. "I prefer that they don't spend time learning to read now," Marion, herself a journalist, tells me. She and her husband say that at this stage it's much more important for children to learn social skills, how to organize their thoughts, and how to speak well.

They're in luck. While reading isn't taught at maternelle, speaking definitely is. In fact, it turns out that the main goal of maternelle is for kids of all backgrounds to perfect their spoken French. A booklet for parents produced by the French government says this French should be "rich, organized, and comprehensible to others" (that is, they need to speak it much better than I do). Charlotte, the teacher, tells me that children of immigrants typically enter maternelle in September speaking bare-bones French or none at all. By March, they're usually competent if not fluent.

The French logic seems to be that if children can speak clearly, they can also think clearly. In addition to polishing their spoken grammar, the government's booklet says a French child learns to "observe, ask questions, and make his interrogations increasingly rational. He learns to adopt a point of view other than his own, and this confrontation with logical thinking gives him a taste of reasoning. He becomes capable of counting, of classifying, ordering, and describing . . ." All those philosophers and intellectuals I see pontificating on evening television in France apparently began their analytical training in preschool.

I'm grateful for the maternelle. I haven't forgotten that my friends back in the United States—even if they're not buying baby-literacy DVDs—are battling to get their kids into private preschools that can cost twelve thousand dollars a year for just half-day sessions. I meet a mother from New Jersey who drives fifty minutes to drop off her twin daughters at their preschool. By the time she gets home, she has enough time to shower and toss in some laundry before she has to go pick them up. It's not just the well-off who are overwhelmed by child-care costs. In a study showing how much money an American couple with two young kids needs for basic economic security, child care is the top expense.[1]

The French maternelle is far from perfect. Teachers effectively have tenure, whether they're any good or not. There are chronic funding problems and the occasional shortage of places. Bean's class has twenty-five kids, which feels like quite a lot but isn't even the maximum. (There's a teacher's assistant who helps with supplies, bathroom runs, and general wrangling.)

On the plus side, the only thing I regularly pay for at maternelle is lunch. (The cost is on a sliding scale ranging from thirteen cents to five euros per day, based on parents' income.) The school is a seven-minute walk from our house. And the maternelle makes it very easy for mothers to work. It's in session from 8:20 to 4:20, four days a week. For another small fee there's a "leisure center" on the premises that can look after kids until the early evening and all day on Wednesdays. The leisure center is also open on many school holidays and during much of the summer, when they take the kids to parks and museums.

Maternelle is clearly a big part of what's turning my little American girl into a French person. It's even making me more French. Unlike at the crèche, the other parents immediately take an interest in Bean and by association in me. They now seem to view our family as part of the cohort that they'll be traveling all through school with (whereas after the crèche, the kids scattered to different schools). A few of the mothers from Bean's class have little babies and are out on maternity leave. When I pick up Bean from school and bring her to the park across the street, I sit with some of these women while our kids play. Gradually, we're even invited over to their homes for birthday parties, afternoon *goûters*, and dinners.

While the maternelle brings us all more into French life, it also makes us realize that French families observe social codes that we don't. After a dinner at the home of my friend Esther and her husband, who have a daughter Bean's age, Esther becomes agitated because the little girl won't come out of her room to say good-bye to us. Esther finally marches into the the girl's room and drags her out.

"*Au revoir*," the four-year-old says, meekly. Esther is soothed.

Of course I'd been making Bean say the magic words, "please" and "thank you." But it turns out that in French there are four magic words: *s'il vous plaît* (please), *merci* (thank you), *bonjour* (hello), and *au revoir* (good-bye). Please and thank you are necessary, but not nearly sufficient. *Bonjour* and *au revoir*—and *bonjour* in particular—are crucial. I hadn't realized that learning to say *bonjour* is a central part of becoming French.

"Me, my obsession is that my children know to say *merci*; *bonjour*; *bonjour, madame*," Audrey Goutard, the French journalist with three kids, tells me. "From the age of one, you can't imagine, I said it to them fifteen times a day."

For some French parents, a simple *bonjour* isn't enough. "They should say it with confidence, it's the first part of a relationship," another mother tells me. Virginie, the skinny stay-at-home mom, demands that her kids heighten the politeness by saying *"bonjour, monsieur"* and *"bonjour, madame."*

My friend Esther insists on *bonjours* at the threat of punishment. "If she doesn't say *bonjour,* she stays in her room, no dinner with guests," Esther explains. "So she says *bonjour.* It's not the most sincere *bonjour,* but it's the repetition, I'm hoping."

Benoît, a professor and father of two, tells me there was a family crisis when he took his kids to stay with their grandparents. His three-year-old daughter would wake up grumpy and didn't want to say *bonjour* to her grandfather until she'd had breakfast. She finally compromised by agreeing to say *pas bonjour, Papi* (not "good morning, Grandpa") to him on the way to the table. "He was happy with that. In a way, she was acknowledging him," Benoît explains.

Adults are supposed to say *bonjour* to one another, too, of course. I think tourists are often treated gruffly in Parisian cafés and shops partly because they don't begin interactions with *bonjour,* even if they switch to English afterward. It's crucial to say *bonjour* upon climbing into a taxi, when a waitress first approaches your table in a restaurant, or before asking a salesperson if the pants come in your size. Saying *bonjour* acknowledges the other person's humanity. It signals that you view her as a person, not just as someone who's supposed to serve you. I'm amazed that people seem visibly put at ease after I say a nice solid *bonjour.* It signals that—although I have a strange accent—we're going to have a civilized encounter.

In the United States, a four-year-old American kid isn't obliged to greet me when he walks into my house. He gets to skulk in under the umbrella of his parents' greeting. And in an American context, that's supposed to be fine with me. I don't need the child's acknowledgment because I don't quite count him as a full person; he's in a separate kids' realm. I might hear all about how gifted he is, but he never actually speaks to me.

When I'm at a family luncheon back in the United States, I'm struck that the cousins and stepcousins at the table, who range in age from five to fourteen, don't say anything at all to me unless I pry it out of them. Some can only muster one-word responses to my questions. Even the teenagers aren't used to expressing themselves with confidence to a grown-up they don't know well.

Part of what the French obsession with *bonjour* reveals is that, in France, kids don't get to have this shadowy presence. The child greets, therefore he is. Just as any adult who walks into my house has to acknowledge me, any child who walks in must acknowledge me, too. "Greeting is essentially recognizing someone as a person," says Benoît, the professor. "People feel injured if they're not greeted by children that way."

These aren't just social conventions; they're a national project. In a meeting for parents at Bean's school, her teacher says that one of the school's goals is for students to remember the names of adults (Bean calls her teachers by their first names) and to practice saying *bonjour, au revoir,* and *merci* to them. The booklet by the French government says that in maternelle kids are supposed to show their grasp of "civility and politeness," including "greeting the teacher at the beginning and the end of the day, responding to questions, thanking the person who helps him, and not cutting someone off when they're speaking."

French children don't always succeed in saying *bonjour*. Often there's a little ritual in which the parent pushes the child to say it ("Come say *bonjour!*"). The adult who's being greeted waits a beat and then tells the parent, in a friendly way, not to worry about it. This seems to satisfy the obligation, too.

Making kids say *bonjour* isn't just for the benefit of grown-ups. It's also to help kids learn that they're not the only ones with feelings and needs.

"It avoids selfishness," says Esther, who dragged out her daughter—

an adorable, doted-on only child—to say good-bye to me. "Kids who ignore people, and don't say *bonjour* or *au revoir*, they just stay in their bubble. Since parents are dedicated to them already, when will they get the sense that they are there to give, not just to receive?"

Saying "please" and "thank you" puts children in an inferior, receiving role. An adult has either done something for them or the child is asking the adult to do something. But *bonjour* and *au revoir* put the child and the adult on more equal footing, at least for that moment. It cements the idea that kids are people in their own right.

I can't help thinking that letting an American kid slink in the door without greeting me could set off a chain reaction in which she then jumps on my couch, refuses to eat anything but plain pasta, and bites my foot while I'm having dinner. If she's exempt from that first rule of civility, she—and everyone else—will be quicker to assume that she's exempt from many other rules, too, or that she's not capable of following these rules. Saying *bonjour* signals to the child, and to everyone else, that she's capable of behaving well. It sets the tone for the whole interaction between adults and children.

Parents acknowledge that greeting someone is in some ways an adult act. "I don't think it's easy to say hello," says Denise, a medical ethicist with two girls, ages seven and nine. But Denise says it fortifies kids to know that their greeting matters to the adult. She explains: "I think the child who doesn't say *bonjour* cannot really feel confident."

Neither can the child's parents. That's because saying *bonjour* is also a strong marker of upbringing. Kids who don't say the French magic words risk being slapped with the label *mal élevé*—badly brought up.

Denise says her younger daughter had a friend over who shouted quite a lot and jokingly called Denise *chérie*—darling. "I told my husband, I will not invite him back," she tells me. "I don't want my child to play with children who are badly brought up."

Audrey Goutard, the journalist, has written a book called *Le Grand Livre de la Famille*, in which she tries to upend some French parenting conventions. But even Goutard doesn't dare question the importance of *bonjour*. "Honestly, in France, a child who arrives somewhere and doesn't say *bonjour, monsieur*; *bonjour, madame* is a child that one rejects," she tells me. "A six-year-old who doesn't look up from the TV when you come in, at a friend's house . . . I'm going to say that he is 'badly raised.' I won't say that it's normal.

"We're a society with a lot of codes. And this code, if you don't follow it, you're excluded from society. It's as stupid as that. So you give [your kids] less of a chance to be integrated, to meet people. I say in my book that it's better that your kids know this code."

Yikes. I'd vaguely noticed French kids saying *bonjour*. But I hadn't realized how much rests on it. It's the sort of signifier that having nice teeth is in the United States. When you say *bonjour*, it shows that someone has invested in your upbringing and that you're going to play by some basic social rules. Bean's cohort of three- and four-year-olds has already had several years' worth of *bonjours* drilled into them. Bean hasn't had any. With only "please" and "thank you" in her arsenal, she's at just 50 percent. She might have already earned the dreaded label "badly brought up."

I try to appeal to the tiny anthropologist in her by explaining that *bonjour* is a native custom she has to respect.

"We live in France, and for French people it's very important to say *bonjour*. So we have to say it, too," I say. I coach her in the elevator before we arrive at birthday parties and at visits to the homes of French friends.

"What are you going to say when we walk in?" I ask anxiously.

"*Caca boudin*," she says.

Usually when we walk in, she says nothing at all. So I go through the ritual of, very publicly, telling her to say *bonjour*. At least I'm acknowledging the convention. Maybe I'm even instilling the habit.

One day while Bean and I are walking to her school, she spontane-

ously turns to me and says, "Even if I'm shy, I have to say *bonjour*."
Maybe it's something she picked up in school. Anyway, it's true. And
it's good that she knows it. But I can't help worrying that she's internalizing the rules a bit too much. It's one thing to play at being French.
It's quite another to really go native.

Although I'm ambivalent about Bean growing up French, I'm thrilled
that she's growing up bilingual. Simon and I speak only English to her.
And at school, she speaks only French. I'm sometimes astonished that
I've given birth to a child who can effortlessly pronounce phrases like
carottes rapées and *confiture sur le beurre*.

I had thought that young kids just "pick up" languages. But it's
more like a long process of trial and error. A few people tell me that
Bean's French still has an American twang. And though Bean has never
lived outside the Paris ring road, thanks to us she evidently radiates
some kind of Americanness. When I take her to her Wednesday-
morning music class one day (the babysitter usually takes her), I discover that the teacher has been speaking to Bean in pidgin English,
though she speaks French to all the other children. Later, a dance
teacher tells the class of little girls, in French, to lie down flat on the
floor "*comme une crêpe*"—like a crepe. Then she turns to Bean and says,
"*comme un* pancake."

At first, even I can tell that Bean is making lots of mistakes in
French and coming up with some bizarre constructions. She usually
says the English "for" instead of its French equivalent, "*pour*." And
she knows only the vocabulary that she's learned in the classroom,
which doesn't really equip her to talk about cars or dinner. One day
she suddenly asks me, "*Avion* is the same as airplane?" She's figuring
it out.

I'm not sure which mistakes come from being bilingual and which come from being three or four years old. One day in the metro, Bean leans into me and says, "You smell like *vomela*." This turns out to be a combination of "vomit" and "Pamela."

A minute later Bean leans into me again.

"What do I smell like now?" I ask.

"Like college," she says.

At home, some French expressions edge out the English ones. We start saying *coucou* instead of "peekaboo," and *guili-guili* when we tickle her, instead of "coochi coochi coo." Bean doesn't play hide-and-seek, she plays *cache-cache*. We put our garbage in the *poubelle*; her pacifier is a *tétine*. No one in our household farts, they make *prouts* (rhymes with "roots").

By the spring of Bean's first year in maternelle, friends tell me that her American twang is gone. She sounds like a genuine *Parisienne*. She's become so confident in French that I overhear her joking around with friends, in French, in an exaggerated American accent (probably mine). She likes to mix up the two accents on purpose, and decides that the French word for "sprinkles" must be "shpreenkels."

Me: How do you say *d'accord* in English?

Bean: You know! [sounding like an Alabaman] Dah-kord.

My father finds the idea of having a "French" grandchild charming. He tells Bean to call him *grand-père*. Bean doesn't even consider doing this. She knows he's not French. She just calls him Grandpa.

At night Bean and I look at picture books. She's excited and re-lieved to confirm that, as with "airplane," certain words in French and English refer to the same thing. When we read the famous line in the Madeline books, "Something is not right!" she translates it into col-loquial French: *"Quelque chose ne va pas!"*

Although Simon has an English accent, Bean's English sounds mostly American. I'm not sure if that's my influence or Elmo's. The other Anglophone kids we know in Paris all have their own accents. Bean's friend with a dad from New Zealand and a mother who's half-Irish sounds full-on British. A boy with a Parisian mother and a Californian dad sounds like a French chef from 1970s American television. The little boy around the corner with a Farsi-speaking father and an Australian mom just sounds like a creaky Muppet.

In English, Bean occasionally emphasizes the wrong syllables of words (the second syllable of "salad," for example). And she sometimes puts English sentences into a French word order ("Me, I'm not going to have an injection, me") or translates literally from French to English ("Because it's like that!"). She tends to say "after" when what she means is "later." (In French they're the same word, *après*.)

Sometimes Bean just doesn't know how native English speakers talk. In a weird appropriation of all the Disney princess DVDs she's been watching, when she wants to know if something looks good on her, she simply asks, "Am I the fairest?" These are all small things. There's nothing that a summer at an American sleepaway camp won't fix.

Another French word that infiltrates our English vocabulary is *bêtise* (pronounced beh-teeze). It means a small act of naughtiness. When Bean stands up at the table, grabs an unauthorized piece of candy, or pitches a pea on the floor, we say that she's "doing a *bêtise*." *Bêtises* are minor annoyances. They're bad, but they're not that bad. The accumulation of many of them may warrant a punishment. But just one *bêtise* on its own probably doesn't.

We've appropriated the French word because there's no good English translation of *bêtise*. In English, you wouldn't tell a child that he's committed a "small act of naughtiness." We tend to label the kid rather than the crime, by telling him that he's being naughty, misbehaving, or just "being bad."

These phrases don't really show the severity of the act. Of course, in English, I know the difference between hitting the table and hitting a person. But being able to label an offense as a misdemeanor—a mere *bêtise*—helps me, as a parent, to respond appropriately. I don't have to freak out and crack down every time Bean does something wrong or challenges my authority. Sometimes it's just a *bêtise*. Having this word calms me down.

I acquire much of my new French vocabulary not just from Bean but from the many French kids' books we somehow end up owning, thanks to birthday parties, impulse purchases, and neighbors' garage sales. I'm careful not to read to Bean in French if there's a native speaker within earshot. I can hear my American accent and the way I stumble over the odd word. Usually I'm trying so hard not to mispronounce anything too egregiously that I grasp the story line only on the third reading.

I soon notice that French and English kids' books and songs aren't just in different languages. Often, they have very different story lines and moral messages. In the American books there's usually a problem, a struggle to fix the problem, and then a cheerful resolution. The spoon wishes that she were a fork or a knife but eventually realizes how great it is to be a spoon. The boy who wouldn't let the other kids play in his box is then excluded from the box himself and realizes that all the kids should play in the box together. Lessons are learned, and life gets better.

It's not just the books. I notice how deliriously hopeful I sound when I sing to Bean about how if you're happy and you know it clap your hands, and, when we're watching a DVD of the musical *Annie*, how the sun'll come out tomorrow. In the English-speaking world, every problem seems to have a solution, and prosperity is just around the corner.

The French books I read to Bean start out with a similar structure. There's a problem, and the characters struggle to overcome that problem. But they seldom succeed for very long. Often the book ends with the protagonist having the same problem again. There is rarely a moment of personal transformation, when everyone learns and grows.

One of Bean's favorite French books is about two pretty little girls who are cousins and best friends. Eliette (the redhead) is always bossing around Alice (the brunette). One day Alice decides she can't take it anymore and stops playing with Eliette. There's a long, lonely stand-off. Finally Eliette comes to Alice's house, begging her pardon and promising to change. Alice accepts the apology. A page later, the girls are playing doctor and Eliette is trying to jab Alice with a syringe. Nothing has changed. The end.

Not all French kids' books end this way, but a lot of them do. The message is that endings don't have to be tidy to be happy. It's a cliché about Europeans, but you can see it in the morals of Bean's French stories: Life is ambiguous and complicated. There aren't bad guys and good guys. Each of us has a bit of both. Eliette is bossy, but she's also lots of fun. Alice is the victim, but she also seems to ask for it, and she goes back for more.

We're to presume that Eliette and Alice keep up their little dysfunctional cycle, because, well, that's what a friendship between two girls is like. I wish I had known that when I was four, instead of finally figuring it out in my thirties. Writer Debra Ollivier points out that American girls pick the petals off daisies saying, "He loves me, he loves me not." Whereas little French girls allow for more subtle varieties of affection, saying, "He loves me a little, a lot, passionately, madly, not at all."[2]

Characters in French kids' books can have contradictory qualities. In one of Bean's Perfect Princess books, Zoé opens a present and declares that she doesn't like it. But on the next page, Zoé is a "perfect princess" who jumps up and says *merci* to the gift giver.

If there were an American version of this book, Zoé would probably overcome her bad habits and morph fully into the perfect princess. The French book is more like real life: Zoé continues to struggle with both sides of her personality. The book tries to encourage princesslike habits (there's a little certificate at the end for good behavior) but takes for granted that kids also have a built-in impulse to do *bêtises*.

There is also a lot of nudity and love in French books for four-year-olds. Bean has a book about a boy who accidentally goes to school naked. She has another about a romance between the boy who accidentally pees in his pants and the little girl who lends him her pants while fashioning her bandana into a skirt. These books—and the French parents I know—treat the crushes and romances of preschoolers as genuine.

I get to know a few people who grew up in France with American parents. When I ask whether they feel French or American, they almost all say that it depends on the context. They feel American when they're in France and French when they're in America.

Bean seems headed for something similar. I'm able to transmit some American traits, like whining and sleeping badly, with little effort. But others require a lot of work. I begin picking off certain American holidays, based mainly on the amount of cooking each one requires. Halloween is a keeper. Thanksgiving is out. Fourth of July is close enough to Bastille Day (July 14) that I sort of feel like we're celebrating both. I'm not sure what constitutes classically "American" food, but I am strangely adamant that Bean should like tuna melts.

Making Bean feel a bit American is hard enough. On top of that, I'd also like her to feel Jewish. Though I put her on the no-pork list at school, this apparently isn't enough to cement her religious identity. She keeps trying to get a grip on what this strange, anti-Santa label means and how she can get out of it.

"I don't want to be Jewish, I want to be British," she announces in early December.

I'm reluctant to mention God. I fear that telling her there's an omnipotent being everywhere—including, presumably, in her room—

would terrify her. (She's already afraid of witches and wolves.) Instead, in the spring, I prepare an elegant Passover dinner. Halfway through the first benediction, Bean begs to leave the table. Simon sits at the far end with a sullen, "I told you so" look. We slurp our matzo-ball soup, then turn on some Dutch football.

Hanukah is a big success. The fact that Bean is six months older probably helps. So do the candles and the presents. What really wins over Bean is that we sing and dance the hora in our living room, then collapse in a dizzy circle.

But after eight nights of this, and eight carefully selected presents, she's still skeptical.

"Hanukah is over, we're not Jewish anymore," she tells me. She wants to know whether Father Christmas—aka the *"Père Noël"* she's been hearing about in school—will be coming to our house. On Christmas Eve, Simon insists on setting out shoes with presents in front of our fireplace. He claims he's loosely following the Dutch cultural tradition, not the religious one (the Dutch put out shoes on December fifth). Bean is ecstatic when she wakes up and sees the shoes, even though the only thing in them is a cheap yo-yo and some plastic scissors.

"Père Noël doesn't usually visit the Jewish children, but he came to our house this year!" she chirps. After that, when I pick her up at school, our conversations usually go something like this:

Me: What did you do at school today?

Bean: I ate pork.

As long as we're foreign, it's not a bad idea to be native English speakers. English is, of course, the language du jour in France. Most Parisians under forty can speak it at least passably. Bean's teacher asks me and a Canadian dad to come in one morning to read some English-language books out loud to the kids in Bean's class. Several of Bean's friends take English lessons. Their parents coo about how lucky Bean is to be bilingual.

But there's a downside to having foreign parents. Simon always reminds me that, as a child in Holland, he cringed when his parents spoke Dutch in public. I'm reminded of that when, at the year-end concert at Bean's preschool, parents are invited to join in for a few songs. Most of the other parents know the words. I mumble along, hoping that Bean doesn't notice.

It's clear that I will have to compromise between the American identity I'd like to give Bean and the French one she is quickly absorbing. I get used to her calling Cinderella *Cendrillon* and Snow White *Blanche-Neige*. I laugh when she tells me that a boy in her class likes *Speederman*—complete with a gutteral "r"—instead of Spider-Man. But I draw the line when she claims that the seven dwarfs sing "Hey ho," as they do in the French voice-over. Some things are sacred.

Luckily, it turns out that bits of Anglophone culture are irresistibly catchy.

As I'm walking Bean to school one morning, through the glorious medieval streets of our neighborhood, she suddenly starts singing "The sun'll come out, tomorrow." We sing it together all the way to school. My hopeful little American girl is still in there.

I finally decide to ask some French adults about this mysterious word, *caca boudin*. They're tickled that I'm taking *caca boudin* so seriously. It turns out that it is a swear word, but one that's just for little kids. They pick it up from one another around the time that they start learning to use the toilet.

Saying *caca boudin* is a little bit of a *bêtise*. But parents understand that that's the joy of it. It's a way for kids to thumb their noses at the world and to transgress. The adults I speak to recognize that since children have so many rules and limits, they need some freedom, too. *Caca boudin* gives kids power and autonomy. Bean's former teacher Anne-Marie smiles indulgently when I ask her about *caca boudin*. "It's part of the environment," she explains. "We said it when we were little, too."

That doesn't mean that children can say *caca boudin* whenever they want. The parenting guide *Votre Enfant* suggests telling kids they can say bad words only when they're in the bathroom. Some parents tell me they ban such words from the dinner table. They don't forbid kids from saying *caca boudin*; they teach them to wield it appropriately.

When Bean and I visit a French family in Brittany, she and their little girl, Leonie, stick out their tongues at the little girl's grandmother. The grandmother immediately sits them down for a talk about when it's appropriate to do such things.

"When you're alone in your room you can. When you're alone in the bathroom you can. . . . You can go barefoot, stick out your tongue, point at someone, say *caca boudin*. You can do all that, when you're by yourself. But when you're at school, *non*. When you're at the table, *non*. When you're with Mommy and Daddy, *non*. In the street, *non*. *C'est la vie*. You must understand the difference."

Once Simon and I learn more about *caca boudin*, we decide to lift our moratorium on it. We tell Bean that she can say it, but not too much. We like the philosophy behind it and even occasionally say it ourselves. A curse word just for kids: How quaint! How French!

In the end, I think the social complexities of *caca boudin* are too subtle for us to master. When the father of one of Bean's school friends comes to fetch his daughter at our house one Sunday afternoon after a playdate, he hears Bean shouting *caca boudin* as she runs down the hall. The father, a banker, looks at me warily. I'm sure he mentions the incident to his wife. His daughter hasn't been back to our house since.

Chapter 10

double entendre

So I finished my book. And for about fifteen glorious minutes before breakfast one morning, I'm within a hundred grams of my target weight. I'm all ready to be pregnant.

And yet, I'm not.

Everyone around me is. There seems to be a last gasp of fertility among my friends who are, like me, in their late thirties. Getting pregnant with Bean was a bit like having a pizza delivered. You want one? Phone up and get one! It worked on the first try.

But this time, there's no pizza. As the months go by, I feel the age gap between Bean and her theoretical, possibly counterfactual sibling widening. I don't feel like I have many months to spare. If I don't have the second baby soon, the third will become physically impossible.

My doctor tells me that my cycle has become too long. She says the egg shouldn't be sitting on the shelf so long before it breaks through to reach a possible mate. She prescribes Clomid, which makes me release more eggs, upping the odds that one will stay fit enough. Meanwhile, more friends call me with their wonderful news: they're pregnant! I'm happy for them. Really, I am.

After about eight months, I get the name of an acupuncturist specializing in fertility. She has long black hair and a storefront in a low-end Parisian business district. (Most cities have one "Chinatown"; Paris has five or six.) The acupuncturist studies my tongue, sticks some needles in my arms, and asks the length of my cycle.

"That's too long," she says, explaining that the egg is withering on the shelf. She writes me a prescription for a liquid potion that tastes like tree bark. I drink it dutifully. I don't get pregnant.

Simon says he'd be happy with just one kid. Out of respect for him, I consider this possibility for about four seconds. Something primal is driving me. It doesn't feel Darwinian. It feels like a carbohydrate high. I want more pizza. I go back to my doctor and tell her I'm ready to up the ante. What else has she got?

She doesn't think we need to go all the way to in vitro fertilization. (France's national insurance pays for up to six rounds of IVF for women under age forty-three.) Instead, she teaches me to inject myself in the thigh with a drug that will force me to ovulate earlier in my cycle, so the egg won't have time to wither. For this to work, I have to take the shot on day fourteen. And in a primitive twist, just after taking the shot, I must have sex.

It turns out that at the next fourteen-day point, Simon will be in Amsterdam for work. For me, there's no question of waiting another month. I book a babysitter for Bean, and arrange to meet Simon in Brussels, which is about halfway between Amsterdam and Paris. We plan to have a leisurely dinner and then retire to our hotel room. At the very least, it'll be a nice escape. He'll return to Amsterdam the next morning.

On day fourteen, there's a massive storm and a freak rail-service breakdown in western Holland. Just as I arrive at the Brussels train station around six P.M., Simon calls to say that his train has been halted in Rotterdam. It's unclear which trains—if any—will leave from there. He might not get to Brussels tonight. He'll call me back. As if on cue, it starts to rain.

I've carried the injection in a portable cooler with a cold pack that lasts only a few hours. What if I get caught in a hot train? I dash into a convenience store at the station, buy a bag of frozen peas, and shove them inside the cooler.

Simon calls back to say there's a train leaving Rotterdam for Antwerp. Can I meet him in Antwerp? On the giant overhead screen I see that there's a train leaving Brussels for Antwerp in a few minutes. In a scene where *The Bourne Identity* meets *Sex and the City*, I grab my pea-wrapped syringe and bolt up to the platform.

I'm in the rain, about to board the train to Antwerp, when Simon calls again. "Don't get on!" he shouts. He's on a train bound for Brussels.

I take a taxi to our hotel, which is cozy and warm and decked out for Christmas with a giant tree. I should be grateful just to be there, but the first room the bellhop brings me to doesn't quite have the conception vibe I'm looking for. He leads me to another room on the top floor, with a slanted ceiling. This one seems like a good place to procreate.

While I wait for Simon to arrive I take a bath, put on a robe, then calmly jab myself with the syringe. I realize I wouldn't make a bad junkie. I hope, however, that I'll make an even better mother of two.

A few weeks later, I'm in London for work. I buy a pregnancy test at a pharmacy. Then I buy a bagel at a deli, for the sole purpose of using its dingy basement bathroom to take the test. (Okay, I also eat the bagel.) To my amazement, the test is positive. I call Simon while I'm pulling my suitcase to a meeting. He immediately starts choosing nicknames. Since the baby was conceived in Brussels, maybe we'll call him "Sprout"?

Simon comes with me to an ultrasound a month later. I lie back on the table watching the screen. The baby looks wonderful: heartbeat, head, legs. Then I notice a dark spot off to the side.

"What's that?" I ask the doctor. She moves the wand over a bit. Suddenly another little body pops onto the screen, with its own heartbeat, head, and legs.

"Twins," she says.

This is one of the best moments of my life. I feel like I've been given an enormous gift: two pizzas. It also seems like a very efficient way for a woman in her late thirties to breed.

When I turn to look at Simon, I realize that the best moment of my life may be the worst moment of his. He appears to be in shock. For once, I don't want to know what he's thinking. I'm giddy from the idea of twins. He's blown over by the enormity of it.

"I'll never be able to go to a café again," he says. Already he foresees the end of his free time.

"You could get one of those home espresso makers," the doctor suggests.

My French friends and neighbors congratulate us on the news. They treat the reason I'm having twins as none of their business. The Anglophones I know are generally less discreet.

"Were you surprised?" a mother in my playgroup asks, when I announce the news. When I offer an unrevealing "yes," she tries again: "Well, was your doctor surprised?"

I'm too busy to be bothered. Simon and I have decided that what we really need isn't a better coffee maker, it's a larger apartment. (Our current one has just two small bedrooms.) This seems even more urgent when we discover that the babies are both boys.

I trek out to see several dozen apartments, all of which are either too dark, too expensive, or have long, scary hallways leading to tiny kitchens. (Apparently in the nineteenth century, it wasn't chic to smell food while the servants were cooking it.) The real-estate agents always boast that the place I'm about to see is "very calm." This seems to be a prized quality in both French apartments and French children.

All the focus on real estate keeps me from worrying too much about the pregnancy. I think I've also absorbed the French idea that there's no need to track the formation of each fetal eyebrow. (Though there are quite a few eyebrows in there to worry about.) I do briefly indulge in some twin-specific angst, like about the babies being born prematurely. But mostly the health system does the worrying for me. Because it's twins, I get extra doctor's visits and sonograms. At each visit, the handsome radiologist points out "Baby A" and "Baby B" on the screen, then makes the same bad joke: you're not obliged to keep those names. I flash him my best microsmile.

This time around, it's Simon who's anxious—about himself, not the babies. He treats each cheese plate as if it's his last. I revel in all the attention. Despite the free IVF, twins are still a novelty in Paris. (I'm told that doctors often implant just one or two embryos.) Within a few weeks, I'm visibly pregnant. By six months, it looks like I'm about to deliver. Even some maternity clothes are too tight. Soon it's clear even to young children that there's more than one baby in there.

I also study up on the nomenclature. In French, twins aren't called identical or fraternal. They're called *vrais* or *faux*—real or fake. I get used to telling people that I'm waiting for two fake twin boys.

I needn't have worried about my fake boys coming out early. At nine months pregnant, I have two full-sized babies inside of me, each weighing nearly as much as Bean did. People point at me from café tables. And I can no longer climb stairs.

"If you want an apartment, go find one," I tell Simon. Less than a week later, after seeing exactly one apartment, he does. The apartment is old, even for Paris. It has no hallways, and a triple-wide sidewalk in front. It needs a lot of work. We buy it. The day before I give birth, I meet with an architect to plan the renovations.

. . . .

The private hospital where I delivered Bean was small and spotless, with an around-the-clock nursery, endless fresh towels, and steak and foie gras on the room-service menu. I barely had to change a diaper.

I've been warned that the public maternity hospital where I'm planning to deliver the twins will be a less rarefied experience. The medicine is excellent at French public hospitals, but the service is supposedly no-frills. They give you a list of things to bring to the birth, which includes diapers. There's no customizing with birth plans, bathtubs, and "walking epidurals." They don't give the baby a chic little hat. People keep saying "conveyor belt" to describe the efficient but impersonal experience.

I opt for Hôpital Armand-Trousseau because it's a ten-minute taxi ride from our house and it's equipped to handle complications with twins. (I later learn that it's attached to the children's hospital where Françoise Dolto did her weekly rounds.) I don't want to give birth in a bathtub anyway. And I figure that when the moment comes, I'll just use my New York chutzpah to customize things. I point out to Simon that we're already enjoying economies of scale: they're going to deliver our two babies for the price of one.

When I go into labor, the epidural isn't optional. The doctor puts me in a sterile operating room, so he can do a C-section instantly if necessary. I'm flat on my back, my legs locked into a retro 1950s harness, surrounded by strangers in shower caps and surgical masks. I ask several times for someone to put pillows under my back, so I can see what's happening. No one even responds. Eventually, in a small concession, someone shoves a folded sheet under me, which just makes me more uncomfortable.

As soon as active delivery starts, my French evaporates. I can't understand anything the doctor says, and I can only speak English. This must have happened before, because a midwife immediately begins interpreting between me and the doctor. Maybe she's summarizing, or maybe her English isn't great. But she mostly just says "push" and "don't push."

When the first baby emerges, the midwife hands him to me. I'm captivated. Here is Baby A at last! We're just getting acquainted when the midwife taps me on the shoulder.

"Excuse me, but you must deliver the other baby," she says, taking Baby A to an undisclosed location. I realize, right then, that having twins is going to be complicated.

Nine minutes later, Baby B emerges. I say a quick hello, and then they whisk him away, too. In fact, soon almost everyone is gone— Simon, the babies, and most of the enormous medical team. I'm still on my back, paralyzed from the waist down. My legs are up in the harness, spread wide apart. On a stainless-steel table in front of me are two red placentas, each the size of a human head. Someone has decided to open the dividing curtains that were the walls of my room, so now anyone who walks past has a bull's-eye view of my five-minutes-post-twins crotch.

The only person still with me is the anesthesia nurse, who also isn't thrilled about being left behind. She decides to mask her irritation by making small talk: Where am I from? Do I like Paris?

"Where are my babies? When can I see them?" I ask. (My French has reappeared.) She doesn't know. And she's not allowed to leave me to find out.

Twenty minutes pass. No one comes for us. Perhaps because of the hormones, none of this bothers me. Though I'm grateful when the nurse finally uses surgical tape to put up a little modesty cloth between my knees. After that, she no longer wants to chat. "I hate my job," she says.

Eventually someone wheels me into a recovery room, where I re-

unite with Simon and the babies. We take pictures, and for the first
and only time I attempt to nurse both boys at once.

An orderly wheels us to the room where the boys and I will be staying for the next few days. A boutique hotel it's not. It's more like a
Motel 6. There's a skeletal staff to help out, and a nursery that's open
from about one to four A.M. Because I have an older child and am thus
deemed unable to mess up too badly, the staff leaves me practically on
my own. At mealtimes someone brings in plastic trays with a parody
of hospital food: limp French fries, chicken nuggets, and chocolate
milk. It takes me a few days to realize that none of the other mothers
are eating this: there's a communal refrigerator down the hall, where
they store groceries.

Simon is home looking after Bean, so most of the time I'm alone
with the boys, who howl for hours at a stretch. I usually wedge one
between my legs, in some approximation of a hug, while I try to
nurse the other. With the constant blur of noise and body parts, it
feels like there are more than two of them. When I finally get them
both to sleep, after hours of wailing and drinking, Simon shows up.
"It's so peaceful in here," he says. I try not to think about the fact that
my belly looks like a giant mound of flesh-colored Jell-O.

Amid all this, we have to name the boys (the city of Paris gives you
three days. By day two, an angry bureaucrat marches into your hospital room holding a clipboard). Simon asks only that "Nelson" is somewhere in the mix, after his hero Nelson Mandela. Mostly he's worried
about selecting the perfect nicknames. He wants to call one boy Gonzo
and the other Chairman. I have a thing for contiguous vowels and am
considering calling them both Raoul.

We settle on Joel—whom we'll only ever call Joey—and Leo, who
defies all attempts at nicknames. They're the most fraternal twins I've
ever seen. Joey looks like me, except with platinum-blond hair. Leo is
a swarthy little Mediterranean man. If they weren't exactly the same

size and constantly together, you wouldn't guess that they were related. I'll later find that a good tip-off that someone has no interest in babies is if they ask whether the boys are identical.

After four long days, we're allowed to leave the hospital. Being at home with the boys is only marginally easier. In the early evenings, they wail for hours. Both wake up all through the night. Simon and I each pick a baby before we go to sleep and are responsible for that one the whole night. We each angle to pick the "better" baby, but who that is keeps changing. Anyway, we haven't yet moved into the larger apartment, so we're all sleeping in the same room. When one baby wakes up, everyone else does, too.

It still feels like there are more than two of them. I never thought I'd dress twins alike, but I'm suddenly tempted to do so just to create a little bit of order, at least visually, like making kids at a tough school wear uniforms.

Amazingly, I still find time to be neurotic. I'm obsessed with the idea that we've given the boys the wrong names, and that I should go back to the town hall and switch them. I spend my few leisure minutes ruminating on this.

Then comes the small matter of the circumcisions. Most French babies aren't circumcised. Mostly, just Jews and Muslims do this. Because it's August in Paris, even the mohels, who do ritual circumcisions, are on vacation. We wait for one who's been recommended (a man who is reassuringly both a mohel and a pediatrician) to come back.

Unlike the birth, the circumcision isn't two for the price of one. There isn't even a package discount. Before the little ceremony, I confess to the mohel that I fear I've given the boys the wrong names and that I may need to switch them. He doesn't offer me any spiritual advice. But being French, he explains that the bureaucracy I'd need to go through to do this would be labyrinthine and excruciating. Somehow this information, plus the consecration of the circumcisions, erases my doubt. After the ceremony, I never worry about their names again.

Thankfully, my mother has arrived from Miami. She, Simon, and I spend most of our time in the living room, holding the boys. One day a woman rings the doorbell. She explains that she's a psychologist from the PMI office in our neighborhood. She says that she pays house calls to all mothers of twins, which I think is a tactful way of saying that she wants to make sure I'm not having a breakdown. A few days later, a midwife from the same PMI stops by and stands with me as I'm changing Joey's diaper. His poop, she declares, is "excellent." I take that to be the official view of the French state.

We're able to put some of what we've learned about French parenting to use on the boys. We slowly nudge them onto the national meal plan, with four feeds a day. From the time they're a few months old, except for the *goûter*, they never snack.

Unfortunately, we don't get to try out The Pause on them. Having newborn twins who don't even have a room of their own—and an older child who's just a few feet away—makes it difficult to try out anything.

So once again, we suffer. After about a month of almost no sleep, Simon and I are zombies. We fall back on our Filipina nanny and her network of cousins and friends. We eventually have four different women to help us, on shifts covering practically twenty-four hours a day. We're bleeding cash, but at least we're sleeping a bit. I start to view mothers of multiples as a persecuted minority, like Tibetans.

Both boys have trouble breastfeeding. So I spend a lot of time upstairs in my bedroom, bonding with my electric breast pump. Bean eventually figures out that she can spend time alone with me if she sits with me while I pump. She learns to assemble the bottles and receptacles, as if she's putting together a rifle. She does a great impression of the *wapa wapa* sound the pump makes.

Most of the time, I look like a stunned animal. I come downstairs to deliver my bottles of milk, or send Bean down with them and go back to sleep. There are so many babysitters around that I feel more like a supporting cast member than a lead actress. I'm convinced the boys don't know that among all these women, I'm their mother. I must seem detached, because at one point a friend grabs me by the shoulders, stares me in the eye, and asks whether I'm okay. This isn't easy for her; she's quite a bit shorter than me.

"I'm okay, but I'm running out of money," I say. I spend so much time singing "Silent Night" to the boys—more as a command than a lullaby—that one of the babysitters asks me if I've become a Catholic.

Meanwhile, our renovations are under way. Between pumping sessions, I dash over to inspect the new apartment. I meet with the head of the building association, an economist in his sixties, to discuss whether we can leave our double stroller in the vestibule downstairs. He won't commit.

"The previous owners were excellent neighbors," he says.

"Excellent how?" I ask.

"They were very discreet," he says.

The apartment itself is an enormous mess. I had approved the plans one night, while the boys were having a full-on fit of colic. It's suddenly clear that I had no idea how to read them. Two-hundred-year-old doors and walls, which I had thought were fine, have been thrown away. They've been replaced with new, flimsy ones. It's only when the renovations are done and we move in that I realize I've turned our nineteenth-century Parisian apartment into what looks like a high-rise condominium in Miami, but with mice. I didn't understand quite how beautiful Paris is—the heavy doors, the intricate moldings—until I destroyed a small part of it, at enormous expense.

Now I spend a lot of time ruminating on this. "You know how

Edith Piaf said, '*Je ne regrette rien?*'" (I regret nothing), I ask Simon. "Well, for me it's '*je regrette tout*'" (I regret everything).

Occasionally our life shifts from expensive and exhausting to merely surreal. When the boys are a bit older, a single girlfriend of mine stops by before bedtime one night. She watches as the boys—in footed pajamas—silently pull themselves up and down the furniture, in a kind of Dadaist dance. Later they'll march around silently while holding their toothbrushes aloft, like talismans. Simon watches them and pretends to narrate a documentary. "To these boys, in their culture, toothbrushes are these curious status symbols," he explains.

Mostly our new life is full of extreme emotions. Simon mopes around in exhaustion and despair, taking little passive-aggressive snips at me. "Maybe in eighteen years I'll get to have a cup of coffee," he says. He describes the dread he feels when he approaches our house and hears the wailing from outside. Three kids under the age of three are a lot, even among our very fertile cohort.

Amid all the crying and complaining, there are hopeful moments. My whole mood lifts one afternoon when Leo is cheerful and calm for five whole minutes. The first night that he sleeps seven straight hours, Simon jumps around the house singing the Frank Zappa song "Titties and Beer."

Even so, I still feel much as I did at the moment of the boys' birth: that my attention is hopelessly divided. I ask my friend Hélène—who also has twins and a singleton—whether she's considering having more. "I don't think so; I'm at the limit of my competence," she says. I know exactly what she means. Only I fear that I've surpassed my competence. Even my mother, who spent years begging for grandchildren, tells me not to have any more kids.

As if to cement my status, Bean comes home from school one day and announces that I'm a *maman crotte de nez*. I immediately type this into Google Translate. It turns out that she has called me a "mommy booger." Given the circumstances, it's a very good description.

i adore this baguette

Friends tell me that parents of twins have a high divorce rate. I'm not sure this is statistically true, but I can certainly understand how the rumor got started.

In the months after the twins are born, Simon and I bicker constantly. During one argument, he tells me that I'm "rebarbative." I have to look up this word, too. The dictionary says, "unattractive and objectionable: a rebarbative modern building." I march back to Simon.

"Unattractive?" I ask. Even in our current state, that's a low blow.

"Okay, you're just objectionable," he says.

To remind myself to be civil, I tape up signs around the apartment that read Don't Snap at Simon. There's one on the bathroom mirror, in plain view of the babysitters. Simon and I are too tired to realize that we're fighting because we're tired. I no longer care what he's thinking about, though it's probably still Dutch football.

During rare moments of leisure, Simon likes to burrow in bed with a magazine. If I dare to interrupt him, he says, "There's nothing you can say to me that's more interesting than this article I'm reading in *The New Yorker*."

One day I have a revelation. "I think we're actually quite compatible," I tell him. "You're irritable, and I'm irritating."

Apparently, we send off a scary vibe. A childless couple we know comes to visit from Chicago and concludes, after four days, that they don't want kids after all. At the end of one weekend *en famille*, Bean decides that she doesn't want to have kids either. "Children are too difficult," she says.

On a positive note for our relationship, we get spots in the crèche for both boys (even my mother is relieved to hear this). Twins are still uncommon enough in France that our application got priority status. The crèche committee took such pity on us that they assigned the boys to a tiny crèche two blocks from our new home, which I'd been told had no vacancies.

The crèche offers some hope for the future. But we still have to survive as a family and, perhaps more dauntingly, as a couple until we hand the boys over in a few months. (We've decided to keep them at home until they're a year old.)

It's not always obvious that Simon and I will make it that long. It seems no coincidence that as "concerted cultivation" has become the de facto parenting style for the American middle-class, research shows that marital satisfaction has fallen[1] and that mothers find it more pleasant to do housework than to take care of their kids.[2] American social scientists now pretty much take for granted that today's parents are less happy than nonparents. Studies show that parents have higher rates of depression and that their unhappiness increases with each additional child[3] (or in Simon's case, with merely seeing those additional children on an ultrasound).

Maybe we just need a date night? While I've been living in France, date nights have become the new penicillin for North American couples with kids. Hate your spouse? Have a date night! Want to strangle your kids? Go out to dinner! The Obamas go on date nights. Even social scientists now study them. A paper on middle-class Canadians[4] found that when couples got leisure time alone together, it "helped them tremendously as a couple, rejuvenated them personally, and re-inspired their parenting." But the couples in the study rarely got this time. "Many [participants] felt pressured by the wider culture to al-ways place the needs of the children above the needs of the partner-ship," the authors conclude. One husband said that while speaking to his wife, "we would be interrupted on a minute-to-minute basis" by the children.

This is, of course, another consequence of "concerted cultivation," which eats up leisure time and makes fomenting the child's develop-ment the family's overwhelming priority. I see this all around me when I visit the United States and the United Kingdom. An American cousin of mine—who's a nurse with four kids—has family nearby who'd be willing to babysit. But after a week of getting everybody to school, gymnastics, track meets, and church, she and her husband—who works nights as a policeman—don't even consider going out alone. They're too tired. A schoolteacher from Manchester, England, tells me that she's taking her toddler on her honeymoon, even though her mother has volunteered to watch him. "I'd just feel too bad leaving him behind," she explains.

Every Anglophone mother I speak to has a cautionary tale about a mother in her social circle who refuses to leave her child with anyone. These moms aren't urban myths; I frequently meet them. At a wed-ding I sit next to a stay-at-home mother from Colorado, who explains that she has a full-time babysitter, but never leaves the sitter alone with her three kids. (Her husband has skipped the wedding to look after them.)

An artist from Michigan tells me that she couldn't bring herself to use a babysitter for her son's whole first year. "He seemed so tiny, he was my first kid. I'm really pretty neurotic. The idea of handing him over to someone . . ."

Some American parents I meet have adopted such specific diets and discipline techniques that it's hard for anyone else—even a grandparent—to take over and follow all the rules. A grandfather from Virginia says his daughter became livid when he pushed her baby's stroller the "wrong" way over a bump. The baby's mom had read that there's a smaller chance of brain damage if babies go over bumps backward.

Obviously, Simon and I aren't against babysitters. We're currently employing half the Philippines. But since the boys were born, I haven't spent more than a few hours away from home. Mostly I do what that mother from Colorado does: I use the babysitter as a kind of assistant who changes diapers and does the laundry. But I'm usually on the premises.

This system has the advantage of both depleting our savings and destroying our relationship, simultaneously. I feel rebarbative much of the time. I realize I'm losing my mind a little bit when—about fifteen minutes before one of our babysitters is supposed to arrive—my phone beeps, indicating that I have a new text message. I panic, fearing that the babysitter is late. In fact, it's a message from a news service that I subscribe to, informing me that there's been a deadly earthquake in South America. For an instant, I'm relieved.

Of course, it's easier to get along with your spouse if your baby sleeps through the night by three months old, your kids play by themselves, and you're not constantly shuttling them from one activity to the next. It also helps that couples in France don't have some of the big financial stressors, like high costs for child care, health care, and college.

In the short term, however, what seems to really help is that French couples view romance differently, even when they have young kids. I get an inkling of this when my gynecologist writes me a prescription for ten sessions of *rééducation périnéale* (perineal reeducation). She did this for the first time after Bean was born and again after the birth of the boys.

Before my first reeducation, I had only been vaguely aware that I had a perineum, or what exactly it is. It turns out to be the hammock-like pelvic-floor area, which often gets stretched out during pregnancy and birth. The stretching loosens the birth canal and can cause mothers to pee a little bit whenever they cough or sneeze.

In the United States, doctors sometimes suggest that women tone their perineums with Kegel squeezes. But often they don't suggest anything. Being a little slack and leaky is just a seldom-mentioned part of being an American mom.

In France, such troubles are *pas acceptable*. Friends tell me that their French obstetricians gauge whether a few sessions of perineal reeducation are needed by asking, "Is *monsieur* happy?"

I think my *monsieur* would be happy to have any access to my perineum. The region hasn't exactly lain fallow in the year or so since the boys were born. But I wouldn't say there's any danger of overuse. For a while, as soon as Simon went anywhere near my breasts, it was like a fire alarm: they began spurting milk. Anyway, sleep is more of a priority for us. Though all three kids now technically "do their nights," somehow I never seem to sleep more than six or seven straight hours.

I'm intrigued enough by perineal reeducation to give it a try. My first reeducator is a slim Spanish woman named Mónica, with an office in the Marais neighborhood. Our introductory session begins with a forty-five-minute interview, during which she asks me dozens of questions about my bathroom habits and my sex life.

Then I disrobe from the waist down and lie on a padded table covered with crinkly paper. Mónica slips on surgical gloves and leads me in what I can best describe as assisted crunches for the crotch, in sets of fifteen ("and up, and release"). It's a bit like Pilates for the below-the-belt region.

Afterward Mónica shows me a slender white wand that she'll introduce in the next phase. It resembles a device you might see for sale in an adults-only shop. The wand will add electrostimulation to my mini sit-ups. By the tenth session we'll be ready to try out a kind of video game, in which sensors on my groin measure whether I'm contracting the muscles enough to stay above a running orange line on the computer screen.

Perineal reeducation is at once extremely intimate and strangely clinical. Throughout the exercises, Mónica and I address each other using the formal *vous*. But she asks me to close my eyes, so I can better isolate the muscles where her hand is.

My doctor writes me a prescription for abdominal reeducation, too. She's noticed that, more than a year after the twins are born, I still have a kind of bulge around my waist that's part fat, part stretch, and part unknown substance. Frankly, I'm not sure what's in there. I decide that it's time to take action when I'm standing up on the Paris metro and a decrepit old woman offers me her seat. She thinks I'm pregnant.

Not all Frenchwomen do reeducation after they give birth. But many do. Why not? France's national insurance picks up most or all of the cost, including the price of the white wand. The state even helps pay for some tummy tucks, usually when the mother's belly hangs below her pubis, or when it's inhibiting her sex life.

Of course, all this reeducation just gets mothers out of the starting gate. What do Frenchwomen do once their bellies and their pelvic floors are back in fighting shape?

Some do focus only on their kids. But unlike in the United States or Britain, the culture doesn't encourage or reward this. Sacrificing your sex life for your kids is considered wildly unhealthy and out of balance. The French know that having a baby changes things, especially at first. Couples typically assume that there's a very intense stretch after the birth, when it's all hands on deck for the baby. After that, gradually, the mother and father are supposed to find their equilibrium as a couple again.

"There's this fundamental assumption [in France] that every human being has desire. It never disappears for very long. If it does it means you're depressed and you need to be treated," explains Marie-Anne Suizzo, the University of Texas sociologist who studied French and American mothers.

The French mothers I meet talk about le couple in a whole different way from the Americans I know. "For me, the couple comes before the children," says Virginie, the stay-at-home mom who taught me to "pay attention" to what I eat.

Virginie is principled, smart, and a devoted mother. She's the only young Parisian I know who's an observant Catholic. But she has no intention of letting her romantic life slacken just because she has three kids.

"The couple is the most important. It's the only thing that you chose in your life. Your children, you didn't choose. You chose your husband. So, you're going to make your life with him. So you have an interest in it going well. Especially when the children leave, you want to get along with him. For me, it's prioritaire."

Not all French parents would agree with Virginie's ranking. But in general, the question for French parents isn't whether they'll resume having full romantic lives again, but when. "No ideology can dictate the moment when the parents will feel truly ready to find each other again," says the French psychosociologist Jean Epstein. "When conditions permit, and when they feel ready, the parents will give the baby his rightful place, outside their couple."

American experts do sometimes mention that parents should take time for themselves. In Dr. Spock's Baby and Child Care (which my friend Dietlind hands off to me before leaving Paris) there's a two-paragraph section called Needless Self-sacrifice and Excessive Preoccupation. It says that today's young parents tend to "give up all their freedom and all their former pleasures, not as a matter of practicality but as a matter of principle." Even when these parents occasionally sneak off by themselves, "they feel too guilty to get full enjoyment." The book urges parents to carve out quality time together, but only after making "all the necessary sacrifice of time and effort to your children."

French experts don't treat having quality time together as an after-thought; they're adamant and unambiguous about it. That's perhaps because they're very sanguine and up-front about how hard babies can be on a marriage. "It isn't for nothing that a good number of couples separate in the first few years, or the first few months following the arrival of a child. Everything changes," one article says.

In the French parenting books I read, *le couple* is treated as a cen-tral and crucial topic. Some French parenting Web sites occasionally have as many articles on *le couple* as they do on pregnancy. "The child must not invade the parents' whole universe . . . for family balance, the parents also need personal space," writes Hélène De Leersnyder, the pediatrician. "The child understands without a clash, and always very young, that his parents need time that's not about work, the house, shopping, children."

Once French parents emerge from the initial cocooning period, they take this call to coupledom seriously. There is actually a time of day in France known as "adult time" or "parent time." It's when the kids go to sleep. Anticipation of "adult time" helps explain why—once the fairy tales are read and the songs are sung—French parents are strict about enforcing bedtime. They treat "adult time" not as an occasional, hard-won privilege, but as a basic human need. Judith, an art historian with three young kids, explains that all three are asleep by eight or eight thirty because "I need a world for myself."

French parents don't just think these separations are good for par-ents. They also genuinely believe that they're important for kids, who must understand that their parents have their own pleasures. "Thus the child understands that he is not the center of the world, and this is essential for his development," the French parenting guide *Votre Enfant* explains.

French parents don't just have their nights to themselves. After Bean starts school, we are confronted with a seemingly endless series of midsemester two-week holidays. During these times I can't even arrange a playdate. Most of Bean's friends have been dispatched to stay with their grandparents in the countryside or the suburbs. Their parents use this time to work, travel, have sex, and just be alone.

Virginie says she takes a ten-day holiday alone with her husband every year. It's nonnegotiable. Her kids, ages four to fourteen, stay with Virginie's parents in a village about two hours by train from Paris. Virginie says guilt doesn't enter into this holiday. "With what you construct between the two of you when you're away for ten days, it has to be good for the kids, too." She says that kids also occasionally need space from their parents. When they all reunite after the trip, it's very sweet.

The French parents I meet grab adult time whenever they can. Caroline, the physical therapist, tells me without a trace of guilt that her mother is picking up her three-year-old son from maternelle on Friday afternoon and looking after him through Sunday. She says that on their weekend off, she and her husband plan to sleep late and go to the movies.

French parents even get pockets of adult time when their kids are home. Florence, forty-two, with three kids ages three to six, tells me that on weekend mornings, "the kids don't have the right to enter our room until we open the door." Until then, miraculously, they've learned to play by themselves. (Inspired by her story, Simon and I try this. To our amazement, it mostly works. Though we have to reteach it to the kids every few weeks.)

I have trouble explaining the concept of a date night to my French colleagues. For starters, there's no "dating" in France. Here, when you start going out with someone, it's automatically supposed to be exclusive. In France, a "date" sounds too tentative and too much like a job interview to be romantic. It's the same once a couple lives together. Date night, with its implied sudden switch from sweatpants to stilettos, sounds contrived to my French friends. They take issue with the implication that "real life" is unsexy and exhausting and that they should schedule romance like it's a trip to the dentist.

When the American movie *Date Night* comes to France, it's titled *Crazy Night*. The couple in the film are supposed to be typical suburban Americans with kids. A reviewer for the Associated Press describes the pair as "tired, ordinary but reasonably content." In an opening scene, they're awakened in the morning when one of their children pounces on their bed. French critics are horrified by such scenes. A reviewer for *Le Figaro* describes the kids in the film as "unbearable."

Despite having kids who don't pounce on them in the morning, Frenchwomen would seem to have more to complain about than American women do. They lag behind Americans in key measures of gender equality, such as the percentage of women in the legislature and heading large corporations. And they have a bigger gap than we do between what men and women earn.[5]

French inequality is especially pronounced at home. Frenchwomen spend 89 percent more time than men doing household work and looking after children.[6] In the United States, women spend 31 percent more time than men on household activities, and 25 percent more time on child care.[7]

Despite all this, my American (and British) girlfriends with kids seem a lot angrier at their husbands and partners than my French girlfriends are.

"I am fuming that he doesn't bother to be competent about a whole slew of stuff that I ask him to do," my friend Anya writes to me in an e-mail about her husband. "He's turned me into a shrewish nag and once I get mad, it's hard for me to cool back down."[8]

American friends—or even acquaintances—regularly pull me aside at dinner parties to grumble about something their husbands have just done. Whole lunches are devoted to such complaints. They're indignant about how, without them, their households would have no clean towels, living plants, or matching socks.

Simon gets many points for effort. He gamely takes Bean across town one Saturday to get some American-sized passport photos. But in a typical twist, he returns with photos that make Bean look like a five-year-old psychopath having a bad-hair day.

Since the boys were born, Simon's incompetence is less charming. I no longer find it adorably mystifying when he breaks the second hands on all his watches or reads our expensive English-language magazines in the shower. Some mornings, our whole marriage seems to hinge on the fact that he doesn't shake the orange juice before he pours it.

For some reason, we mostly fight about food. (I put up a Don't Snap at Simon sign in the kitchen.) He leaves his beloved cheeses unwrapped in the refrigerator, where they quickly dry out. When the boys are a bit older, Simon gets a phone call while he's brushing their teeth. I take over, only to discover that Leo still has an entire dried apricot in his mouth. When I complain, Simon says he feels disempowered by my "elaborate rules."

When I get together with my Anglophone girlfriends, it's just a matter of time before we start venting about such things. At one dinner in Paris, three of the six women at the table discover—in a ricochet of me-toos—that their husbands all retreat to the bathroom for a long session, just when it's time to put the kids to bed. Their complaining is so intense, I have to remind myself that these are women in solid marriages and not on the verge of divorce.

When I get together with Frenchwomen of the same social class, this type of complaining doesn't happen. When I ask, Frenchwomen acknowledge that they sometimes have to prod their husbands to do more around the house. Most say they've had their sulky moments, when it felt like they were carrying the whole household while their husbands were lying on the couch.

But somehow, in France, this imbalance doesn't lead to what a writer in the bestselling American anthology *The Bitch in the House* calls "the awful, silent process of tallying up and storing away and keeping tabs on what he helped out with and what he did not." Frenchwomen are no doubt tired from playing mother, wife, and worker simultaneously. But they don't reflexively blame their husbands for this, or at least not with the venom that American women often do.

Possibly, Frenchwomen are just more private. But even the mothers I get to know well don't seem to be secretly boiling over with the belief that the life they have isn't the one they deserve. Their unhappiness seems like normal unhappiness. No matter how much I dig, I don't find rage.

Partly, this is because Frenchwomen don't expect men to be their equals. They view men as a separate species that by nature isn't good at booking babysitters, buying tablecloths, or remembering to schedule checkups with the pediatrician. "I think Frenchwomen accept more the differences between the sexes," says Debra Ollivier, author of *What French Women Know.* "I don't think that they expect men to rise to the plate with the same kind of meticulous attention and sense of urgency."

When the Frenchwomen I know mention their partners' inadequacies, it's to laugh about how adorably inept the men are. "They're just not capable; we're superior!" jokes Virginie, as her girlfriends chuckle. Another mother breaks into peals of laughter when she describes how her husband blow-dries her daughter's hair without brushing it first, so the little girl goes to school "looking like Don King."

This outlook creates a virtuous cycle. Frenchwomen don't harp on

men about their shortcomings or mistakes. So the men aren't demor-
alized. They feel more generous toward their wives, whom they praise
for their feats of micromanagement and their command of household
details. This praise—instead of the tension and resentment that builds
in Anglophone households—seems to make the inequality easier to
bear. "My husband says, 'I can't do what you do,'" another Parisian
mom, Camille, proudly tells the group. None of this follows the
American feminist script. But it seems to go a lot more smoothly.

Fifty-fifty equality just isn't the gold standard for most Parisian
women I know. Maybe this will change one day. But for now, the mothers I meet care more about finding a balance that works. Laurence, a
management consultant with three kids, has a husband who works
long hours during the week. (She has switched to part time.) The couple used to fight all weekend about who does what. But lately Laurence
has been urging her husband to go to his aikido class on Saturday
mornings, since he's more relaxed afterward. She'd rather do a bit
more child care in exchange for a husband who's cheerful and calm.

French mothers also seem better at giving up some control and
lowering their standards in exchange for more free time and less stress.
"You just have to say, I'm going to come home, and there's going to
be a week's worth of laundry in a pile," Virginie tells me, when I mention that I'm taking Bean to the United States for a week and leaving
Simon in Paris with the boys.[9]

There are structural reasons why Frenchwomen seem calmer than
American women. They take about twenty-one more vacation days
each year.[10] France has less feminist rhetoric, but it has many more
institutions that enable women to work. There's the national paid
maternity leave (the United States has none), the subsidized nannies
and crèches, the free universal preschool from age three, and myriad
tax credits and payments for having kids. All this doesn't ensure
that there's equality between men and women. But it does ensure that
Frenchwomen can have both a career and kids.

If you drop the forlorn hope of fifty-fifty equality, it becomes easier to enjoy the fact that some urban French husbands do quite a lot of child care, cooking, and dishwashing. A 2006 French study[11] found that just 15 percent of fathers of infants participated equally in the babies' care and 11 percent took primary responsibility. But 44 percent played very active supporting roles. You see these dads, adorably scruffy, pushing strollers to the park on Saturday mornings and bringing home bags of groceries afterward.

This latter category of dads often focused on housework and cooking, in particular. The French mothers I meet often say their husbands handle specific domains, like homework or cleaning up after dinner. Perhaps having this clear division of labor is the secret. Or maybe French couples are just more fatalistic about marriage.

"One of the great feelings of a couple and of marriage is gratitude to the person who hasn't left," says Pascal Bruckner, the raffish and professionally provocative French philosopher. He's speaking to Laurence Ferrari, the anchorwoman of France's top nightly news program. She's a pretty blonde, six months pregnant with her second husband's baby. The two are discussing "Love and Marriage: Are They a Good Combination?" for a French magazine.

Bruckner and Ferrari are part of the French elite—a rarified circle of journalists, politicians, academics, and businesspeople who socialize with and marry one another. Their views represent an exaggerated, perhaps aspirational version of how ordinary French people think.

"Today, marriage no longer has a bourgeois connotation. To the contrary, for me, it's an act of bravado," Ferrari says.

Marriage is a "revolutionary adventure," Bruckner replies. "Love is an indomitable feeling. The tragedy of love is the fact that it changes, and we're not the masters of this change."

Ferrari concurs. "It's because of that that I persist in saying, marriage for love is a magnificent risk."

. . . .

In a sign of how far we've come socially, Simon and I are invited away for the weekend—with kids—to the country home of my French friend Hélène and her husband, William. They, too, have twins and a singleton. Hélène, who's tall with a heart-shaped face and ethereal blue eyes, grew up in Reims, the capital of the Champagne region. Her family's vacation home is nearby in the Ardennes, close to the Belgian border.

Many of World War I's battles took place in the Ardennes. For four years, French and German soldiers dug trenches on opposite sides of a narrow stretch of territory called no-man's-land and fired artillery and machine guns at one another. The two sides lived in such close proximity that they knew one another's work shifts and habits, the way neighbors do. Sometimes they'd hold up handwritten signs for the other side to read.

In the small town where Hélène's family home is, it feels as if the fighting only recently stopped. Farmers still find exploded shell fragments in the soil. Many of the homes and buildings destroyed in the war were never rebuilt, leaving a lot of the landscape covered in fields.

Hélène and William are ultradedicated parents all day long. But I notice that each night we're there, as soon as the kids are down, they bring out the cigarettes and the wine, turn on the radio, and have what is obviously adult time. They want to *profiter*—to take advantage of the company and the warm summer night. (Hélène is so keen to *profiter* one afternoon when we're driving with the kids that she pulls over to a field in the late afternoon, whips out a blanket from the trunk, and produces cake for our *goûter*. The setting is so picture perfect, it's almost more pleasure than I can handle.)

On weekends, William gets up early with the kids. One morning he pops out of the house—while Simon babysits—to fetch some fresh *pain au chocolat* and a crusty baguette. Hélène eventually wanders downstairs in her pajamas, her hair adorably mussed, and plops down at the breakfast table.

"*J'adore cette baguette!*" (I adore this baguette!) she says to William, as soon as she sees the bread he's bought.

It's a very simple, sweet, honest thing to say. And I can't imagine saying anything like it to Simon. I usually say that he's bought the wrong baguette or worry that he's left a mess that I'll have to clean up. I tend not to wake up feeling very generous toward him. He doesn't make me beam with delight, at least not first thing in the morning. That sheer girlish pleasure—*j'adore cette baguette*—sadly doesn't exist between us anymore.

I tell Simon the baguette story as we're driving home from the Ardennes, past fields of yellow flowers and the occasional stone war memorial. "We need more of that *j'adore cette baguette*," he says. He's right; we absolutely do.

Chapter 12

you just have to taste it

The main question people ask about twins, besides how they were conceived, is how they're different from each other. Some mothers of twins have this all figured out: "One's a giver and one's a taker," the mother of two-year-old girls cooed, when I met her in a park in Miami. "They get along perfectly!"

It's not quite that smooth with Leo and Joey. They seem like an old married couple—inseparable, but always bickering. (Perhaps they've learned that from Simon and me.) The differences between them become clearer when they start to talk. Leo, the swarthy one, says nothing but the odd noun for several months. Then suddenly at dinner one night, he turns to me and says, in a kind of robot voice, "I am eating."

It's no accident that Leo has mastered the present progressive. He lives in the present progressive. He's in constant, rapid motion. He doesn't walk anywhere; he runs. I can tell who's approaching by the speed of the footsteps.

Joey's preferred grammatical form is the possessive: my rabbit, my mommy. He moves slowly, like an old man, because he's trying to carry his key possessions with him at all times. His favored items vary, but there are always many of them (at one point he sleeps with a small kitchen whisk). He eventually puts everything into two briefcases, which he drags from room to room. Leo likes to swipe these, then run away. If I had to sum up the boys in a sentence, I'd say one's a taker and one's a hoarder.

Bean's preferred grammatical form is still the command. We can no longer blame her teachers; it's clear that giving orders suits her. She's constantly advocating for a cause, usually her own. Simon refers to her as "the union organizer," as in: "The union organizer would like spaghetti for dinner."

It was hard enough trying to instill Bean with French habits when she was an only child. Now that there are three kids in the house— and just two of us—creating some French *cadre* is even harder. But it's also a lot more urgent. If we don't control the kids, they're going to control us.

One realm in which we're succeeding is with food. Food is of course a source of national pride in France and something that French people love to talk about. My French colleagues in the office where I rent a desk spend most of lunch discussing what they had for dinner. When Simon goes out for post-game beers with his French soccer team, he says they talk about food, not girls.

It becomes clear how French our kids' eating habits have become when we visit America. My mom is excited to introduce Bean to that American classic, macaroni and cheese from a box. But Bean won't eat more than a few bites. "That's not cheese," she says. (I think I detect her first sneer.)

We're on vacation when we visit America, so we end up eating out a lot. On the plus side, American restaurants are a lot more kid-friendly than those in France. There are unheard-of conveniences like high chairs, crayons, and changing tables in the bathrooms. (You might occasionally find one of these in Paris but almost never all three at once.)

But I grow to dread the ubiquitous "kids' menus" in American restaurants. It doesn't matter what type of restaurant we're in—seafood,
Italian, Cuban. The kids' menus all have practically identical offerings:
hamburgers, fried chicken fingers (now euphemistically called chicken
"tenders"), plain pizza, and perhaps spaghetti. There are almost never
any vegetables, unless you count French fries or potato chips. Occasionally, there's fruit. Kids aren't even asked how they want their hamburgers cooked. Perhaps for legal reasons, all the burgers come out a
depressing shade of gray.

It isn't just restaurants that treat kids as if they don't have fully
developed taste buds. On one trip home I sign up Bean for a few days
of tennis camp, which includes lunch. "Lunch" for ten children turns
out to be a bag of white bread and two packages of American cheese.
Even Bean, who'd eat pasta or hamburgers for every meal if I let her,
is taken aback. "Tomorrow is pizza!" one of the coaches chirps.

The reigning view in America seems to be that kids have finicky,
limited palates, and that adults who venture beyond grilled cheese do
so at their peril. This belief is, of course, self-fulfilling. Many of the
American kids I meet do have finicky and limited palates. Frequently
they spend a few years on a kind of mono-diet. A friend in Atlanta
has one son who eats only white foods like rice and pasta. Her other
son eats only meat. Another friend's baby nephew in Boston was supposed to start eating solid foods around Christmas. When the boy
refused to eat anything but foil-wrapped chocolate Santas, his parents
hoarded bags of them, afraid they'd be out of stock after the holidays.

Catering to picky kids is a lot of work. A mother I know in Long
Island makes a different breakfast for each of her four kids, plus a fifth
one for her husband. An American father who's visiting Paris with his
family informs me in reverent tones that his seven-year-old is very
particular about textures. He says the boy likes cheese and tortillas
separately, but refuses to eat them when they're cooked together be-

cause the tortilla becomes—he whispers this while looking at his son—"*too crispy.*"

Instead of resisting this pickiness, the parenting establishment is capitulating to it. *What to Expect: The Toddler Years* says: "Letting a young child go for months on nothing but cereal, milk and pasta, or bread and cheese (assuming a few well-chosen fruits and/or vegetables are thrown in for good balance) isn't indulgent or unacceptable, but perfectly respectable. In fact, there's something inherently unfair about insisting that children eat what's put in front of them when grown-ups enjoy a great deal of freedom of choice at the table."

And then there are snack foods. When I'm with friends and their kids in America, little bags of pretzels and Cheerios just seem to appear all the time in between meals. Dominique, a French mother who lives in New York, says at first she was shocked to learn that her daughter's preschool feeds the kids every hour all day long. She was also surprised to see parents giving their kids snacks all throughout the day at the playground. "If a toddler starts having a tantrum, they will give food to calm him down. They use food to distract them from whatever crisis," she says.

The whole picture is different in France. In Paris, I mostly shop at the local supermarket. But just by going with the middle-class flow, my kids have never tasted high-fructose corn syrup or long-life bread. Instead of Fruit Roll-Ups, they eat fruit. They're so used to fresh food that processed food tastes strange to them.

As I've mentioned, French kids typically eat only at mealtimes and at the afternoon *goûter*. I've never seen a French child eating pretzels (or anything else) in the park at ten A.M. There are kids' menus at some French restaurants—usually at corner bistros or pizza places. These menus don't always have haute cuisine either. There's often steak with *frites*—French fries. ("At home we never have *frites*; my kids know it's their only way of getting them," my friend Christine says.)

But at most restaurants, kids are expected to order from the regular menu. When I ask for spaghetti with tomato sauce for Bean at a nice Italian restaurant, the French waitress very gently suggests that I order her something a bit more adventuresome—say the pasta dish with eggplant.

McDonald's does a thriving business in France, and you can certainly find processed foods to eat if you want them. But a government campaign reminding people to eat at least "five fruits and vegetables per day" has become a national catchphrase. (A lunch restaurant near my office is called 5 Fruits et Légumes Chaque Jour [five fruits and vegetables every day].)

Though French kids eat hamburgers and fries sometimes, I've never met a French child who ate just one type of food or a parent who allowed this. It's not that French kids are clamoring for more vegetables. Of course they like certain foods more than others. And there are plenty of finicky French three-year-olds. But these children don't get to exclude whole categories of textures, colors, and nutrients just because they want to. The extreme pickiness that's come to seem normal in America and Britain looks to French parents like a dangerous eating disorder or, at best, a wildly bad habit.

The consequences of these differences are important. Just 3.1 percent of French five- and six-year-olds are obese.[1] In America, 10.4 percent of kids between two and five are obese.[2] This gap is much wider for older French and American kids. Even in prosperous American neighborhoods, I see fat children all the time. But in five years of hanging out at French playgrounds, I've seen exactly one child who might qualify as obese (and I suspect she was just visiting).

With food in particular, I can't help but ask the same question that I've been asking about so many other aspects of French parenting: How do French parents do it? How do they make their kids into little gourmets? And in the process, why don't French kids get fat? I see the results all around me, but how do French kids get to be this way?

. . . .

I suspect that it starts with babies. When Bean is around six months old and I'm ready to feed her solid foods, I notice that French supermarkets don't sell the ground rice that my mother and all my Anglophone friends say should be a baby's first food. I have to trek to health food stores to buy an expensive, organic version imported from Germany, tucked away below the recycled diapers.

It turns out that French parents don't start their babies off on bland, colorless grains. From the first bite, they serve babies flavor-packed vegetables. The first foods that French babies typically eat are steamed and pureed green beans, spinach, carrots, peeled zucchini, and the white part of leeks.

American babies eat vegetables, too, of course, sometimes even from the start. But we Anglophones tend to regard vegetables as obligatory vitamin-delivery devices and mentally group them in a dull category called "vegetables." Although we're desperate for our kids to eat vegetables, we don't always expect them to. Bestselling cookbooks teach parents how to sneak vegetables into meatballs, fish sticks, and macaroni and cheese, without kids even noticing. I once watched as friends of mine urgently spooned vegetables coated in yogurt into their kids' mouths after a meal, while the kids watched television, seemingly oblivious to what they were eating. "Who knows how much longer we'll be able to do this," the wife said.

French parents treat their *légumes* with a whole different level of intention and commitment. They describe the taste of each vegetable and talk about their child's first encounter with celery or leeks as the start of a lifelong relationship. "I wanted her to know the taste of carrot by itself. Then I wanted her to know the taste of zucchini," swoons Samia, the mother who showed me topless pictures of herself. Like other French parents I spoke to, Samia views vegetables—and also fruits—as the building blocks of her daughter's incipient culinary *éducation* and a way of initiating her into the richness of taste.

My American baby books recognize that certain foods are an acquired taste. They say that if a baby rejects a food, parents should wait a few days and then offer the same food again. My Anglophone friends and I all do this. But we assume that if it doesn't work after a few tries, our babies just don't like avocado, sweet potatoes, or spinach.

In France, the same advice to keep reproposing foods to babies is elevated to a mission. Parents take for granted that, while kids will prefer certain tastes over others, the flavor of each vegetable is inherently rich and interesting. Parents see it as their job to bring the child around to appreciating this. They believe that just as they must teach the child how to sleep, how to wait, and how to say *bonjour*, they must teach her how to eat.

No one suggests that introducing all these foods will be easy. The French government's free handbook on feeding kids says all babies are different. "Some are happy to discover new foods. Others are less excited, and diversification takes a little bit longer." But the handbook urges parents to be dogged about introducing kids to new foods and not giving up even after a child has rejected a food three or more times.

French parents advance slowly. "Ask your child to taste just one bite, then move on to the next course," the handbook suggests. The authors add that parents should never offer a different food to replace the rejected one. And they should react neutrally if the child won't eat something. "If you don't react too much to his refusal, your child will truly abandon this behavior," the authors predict. "Don't panic. You can keep giving him milk to be sure he's getting enough food."

This long-term view of cultivating a child's palate is echoed in Laurence Pernoud's legendary parenting book *J'élève mon enfant*. Her section on feeding solids to babies is called How Little by Little a Child Learns to Eat Everything.

"He refuses to eat artichokes?" Pernoud writes. "Here again, you have to wait. When, a few days later, you try again, try putting a little bit of artichoke into a lot of puree," for instance, of potatoes.

The government food guide tells parents to offer the same ingredients prepared many different ways. "Try steaming, baking, in parchment, grilled, plain, with sauce or seasoned." The handbook's authors say, "Your child will discover different colors, different textures and different aromas."

The guide also suggests a talking cure, à la Dolto. "It's important to reassure him, and to talk to him about this new food," it says. The conversation about food should go beyond "I like it" or "I don't like it." They suggest showing kids a vegetable and asking, "Do you think this is crunchy, and that it'll make a sound when you bite it? What does this flavor remind you of? What do you feel in your mouth?" They suggest playing flavor games like offering different types of apples and having the child decide which is the sweetest and which is the most acidic. In another game, the parent blindfolds the child and has him eat and identify foods he already knows.

All the French baby books I read urge parents to stay calm and cheerful at mealtimes, and above all to stay the course, even if their child doesn't take a single bite. "Don't force him, but don't give up on proposing it to him," the government handbook explains. "Little by little, he'll get more familiar with it, he'll taste it . . . and without a doubt, he'll end up appreciating it."

To get more insight into why French children eat so well, I attend the Commission Menus in Paris. It's here that those sophisticated menus posted at Bean's crèche every Monday get their final imprimatur. The commission decides what the crèches of Paris will be serving for lunch for the subsequent two months.

I'm probably the first foreigner to ever attend this meeting. It's held in a windowless conference room inside a government building on the banks of the Seine. Heading the meeting is Sandra Merle, the chief nutritionist of Parisian crèches. Merle's deputies are also there, along with a half dozen chefs who work in crèches.

The commission is a microcosm of French ideas about kids and food. Lesson number one is that there's no such thing as "kids' food." A dietician reads out the proposed menus, including all four courses for each lunch, as if she's entering them into the official record. There is no mention of French fries, chicken nuggets, pizza, or even ketchup. The proposed menu for one Friday is a salad of shredded red cabbage and *fromage blanc*. This is followed by a white fish called *colin* in dill sauce and a side of organic potatoes *à l'anglaise*. The cheese course is a Coulommiers cheese (a soft cheese similar to Brie). Dessert is a baked organic apple. Each dish is cut up or pureed according to the age of the kids.

The commission's second lesson is the importance of variety. Members take a leek soup off the menu when someone points out that the children will have eaten leeks the previous week. Merle scratches a tomato dish she had planned for late December—another repeat—and replaces it with a boiled-beet salad.

Merle stresses visual and textural variety, too. She says that if foods are all the same color one day, she inevitably gets complaints from crèche directors. She reminds the crèche chefs that if the older kids (meaning two- and three-year-olds) have a pureed vegetable as a side dish, they should have a whole fruit for dessert, since they might find two pureed dishes too babyish.

Some of the chefs boast about their recent successes. "I served mousse of sardines, mixed with a little cream," says a chef with curly black hair. "The kids loved it. They spread it on bread."

There is much praise of soup. "They love soup; it doesn't matter which beans or which vegetables," another chef says. "The soup with leeks and coconut milk, they really like it," a third chef adds.

When someone mentions *fagots de haricots verts*, everyone laughs.

It's a traditional Christmas dish that all the crèches were supposed to prepare the previous year. The dish requires blanching green beans, wrapping clusters of the beans in thin slices of smoked pork, piercing the combination with a toothpick, and then grilling it. Apparently this was too much even for the aesthetics-obsessed crèche chefs (though they don't balk at being told to cut a kiwi into the shape of a flower).

Another driving principle of the Commission Menus is that if at first the kids don't like something, they should try it repeatedly. Merle reminds the chefs to introduce new foods gradually and to prepare the foods all different ways. She suggests introducing berries first as a puree, since kids will already be familiar with that texture. After that, the chefs can serve the berries cut into pieces.

One chef asks what to do about grapefruit. Merle suggests serving a thin slice sprinkled with sugar, then gradually serving it on its own. The same goes for spinach. "Our kids don't eat spinach at all. It all goes in the garbage," one chef grumbles. Merle tells her to mix it with rice to make it more appetizing. She says she'll send out a "technical sheet" to remind everyone how to do this. "You repropose spinach in different ways throughout the year; eventually they will like it," she promises. Merle says that once one child starts eating spinach, the others will follow. "It's the principle of nutritional education," she says.

Vegetables are a big concern for the group. One cook says her kids won't eat green beans unless they're slathered in crème fraîche or béchamel sauce. "You need to strike a balance; sometimes with sauce, sometimes without," Merle suggests. Then there's a long discussion of rhubarb.

After about two hours under the fluorescent lights, I'm fading a bit. I'd like to go home and have dinner. But the commission hasn't even gotten to the menu for the upcoming Christmas meal.

"The foie gras, no?" one chef suggests as an appetizer. Another counters with duck mousse. At first I assume that they're both joking, but no one laughs. The group then debates whether to have salmon or tuna for the main course (their first choice is monkfish, but Merle says it's too expensive).

And what about the cheese course? Merle vetoes goat cheese with herbs, because the kids had goat cheese at their fall picnic. The group finally settles on a menu that includes fish, broccoli mousse, and two kinds of cow's milk cheese. Dessert is an apple-cinnamon cake, a yogurt cake with carrots, and a traditional Christmas galette with pears and chocolate. ("You can't veer too much from tradition. Parents will want a galette," someone says.) For the afternoon *goûter* that day, Merle worries that a mousse made of "industrial chocolate" won't be sufficiently festive. They settle on a more elaborate *chocolat liégeois*—a chocolate mousse sundae in a glass, topped with whipped cream.

Not once does anyone suggest that a flavor might be too intense or complicated for a child's palate. None of the foods are outrageously strong—there are a lot of herbs, but no mustards, pickles, or olives. But there are mushrooms, celery, and every other manner of vegetable in abundance. The point isn't that every kid will like everything. It's that he'll give each food a chance.

Not long after I sit in on the Commission Menus, a friend loans me a book called *The Man Who Ate Everything* by the American food writer Jeffrey Steingarten.

Steingarten writes that when he was named food critic for *Vogue*, he decided that his personal food preferences made him unfairly biased. "I feared that I could be no more objective than an art critic who detests the color yellow," he writes. He embarks on a project to see if he can make himself like the foods he despises.

Steingarten's hated foods include kimchi (the fermented cabbage that's a national dish of Korea), swordfish, anchovies, dill, clams, lard, and desserts in Indian restaurants—which he says have "the taste and texture of face creams." He reads up on the science of taste and concludes that the main problem with new foods is simply that they're new. So just having them around should chip away at the eater's innate resistance.

Steingarten bravely decides to eat one of his hated foods each day. He also tries to eat very good versions of each food: chopped anchovies in garlic sauce in northern Italy; a perfectly done capellini in white clam sauce at a restaurant on Long Island. He spends an entire afternoon cooking lard from scratch and eats kimchi ten times, at ten different Korean restaurants.

After six months, Steingarten still hates Indian desserts. ("Not every Indian dessert has the texture and taste of face cream. Far from it. Some have the texture and taste of tennis balls.") But he comes to like, and even crave, nearly all of his other formerly detested foods. By the tenth portion of kimchi, it "has become my national pickle, too," he writes. He concludes that "no smells or tastes are innately repulsive, and what's learned can be forgot."

Steingarten's experiment sums up the French approach to feeding kids: if you keep trying things, you eventually come around to liking most of them. Steingarten discovered this by reading up on the science of taste. But middle-class French parents seem to know it intuitively and do it automatically. In France, the idea of reintroducing a broad range of vegetables and other foods isn't just one idea among many. It's the guiding culinary principle for kids. The ordinary, middle-class French parents I meet are evangelical about the idea that there is a rich world of flavors out there, which their children must be educated to appreciate.

This isn't just some theoretical ideal that can only play out in the controlled environment of the crèche. It actually happens in the kitchens and dining rooms of ordinary French families. I see it firsthand when I visit the home of Fanny, the publisher who lives in a high-ceilinged apartment in eastern Paris with her husband, Vincent, four-year-old Lucie, and three-month-old Antoine.

Fanny has pretty, rounded features and a thoughtful gaze. She usually arrives home from work by six and serves Lucie dinner at six thirty, while Antoine sits in a bouncy chair drinking his bottle. On weeknights, Fanny and Vincent eat together once the kids are asleep.

Fanny says she rarely makes anything as complex as the braised endive and chard that Lucie used to eat at the crèche. Still, she views each night's dinner as part of Lucie's culinary education. She doesn't worry too much about how much Lucie eats. But she insists that Lucie has at least a bite of every dish on her plate.

"She has to taste everything," Fanny says, echoing a rule I hear from almost every French mother I speak to about food.

One extension of the tasting principle is that, in France, everyone eats the same dinner. There are no choices or substitutions. "I never ask, 'What do you want?' It's 'I'm serving this,'" Fanny tells me. "If she doesn't finish a dish, it's okay. But we all eat the same thing."

American parents might see this as lording it over their helpless offspring. Fanny thinks it empowers Lucie. "She feels bigger when we all eat, not the same portions, but the same thing." Fanny says American visitors are amazed when they see Lucie at a meal. "They say, 'How come your daughter already knows the difference between Camembert, Gruyère, and chèvre?'"

Fanny also tries to make the meal fun. Lucie already knows how to make cakes, since she and her mother bake together most weekends. Fanny has Lucie play some role in making dinner, too, by preparing some of the food or setting the table. "We help her, but we make it playful. And it's every day," she says.

When it's time to eat, Fanny doesn't austerely wave her finger at Lucie and order her to taste things. They talk about the food. Often they discuss the flavor of each cheese. And having participated in preparing the meal, Lucie is invested in how it turns out. There's complicity. If a certain dish is a flop, "we all have a laugh about it," Fanny says.

Part of keeping the mood light is keeping the meal brief. Fanny says that once Lucie has tasted everything, she's allowed to leave the table. The book *Votre Enfant* says a meal with young kids shouldn't last more than thirty minutes. French kids learn to linger over longer meals as they get older. And as they start going to bed later, they eat more weeknight dinners with their parents.

Planning the dinner menu is a lesson in balance. I'm struck by how French mothers like Fanny seem to have the day's culinary rhythm mapped out in their heads. They assume that their kids will have their one big protein-heavy meal at lunchtime. For dinner, they mostly serve carbohydrates like pasta, along with vegetables.

Fanny may have just raced home from the office, but, as they do at the crèche, she calmly serves dinner in courses. She gives Lucie a cold vegetable starter, such as shredded carrots in a vinaigrette. Then there's a main course, usually pasta or rice with vegetables. Occasionally she'll cook a bit of fish or meat, but usually she expects Lucie to have had most of her protein at lunch. "I try to avoid proteins [at night] because I think I've been educated like that. They say once per day is enough. I try to focus on vegetables."

Some parents tell me that, in winter, they often serve soup for dinner, along with a baguette or maybe a bit of pasta. It's a filling meal that relies heavily on grains and vegetables. A lot of parents puree these soups. And that's dinner. Kids might drink some juice at breakfast or at the afternoon *goûter*. But at lunch and dinner they drink water, usually at room temperature or slightly chilled.

Weekends are for family meals. Almost all the French families I know have a large lunch *en famille* on both Saturday and Sunday. The kids are usually involved in cooking and setting up these meals. On weekends "we bake, we cook. I have cookbooks for children; they have their own recipes," says Denise, the medical ethicist and mother of two girls.

After all these preparations, they sit down to eat. The French sociologists Claude Fischler and Estelle Masson, authors of the book *Manger*, say that a French person who eats a sandwich on the fly for lunch doesn't even count this as "having eaten." For the French, "eating means sitting at the table with others, taking one's time and not doing other things at the same time." Whereas for Americans, "health is seen as the main reason for eating."[3]

At Bean's fifth birthday party, I announce that it's time for the cake. Suddenly the kids—who've been raucously playing—file into our dining room and sit down calmly at the table. They're all *sage* at once. Bean sits at the head of the table and hands out plates, spoons, and napkins. Except for lighting the candles and carrying out the cake, I don't have much of a role. By five years old, sitting calmly at the table for any kind of eating is an automatic reflex for French kids. There's no question of eating on the couch, in front of the television, or while looking at the computer.

Of course, one of the benefits of having some *cadre* in your home is that you can go outside of the *cadre* without worrying that it will collapse. Denise tells me that once a week she lets her two girls—who are seven and nine—have dinner in front of the television.

On weekends and during those ubiquitous school holidays, French parents are more relaxed about what time their kids eat and go to bed. They trust the *cadre* to be there when they need it again. Magazines run articles about easing your kids back onto an earlier schedule, once you get back from vacation. When we're on holiday with Hélène and William, I panic a bit when it's one thirty and William still hasn't gotten home with some of the ingredients for our lunch.

But Hélène figures that the kids can adapt. They are people, after all, who like us are capable of coping with a bit of frustration. She breaks open a bag of potato chips, and the six kids all gather at the kitchen table to eat them. Then they pile outside to play again until lunch is ready. It's no big deal. We all cope. A little while later we all have a long, lovely meal at the table that we've set up under a tree.

If overparenting was an airline, Park Slope, Brooklyn, would be its hub. Every parenting trend and new product seems to originate or refuel there. Park Slope is home to "New York's first baby wearing and breast-feeding boutique," and to a fifteen-thousand-dollar-per-year preschool where teachers "actively discourage and stop superhero play." If you live in Park Slope, Baby Bodyguards will kid-proof your duplex for six hundred dollars. (The company's founder explains that "once I gave birth and my son became part of the external world, my fear and anxiety kicked in.")

Despite Park Slope's reputation for zealous parenting, I'm unprepared for what I witness in a playground there on a sunny Sunday morning. At first, the father and son I spot just seem to be doing a particularly energetic version of narrated play. The boy looks about six. The father—in expensive jeans and a stylish weekend stubble—has followed him to the top of the jungle gym. In a bilingual twist, he's giving the boy a running commentary in both English and what sounds like American-accented German.

The son seems used to his father heading down the slide behind him. When they move to the swings, the father continues his bilingual soliloquy, while pushing. This is all still within the bounds of what I've seen elsewhere. But then the mother arrives. She's a rail-thin brunette in her own pair of expensive jeans, carrying a bag of produce from the farmer's market next door.

"Here's your parsley snack! Do you want your parsley snack?" she says to the boy, handing him a green sprig.

Parsley? A snack? I think I understand the intention: These parents don't want their son to be fat. They want him to have a varied palate.

They see themselves as original thinkers who can provide him with unusual experiences, German and parsley surely being just a small sampling. And I grant them that parsley doesn't run the risk of ruining their son's—or frankly anyone's—appetite.

But there's a reason why parsley has never caught on as a snack. It's a seasoning. It doesn't taste good all by itself. I get the feeling that these parents are trying to remove their son from the collective wisdom of our species and the basic chemistry of what tastes good. I can only imagine the effort this requires. What happens when he discovers cookies?

When I mention the "parsley snack" incident to American parents, they're not surprised. They concede that parsley isn't a snack. But they admire the effort. At that impressionable age, why not try? In the hothouse environment of Park Slope, some parents have gone beyond the American Question: How do we speed up the stages of development? They're now asking how they can override basic sensory experiences.

I realize I'm guilty of this, too, when I take Bean to her first Halloween party, when she's about two. The French don't widely celebrate the holiday. (I go to one adult Halloween party where all the women are dressed as sexy witches and most of the men are Draculas.) So each year a group of Anglophone mothers in Paris takes over the top floor of a Starbucks near the Bastille and sets up little trick-or-treat stations around the room.

As soon as Bean grasps the concept—all these people are *giving her candy*—she begins to eat it. She doesn't just eat a few pieces; she tries to eat all the candy in her bag. She sits in a corner of the room stuffing pink, yellow, and green gooey masses into her mouth. I have to intervene to slow her down.

It occurs to me then that I've taken the wrong approach to sweets. Before this Halloween, Bean had barely ever eaten refined sugar. To my knowledge, she hadn't had a single gummy bear. Like the parsley parents, I'd tried to pretend that such things didn't exist.

I've watched other Anglophone parents agonize about giving their kids sweets. One afternoon a British mother I know tells me her little girl can't have a cookie, although all the other kids are having them, explaining, "She doesn't need to know about that." Another mom I know—a psychologist—looks to be in agony over whether to let her eighteen-month-old have a Popsicle, even though it's the end of a hot summer day and all our kids are playing outside. (She finally concedes.) I see a couple with three advanced degrees between them convene a nervous meeting over whether their four-year-old can have a lollipop.

But sugar does exist. And French parents know it. They don't try to eliminate all sweets from their children's diets. Rather, they fit sweets inside the *cadre*. For a French kid, candy has its place. It's a regular-enough part of their lives that they don't gorge on it like freed prisoners the moment they get their hands on it. Mostly, children seem to eat it at birthday parties, school events, and as the occasional treat. At these occasions, they're usually free to eat all they want. When I try to limit the boys' intake of candy and chocolate cake at the crèche's Christmas party, one of their caregivers intervenes. She tells me I should just let them enjoy the party and be free. I think of my skinny friend Virginie, who pays strict attention to what she eats on weekdays, then eats whatever she wants on weekends. Kids, too, need moments when the regular rules don't apply.

But parents decide when these moments are. When I drop Bean off at a birthday party for Abigail, a little girl in our building, she's the first guest to arrive. (We haven't yet figured out that you're not supposed to be punctual for kids' birthdays.) Abigail's mom has just set out plates of cookies and candy on a table. Abigail asks her mom if she can have some of the candy. Her mom says "*non*," and explains that it isn't yet time to eat it. In what seems to me like a minor miracle, Abigail looks longingly at the candy, then runs off with Bean to play in another room.

Chocolate has a more regular place in the lives of French kids. Middle-class French parents talk about chocolate as if it's just another food group, albeit one to eat in moderation. When Fanny describes what Lucie eats in a typical day, the menu includes a bit of cookies or cake. "And obviously she'll want chocolate in there somewhere," Fanny says.

Hélène gives her kids hot chocolate when it's cold outside. She serves it for breakfast, along with a hunk of baguette, or makes it their afternoon *goûter*, along with some cookies. My kids love reading books about T'choupi, a French children's-book character modeled on a penguin. When he's sick, his mom lets him stay home and drink hot chocolate. I take my kids to see a performance of *Goldilocks and the Three Bears* at a theater near our house. The bears don't eat oatmeal; they eat *bouillie au chocolat* (hot chocolate thickened with flour).

"It's a compensation for going to school, and I guess it gives them some energy," explains Denise, the medical ethicist. She shuns McDonald's and makes her daughters' dinner from scratch each night. But she gives each girl a bar of chocolate for breakfast, along with some bread and a bit of fruit.

French kids don't get a huge amount of chocolate; it's a small bar, or a drink's worth, or a strip in a *pain au chocolat*. They eat it happily and don't expect a second helping. But chocolate is a nutritional fixture for them, rather than a forbidden treat. Bean once comes home from the summer camp at her school with a chocolate sandwich: a baguette with a bar of chocolate inside. I'm so surprised I take a picture of it. (I later learn that the chocolate sandwich—usually made with dark chocolate—is a classic French *goûter*.)

With sweets, too, the *cadre* is key. French parents aren't afraid of sugary foods. In general, they will serve cake or cookies at lunch or at the *goûter*. But they don't give kids chocolate or rich desserts with dinner. "What you eat in the evening just stays with you for years," Fanny explains.

After dinner, Fanny typically serves fresh fruit or a fruit compote—those ubiquitous little tubs of applesauce with other pureed fruits mixed in. (These come with or without added sugar.) There's a *compotes* section in French supermarkets. Fanny says she also buys all different types of plain yogurt and then gets jams for Lucie to mix in.

As in most realms, French parents aim at mealtimes to give kids both firm boundaries and freedom within those boundaries. "It's things like sitting at the table and tasting everything," Fanny explains. "I'm not forcing her to finish, just to taste everything and sit with us."

I'm not sure exactly when I started serving my kids meals in courses. But I now do it at every meal. It's a stroke of French genius. This starts with breakfast. When the kids sit down, I put plates of cut-up fruit on the table. They nibble on this while I'm getting their toast or cereal ready. They can have juice at breakfast, but they know that for lunch and dinner we drink water. Even the union organizer doesn't complain about that. We talk about how clean water makes us feel.

At lunch and dinner I serve vegetables first, when the kids are hungriest. We don't move on to the main course until they at least make a dent in the starter. Usually they finish it. Except when I introduce an entirely new dish, I rarely have to resort to the tasting rule. If Leo won't eat a food the first time I serve it, he'll usually agree to at least smell it, and he'll take a nibble soon after that.

Bean sometimes exploits the letter of the rule by eating a single piece of zucchini and then insisting that she has fulfilled her obligation. She recently declared that she will taste everything "except salad," by which she means the actual green lettuce leaves. But for the most part, she quite likes the starters we serve. These include sliced avocado, tomato in a vinaigrette, or steamed broccoli with a bit of soy sauce. We all have a good chuckle when I serve *carottes rapées*— shredded carrots in a vinaigrette—and try to pronounce it.

My kids come to the table hungry because, except for the *goûter*, they don't snack. It helps that other kids around them aren't snacking either. But even so, getting to this point required a steely will. I simply don't cave in to demands for a filling piece of bread or a whole banana between meals. And as the kids have gotten older, they've mostly stopped asking. If they do, I just say "no, you're having dinner in thirty minutes." Unless they're very tired, they're usually fine with that. I feel a swell of accomplishment when I'm in the supermarket with Leo, and he points to a box of cookies and says, "*Goûter.*"

I try not to be too fanatical about this (or as Simon describes it, "more French than the French"). When I'm cooking I occasionally give the kids a little preview of dinner—a piece of tomato or a few chickpeas. When I'm introducing a new ingredient, like pine nuts, I'll offer them a few bites of it while I'm cooking, to get them in the mood. I might even give them a sprig of parsley (though I wouldn't call it a snack). Obviously they drink water whenever they want.

Sometimes keeping my kids in the food *cadre* feels like a lot of work. Especially when Simon travels, I'm often tempted to skip the starter, plop a bowl of pasta in front of them, and call it dinner. When I occasionally do this, they're quite happy to gobble it down. There's certainly no clamoring for salad and vegetables.

But the kids don't have a choice. Like a French mom, I've accepted that it's my duty to teach them to like a variety of tastes and to eat meals that are *équilibrés*. Also like a French mom, I try to keep the whole day's menu balanced in my head. We mostly stick to the French formula of having large, protein-heavy lunches and lighter, carbohydrate-driven dinners with vegetables. The kids do eat a lot of pasta, though I try to vary the shape and the sauce. Whenever I have time, I make a big pot of soup for dinner (though I can't bring myself to puree it) and serve it with rice or bread.

It's no surprise that the kids find the food more appetizing when it's made with fresh ingredients and it looks good. I consider the balance of colors on their plates and occasionally slip in some slices of tomato or avocado if dinner looks monotone. We have a collection of colorful melamine plates. But for dinner I use white, which makes the colors of the food pop and signals to the kids that we're having a grown-up meal.

I try to let them help themselves as much as possible. Beginning when the boys were quite young, I passed around a bowl of grated Parmesan on pasta nights and let them sprinkle it on all by themselves. They get to put a spoonful of sugar in their hot chocolates and occasionally in their yogurts. Bean frequently asks for a slice of Camembert, or a hunk of whatever cheese we've got, at the end of the meal. Except for special occasions, we don't do cake or ice cream at night. I still won't serve them chocolate sandwiches.

It's taken a while to make all this second nature. It helps that the boys in particular really like to eat. One of their teachers at the crèche calls them gourmands, which is a polite way of saying that they eat a lot. She says their favorite word is *encore* (more). They've developed the annoying habit, possibly learned at the crèche, of holding up their plates at the end of the meal to show that they've finished. Whatever sauce or liquid is left spills onto the table. (I think at the crèche they've already mopped up the liquid with slices of baguette.)

Sweets are no longer non grata in our house. Now that we offer them in moderation, Bean doesn't treat each piece of candy as if it's her last. When it's really cold out, I make the kids hot chocolate in the morning. I serve it with yesterday's baguette, softened slightly in the microwave, and slices of apple, which the kids dip in their drinks. It feels like a very French breakfast.

hélène's recipe
for *chocolat chaud*

(makes about 6 cups)

1–2 teaspoons cocoa powder
1 liter low-fat milk
sugar to taste

In a saucepan, mix one to two heaping teaspoons unsweetened cocoa powder with a small splash of cold or room-temperature milk. Over low heat, blend well to form a thick paste. Add the rest of the milk and stir (the chocolate should spread evenly into the milk). Cook over medium heat until the mixture boils. Allow the hot chocolate to cool, skim off any skin that has formed, then pour it into mugs with spoons. Let kids add their own sugar at the table.

Quick breakfast version

In a large mug, mix 1 teaspoon cocoa powder and a small splash of milk; blend into a paste. Fill the rest of mug with milk and mix. Heat the mug in the microwave for two minutes, or until very hot. Stir in a teaspoon of sugar. Pour a bit of this hot cocoa concentrate into several mugs. Add cold or room-temperature milk to each mug. Serve with a crusty baguette or any toasted bread.

Chapter 13

it's me who decides

Leo, the swarthy twin, does everything quickly. I don't mean that he's gifted. I mean that he moves at twice the speed of ordinary humans. By age two, he's developed a runner's physique from dashing from room to room. He even speaks quickly. As Bean's birthday approaches, he begins singing "Happybirthdaytoya!" in a high-pitched squeak; the whole song is over in a few seconds.

It's very hard to wrangle this little tornado. Already, he can practically outrun me. When I go to the park with him, I'm in constant motion, too. He seems to regard the gates around play areas as merely an invitation to exit.

One of the most impressive parts of French parenting—and perhaps the toughest one to master—is authority. Many French parents I meet have an easy, calm authority with their children that I can only envy. Often, their kids actually listen to them. French children aren't constantly dashing off, talking back, or engaging in prolonged negotiations. But how exactly do French parents pull this off? And how can I acquire this magical authority, too?

One Sunday morning, my neighbor Frederique witnesses me trying to cope with Leo when we bring our kids to the park. Frederique is a travel agent from Burgundy. She's in her midforties, with a raspy voice and a no-nonsense manner. After years of paperwork she adopted Tina, a beautiful redheaded three-year-old, from a Russian orphanage. At the time of our outing, she's been a mother for all of three months.

But already Frederique is teaching me about *éducation*. Just by virtue of being French, she has a whole different vision of what's *possible* and *pas possible*. This becomes clear in the sandbox. Frederique and I are sitting on a ledge at its perimeter, trying to talk. But Leo keeps dashing outside the gate surrounding the sandbox. Each time he does this, I get up to chase him, scold him, and drag him back while he screams. It's irritating and exhausting.

At first, Frederique watches this little ritual in silence. Then, without any condescension, she says that if I'm running after Leo all the time, we won't be able to indulge in the small pleasure of sitting and chatting for a few minutes.

"That's true," I say. "But what can I do?"

Frederique says I should be sterner with Leo, so he knows that it's not okay to leave the sandbox. "Otherwise you're running after him all the time, it doesn't work," she says. In my mind, spending the afternoon chasing Leo is inevitable. In her mind, it's *pas possible*.

Frederique's strategy doesn't seem to hold out much promise for me. I point out that I've been scolding Leo for the last twenty minutes. Frederique smiles. She says I need to make my "no" stronger, and to really believe in it.

The next time Leo tries to run outside the gate, I say "no" more sharply than usual. He leaves anyway. I follow and drag him back.

"You see?" I say to Frederique. "It's not possible."

Frederique smiles again and says I need to make my "no" more convincing. What I lack, she says, is the belief that he's really going to listen. She tells me not to shout but rather to speak with more conviction.

I'm scared that I'll terrify him.

"Don't worry," Frederique says, urging me on.

Leo doesn't listen the next time either. But I gradually feel my "no's" coming from a more convincing place. They're not louder, but they're more self-assured. I feel like I'm impersonating a different sort of parent.

By the fourth try, when I'm finally brimming with conviction, Leo approaches the gate but—miraculously—doesn't open it. He looks back and eyes me warily. I widen my eyes and try to look disapproving.

After about ten minutes, Leo stops trying to leave altogether. He seems to forget about the gate and just plays in the sandbox with Tina, Joey, and Bean. Soon Frederique and I are chatting, with our legs stretched out in front of us.

I'm shocked that Leo suddenly views me as an authority figure.

"See that," Frederique says, not gloating. "It was your tone of voice."

She points out that Leo doesn't appear to be traumatized. For the moment—and possibly for the first time ever—he actually seems like a French child. With all three kids suddenly *sage* at once, I can feel my shoulders falling a bit. It's an experience I've never really had in the park before. Maybe this is what it's like to be a French mother?

I feel relaxed, but also foolish. If it's that easy, why haven't I been doing this for years? Saying no isn't exactly a cutting-edge parenting technique. What's new is Frederique's coaching me to drop my ambivalence and be certain about my own authority. What she tells me springs from her own upbringing and deepest beliefs. It comes out sounding like common sense.

Frederique has the same certainty that what's most pleasant for us parents—being able to have a relaxing chat at the park while the kids play—is also best for children. This seems to be true. Leo is a lot less stressed than he was half an hour earlier. Instead of a constant cycle of escape and reimprisonment, he's playing happily with the other kids.

I'm ready to bottle my new technique—the fully felt "no"—and sell it off the back of a wagon. But Frederique warns me that there's no magic elixir for making kids respect your authority. It's always a work in progress. "There are no fixed rules," she says. "You have to keep changing what you do."

That's unfortunate. So what else explains why French parents like Frederique have so much authority with their kids? How exactly do French parents summon this authority, day after day, dinner after dinner? And how can I get some more of it?

A French colleague of mine says that if I'm interested in authority, I must speak to her cousin Dominique. She says that Dominique, a French singer who's raising three kids in New York, is an unofficial expert in the differences between French and American parents.

Dominique, forty-three, looks like the heroine of a *nouvelle vague* film. She has dark hair, delicate features, and an intense, gazellelike gaze. If I were thinner, better looking, and could sing, I'd say that she and I were living mirror-image lives: She's a Parisian who's raising her children in New York. I'm an ex–New Yorker who's raising kids in Paris. Living in France has made me calmer and less neurotic. Whereas despite Dominique's sultry good looks, she has adopted the bubbly self-analysis that comes from living in Manhattan. She speaks enthusiastic French-accented English, peppered with "like" and "oh my God."

Dominique arrived in New York as a twenty-two-year-old student. She planned to study English for six months, then go home. But New York quickly became home. "I felt really good and stimulated and had great energy, something I hadn't felt in a long, long time in Paris," she says. She married an American musician.

Beginning when she first got pregnant, Dominique was also enchanted with American parenting. "There's a great sense of community that, in a way, you don't have as much in France. . . . If you like yoga and you're pregnant, boom! You get into this group of pregnant women doing yoga."

She also started to notice the way kids are treated in the United States. At a big Thanksgiving with her husband's family, she was astonished to see that when a three-year-old girl arrived, all twenty adults at the table stopped talking and focused on the child.

"I thought, oh, this is incredible, this culture. It's like the kid is a God, it's really amazing. I'm like, no wonder Americans are so confident and so happy, and the French are so depressed. Here we are—just look at the attention."

But over time Dominique started to view this type of attention differently. She noticed that the same three-year-old girl who'd stopped conversation at Thanksgiving was developing an oversized sense of entitlement.

"I was like, 'that's it, this kid really annoys me.' She's coming and she's thinking that because she's here, everyone has to stop their life and pay attention."

Dominique, whose own kids are eleven, eight, and two, says her doubts grew when she overheard students at her children's preschool responding to teachers' instructions with, "You are not the boss of me." ("You would never see that in France, never," she says.) When she and her husband were invited for dinner at the homes of American friends with young kids, she often ended up doing most of the cooking, because the hosts were busy trying to make their children stay in bed.

"Instead of just being firm and saying, 'No more of that, I'm not giving you more attention, this is bedtime, and this is parents' time, now it's my time as an adult with my friends, you've had your time, this is our time. And go to bed, that's it,'—well, they don't do that. I don't know why they don't do that, but they don't do that. They can't do it. They keep just serving the kids. And I see that and I'm just blown away."

Dominique still adores New York and much prefers American schools to French ones. But in matters of parenting, she has increasingly reverted to French habits, with their clear rules and boundaries.

"The French way sometimes is too harsh. They could be a little more gentle and friendly with kids, I think," she says. "But I think the American way takes it way to the extreme, of raising kids as if they are ruling the world."

I find it hard to argue with my would-be doppelgänger. I can picture those dinner parties she's describing. American parents—myself included—are often deeply ambivalent about being in charge. In theory, we believe that kids need limits. This is a truism of American parenting. However, in practice, we're often unsure where these limits should be or we're uncomfortable policing them.

"I feel more guilty for getting angry than I feel angry," is how a college friend of Simon's justifies his three-year-old daughter's bad behavior. A girlfriend of mine says her three-year-old son bit her. But she "felt bad" yelling at him because she knew that it would make him cry. So she let it go.

Anglophone parents worry that being too strict will break their kids' creative spirits. A visiting American mother was shocked when she saw a playpen in our apartment in Paris. Apparently, back home, even playpens are now seen as too confining. (We didn't know. In Paris they're de rigueur.)

A mother from Long Island tells me about her badly behaved nephew, whose parents were—in her view—alarmingly permissive. But she says the nephew has since grown up to become head of oncology at a major American medical center, vindicating the fact that he was an unbearable child. "I think kids who are very intelligent and not much disciplined are insufferable when they're kids. But I think they are less stifled creatively when they're older," she says.

It's very hard to know where the correct limits lie. By forcing Leo to stay in a playpen or in the sandbox, am I preventing him from one day curing cancer? Where does his free expression end and pointless bad behavior begin? When I let my kids stop and study every manhole cover we pass on the sidewalk, are they following their bliss, or turning into brats?

A lot of Anglophone parents I know find themselves in an awkward in-between zone, where they're trying to be both dictator and muse to their children. The result is that they end up constantly negotiating. I get my first taste of this when Bean is about three. Our new house rule is that she's allowed to watch forty-five minutes of television per day. One day, she asks to watch a bit more.

"No. You've already had your TV time for today," I say.

"But when I was a baby I didn't watch any TV," she says.

Like us, most Anglophone parents I know have at least some limits. But with so many different parenting philosophies in play, there are other parents who oppose authority altogether. I meet one of them on a visit to the United States.

Liz is a graphic designer in her midthirties, with a five-year-old daughter named Ruby. She easily ticks off her main parenting influences: the pediatrician William Sears, the author Alfie Kohn, and the behaviorist B. F. Skinner.

When Ruby acts up, Liz and her husband try to convince the girl that her behavior is morally wrong. "We want to extinguish unacceptable behaviors without resorting to power plays," Liz tells me. "I try not to exploit the fact that I'm larger and stronger than she by physically restraining her. Similarly, I try not to resort to the fact that I have all the money by saying, 'You can have this thing or not.'"

I'm touched by the exacting effort that Liz has put into constructing her approach to parenting. She hasn't merely adopted someone else's rules; she has carefully digested the work of several thinkers and come up with a thoughtful hybrid. The new way of parenting that she's created is, she says, a complete break from the way that she herself grew up.

But there are costs. Liz says that this eclectic style, and her desire not to be judged for it, have isolated her from many of her neighbors and peers, and even from her own parents. She says her parents are bewildered and overtly disapproving of how she's raising Ruby and that she can no longer discuss it with them. Visits home are tense, especially when Ruby acts up.

Nevertheless, Liz and her husband remain determined not to flaunt their authority. Lately Ruby has been hitting them both. Each time, they sit her down and discuss why hitting is wrong. This well-intentioned reasoning isn't helping. "She still hits us," Liz says.

France feels like a different planet. Even the most bohemian parents boast about how strict they are and seem unequivocal about being at the top of the family hierarchy. In a country that reveres revolution and climbing the barricades, there are apparently no anarchists at the family dinner table.

"It's paradoxical," admits Judith, the art historian and mother of three in Brittany. Judith says she's "antiauthority" in her political views, but that when it comes to parenting she's the boss, full stop. "It's parents, then children," she says of the family pecking order. In France, she explains, "sharing power with a child doesn't exist."

In the French media and among the older generation, there's talk of that encroaching "child-king" syndrome. But when I talk to parents in Paris, what I hear all the time is *"C'est moi qui décide"*—It's me who decides. There's another slightly more militant variation, *"C'est moi qui commande"*—it's me who commands. Parents say these phrases to remind both their kids and themselves who's the boss.

To Americans, this hierarchy can look like tyranny. Robynne is an American who lives just outside Paris with her French husband and their two kids, Adrien and Lea. Over a family dinner at her apartment one night, she tells me about taking Adrien to the pediatrician when he was a toddler. Adrien cried and refused to step on the scale, so Robynne knelt down to persuade him.

The doctor interrupted. "He said, 'Don't explain to him why. Just say 'That's why. That's what you're doing, you're going on the scale, that's it, there's no discussion.'" Robynne was shocked. She says she eventually changed pediatricians because she found this one too severe.

Robynne's husband, Marc, has been listening to this story. "No, no, that's not what he said!" Marc interjects. Marc is a professional golfer who grew up in Paris. He's one of those French parents who seem to wear their authority quite effortlessly. I notice the way his kids listen carefully when he speaks to them and respond immediately.

Marc says the doctor wasn't being wantonly bossy. To the contrary, he was helping with Adrien's *éducation*. Marc remembers the incident quite differently:

"He said that you have to be sure of yourself, that you have to take your kid and put him on the scale. . . . If you give him too many choices, he doesn't feel reassured. . . . You have to show him that's the way it is and it's not a bad way or a good way, it's just the way.

"It's a simple gesture but it's the start of everything," Marc adds. "You have certain things that don't need explanation. You need to weigh the kid so you take the kid and put the kid on the scale. Period. Period!"

He says the fact that Adrien found the experience unpleasant was part of the lesson. "Sometimes there are things in life you don't really like, and you have to do them," he says. "You don't always do what you love or what you want to."

When I ask Marc how he got his authority, it's clear that it's not as effortless as it looks. He has put enormous effort into establishing this dynamic with his kids. Having authority is something that he thinks very hard about and considers a priority. All this effort springs from his belief that having a parent who's confident is reassuring to kids.

"For me it's better to have a leader, someone who shows the way," he says. "A kid has to feel like the mom is in control, or the dad."

"Just like when you're on a horse," Adrien, now age nine, chimes in.

"Good comparison!" Robynne says.

Marc adds, "We have a saying in French: it's easier to loosen the screw than to tighten the screw, meaning that you have to be very tough. If you're too tough, you loosen. But if you are too lenient . . . afterward to tighten, forget about it."

Marc is describing the *cadre* that French parents spend the early years of a child's life constructing. They construct it in part by establishing their own right to say, sometimes, "Just get on the scale."

American parents like me just assume that we'll have to chase our kids around the park all afternoon or spend half a dinner party putting them to bed. It's irritating, but it's come to seem normal.

For French parents, living with a child-king seems wildly out of balance and bad for the whole family. They think it would drain much of the pleasure from daily life, for both the parents and the kids. They know that building this *cadre* requires enormous effort, but they believe that the alternative is unacceptable. It's obvious to French parents that the *cadre* is the only thing standing between them and two-hour "good nights."

"In America, it's accepted that when you have kids, your time is not your own," Marc tells me. In his view, "The kids need to understand that they're not the center of attention. They need to understand that the world doesn't revolve around them."

So how do parents build this *cadre*? The process of constructing it does occasionally seem harsh. But it isn't just about saying no and establishing that "it's me who decides." Another way that French parents and educators build the *cadre* is simply by talking a lot about the *cadre*. That is, they spend a lot of time telling their kids what's permissible and what's not. All this talk seems to will the *cadre* into existence. It starts to take on an almost physical presence, much like a good mime convinces you there's actually a wall.

This ongoing conversation about the *cadre* is often very polite. Parents say please a lot, even to babies. (They require politeness, too, of course, since they understand what's being said.) In defining limits for kids, French parents often invoke the language of rights. Rather than saying "Don't hit Jules," they typically say, "You don't have the right to hit Jules." This is more than a semantic difference. It feels different to say it this way. The French phrasing suggests that there's a fixed and coherent system of rights, which both children and adults can refer to. It also makes clear that the child *does* have the right to do other things.

Kids pick up this phrase and police one another. A schoolyard chant for little kids is the rhyming "*Oh la la, on a pas le droit de faire ça!*" (Oh la la, we don't have the right to do that!)

Another phrase that adults use a lot with children is "I don't agree," as in, "I don't agree with you pitching your peas on the floor." Parents say this in a serious tone, while looking directly at the child. "I don't agree" is also more than just "no." It establishes the adult as another mind, which the child must consider. And it credits the child with having his own view about the peas, even if this view is being overruled. Pitching the peas is cast as something the child has rationally decided to do, so he can decide to do otherwise, too.

This may help explain why mealtimes in France are so calm. Instead of waiting for a big crisis and resorting to dramatic punishments, parents and caregivers focus on making lots of small, polite, preventative adjustments, based on well-established rules.

I see this at the crèche, when I sit in with the eighteen-month-olds for another fabulous, four-course lunch. Six little kids, wearing

matching pink terrycloth bibs, are sitting around a rectangular table
as Anne-Marie oversees the meal. The atmosphere is extremely calm.
Anne-Marie describes the foods in each course and tells the children
what's coming out next. I notice that she also closely watches everything they do and—without raising her voice—comments on small
infractions.

"*Doucement*—gently—we don't do that with a spoon," she says to
a boy who has started banging his spoon on the table. "No, no, no, we
don't touch the cheese, it's for later," she tells another. When she
speaks to a child, she always makes eye contact with him.

French parents and caregivers don't always resort to this level of
micromanagement. I've noticed that they tend to do it more at mealtimes, when there are more small gestures and rules, and more risk of
chaos if things go wrong. Anne-Marie does this combination of conversation and corrections throughout the thirty-minute meal. By the
end, the kids' faces are smeared with food. But there is just a crumb
or two on the floor.

Like Marc and Anne-Marie, the French parents and caregivers I
meet have authority without seeming like dictators. They don't aspire
to raise obedient robots. To the contrary, they listen and talk to their
kids all the time. In fact, the adults I meet who have the most authority all speak to children not as a master to a subject but as one equal
to another. "You must always explain the reason" for something that's
forbidden, Anne-Marie tells me.

When I ask French parents what they most want for their children,
they say things like "to feel comfortable in their own skin" and "to
find their path in the world." They want their kids to develop their
own tastes and opinions. In fact, French parents worry if their kids are
too docile. They want them to have character.

But they believe that children can achieve these goals only if they
respect boundaries and have self-control. So alongside character, there
has to be *cadre*.

. . . .

It's hard to be around so many well-behaved kids and around parents with such high expectations. Day after day, I am embarrassed when the boys start shouting loudly or whining, practically every time we walk through the courtyard between our elevator and the main entrance to our building. It's like an announcement to the dozens of people whose apartments open onto the courtyard: the Americans have arrived!

Bean and I are invited to one of her schoolmates' homes for a *goûter* one afternoon during the Christmas holidays. The kids are served hot chocolate and cookies (I'm given tea). Once we're all sitting around the table, Bean decides that it's a good moment to do some *bêtises*. She takes a swig of her hot chocolate, then spits it back into her mug.

I'm mortified. I'd kick Bean under the table if I could be sure which set of legs was hers. I do hiss at her to stop, but I don't want to ruin the moment by making too much of a fuss. Meanwhile, our hostess's three daughters are sitting *sagely* around the table, nibbling on their cookies.

I see how French parents construct *cadres*. What I don't understand is how they calmly keep their kids in the *cadre*. I can't help but think of that adage: if you want to keep a man in a ditch, you have to get in the ditch with him. It's a bit like that at our house. If I send Bean to her room, I have to stay in the room with her, otherwise she'll come out again.

Empowered by that episode in the park with Leo, I'm trying to be strict all the time. But this doesn't always work. I'm not sure when to tighten the screw and when to loosen it.

For some guidance, I make a lunch date with Madeleine, a French nanny who worked for Robynne and Marc. She lives in a small city in Brittany, in western France, but is currently working the overnight shift with a new baby in Paris. (The child is "searching for his nights," Madeleine says.)

Madeleine, sixty-three, is the mother of three boys. She has short graying brown hair and a warm smile. She radiates that total certainty I see in Frederique and other French parents I meet. Like them, she has a calm conviction about her methods.

"The more spoiled a child is, the more unhappy he is," she tells me, almost as soon as we sit down.

So how does she keep her charges in line?

"*Les gros yeux*," she says. This means "the big eyes." Madeleine demonstrates these for me at the table. As she does, she suddenly morphs from a grandmotherly lady in a matching pink scarf and sweater into a scary-looking owl. Even just for show, she has a lot of conviction.

I want to learn "the big eyes," too. When our salads arrive, we practice. At first, I have trouble doing the owl without cracking up. But as with Frederique in the park, when I finally hit the point of real conviction, I can feel the difference. Then, I don't feel like laughing.

Madeleine says that she's not just trying to frighten children into submission. She says "the big eyes" work best when she has a strong connection with the child, and when there's mutual respect. Madeleine says the most satisfying part of her job is developing "complicity" with a child, as if they're seeing the world the same way, and when she almost knows what the child is about to do before he does it. Getting to this point requires carefully observing him, talking with him, and trusting him with certain freedoms.

Indeed, to build a relationship with a child in which the big eyes work, she says strictness must come with flexibility, including giving kids autonomy and choices. "I think you need to leave [kids] a bit of liberty, let their personalities show," she says.

Madeleine doesn't see any contradiction between having this strong reciprocal relationship and also being very firm. Her authority seems to come from inside the relationship with children, not from above it. She's able to balance complicity and authority. "You must listen to the child, but it's up to you to fix the limits," she says.

The big eyes are famous in France. Bean was scared of getting them at the crèche. Many French adults still remember being on the receiving end of the big eyes and other similar expressions.

"She had this look," Clotilde Dusoulier, the Parisian food writer, says of her mother. With both her parents, "There was this tone of voice they used when all of a sudden they felt you had stepped over a line. They had a facial expression that was stern and annoyed and not happy. They would say, 'No, you don't say that.' You would feel chastised and a bit humiliated. It would pass."

What's interesting to me is that Clotilde remembers *les gros yeux*—and the *cadre* the look enforced—very fondly. "She's always been very clear on what was okay and what wasn't," she says of her mother. "She managed to be both affectionate and have authority without ever raising her voice."

Speaking of voice raising, I seem to do it quite a lot. Shouting does sometimes succeed in getting the kids to brush their teeth, or wash their hands before dinner. But it takes a lot out of me and creates an awful ambience. The louder I yell, the worse I feel about it afterward, and the more tired I am.

French parents do speak sharply to their kids. But they prefer surgical strikes to constant carpet-bombing. Shouting is saved for important moments, when they really want to make a point. When I shout at my kids in the park or at home when we have French friends over, the parents look alarmed, as if they think that there's been a serious offense.

American parents like me often view imposing authority in terms of discipline and punishment. French parents don't talk much about these things. Instead, they talk about the *éducation* of kids. As the word suggests, this is about gradually teaching children what's acceptable and what's not.

This idea that you're teaching, not policing, makes the tone a lot gentler in France. When Leo refuses to use his silverware at dinner, I try to imagine that I'm teaching him to use a fork, much like I'd teach him a letter of the alphabet. This makes it easier for me to be patient and calm. I no longer feel disrespected and angry when he doesn't immediately comply. And with some of the stress off the situation, he's more amiable about trying. I don't yell, and dinner is more pleasant for everyone.

It takes me a while to realize that French and American parents also use the word "strict" quite differently. When Americans describe someone as strict, they typically mean that the person has an all-encompassing authority. The image of a stern, joyless schoolteacher comes to mind. I don't know many American parents who use this word to describe themselves. But almost all the French parents I know do.

French parents, however, mean something different than American parents do when they call themselves "strict." They mean that they're very strict about a few things and pretty relaxed about everything else. That's the *cadre* model: a firm frame, surrounding a lot of freedom.

"We should leave the child as free as possible, without imposing useless rules on him," Françoise Dolto says in *The Major Stages of Childhood*. "We should leave him only the *cadre* of rules that are essential for his security. And he'll understand from experience, when he tries to transgress, that they are essential, and that we don't do anything just to bother him." In other words, being strict about a few key things makes parents seem more reasonable and thus makes it more likely that children will obey.

True to Dolto's spirit, middle-class Parisian parents tell me that they don't usually get worked up about minor *bêtises*—those small acts of naughtiness. They assume that these are just part of being a kid. "I think if every misbehavior is treated on the same level, how will they know what's important?" my friend Esther tells me.

But these same parents say that they immediately jump on certain types of infractions. Their zero-tolerance areas vary. But almost all the parents I know say that their main nonnegotiable realm is respect for others. They're referring to all those *bonjour*'s, *au revoir*'s, and *merci*'s, and also about speaking respectfully to parents or other adults.

Physical aggression is another common no-go area. American kids often seem to get away with hitting their parents, even though they know they're not supposed to. The French adults I know don't tolerate this at all. Bean hits me once in front of our neighbor Pascal, a bohemian fiftyish bachelor. Pascal is normally an easygoing guy, but he immediately launches into a stern lecture about how "one does not do that." I'm awed by his sudden conviction. I can see that Bean is awed, too.

At bedtime you can really see the French balance between being very strict about a few things and very relaxed about most others. A few parents tell me that at bedtime, their kids must stay in their rooms. But within their rooms, they can do what they want.

I introduce this concept to Bean and she really likes it. She doesn't focus on the fact that she's confined to her room. Instead she keeps saying, proudly, "I can do whatever I want." She usually plays or reads for a while, then puts herself to bed.

When the boys are about two and they're sleeping in beds rather than cribs, I introduce this same principle. Since they're sharing a room, things tend to get a bit more boisterous. I hear a lot of crashing LEGOs. Unless it sounds dangerous, however, I avoid going back in after I've said good night. Sometimes, if it's getting late and they're still going strong, I come in and tell them that it's bedtime, and that I'm turning off the lights. They don't seem to view this as a violation

of the do-what-you-want principle. By that point they're usually exhausted and they climb into bed.

To pry myself further out of my black-and-white way of looking at
authority, I visit Daniel Marcelli. Marcelli is head of child psychiatry
at a large hospital in Poitiers and the author of more than a dozen
books, including a recent one called *Il est permis d'obéir* (*It Is Permissible
to Obey*). The book is meant for parents, but typically, it's also a med-
itation on the nature of authority. Marcelli develops his arguments in
long expositions, quoting Hannah Arendt and delighting in paradoxes.

His favorite paradox is that in order for parents to have authority,
they should say yes most of the time. "If you always forbid, you're
authoritarian," Marcelli tells me, over coffee and chocolates. He says
the main point of parental authority is to authorize children to do
things, not to block them.

Marcelli gives the example of a child who wants an orange or a glass
of water or to touch a computer. He says the current French "liberal
education" dictates that the child should ask before touching or taking
these things. Marcelli approves of this asking, but he says the parents'
response should almost always be yes.

Parents "should only forbid him every once in a while . . . because
it's fragile or dangerous. But fundamentally, [the parent's job] is to
teach the child to ask before taking."

Marcelli says that embedded in this dynamic is a longer-term goal,
with its own paradox: if all is done right, the child will eventually
reach a point where he can choose to disobey, too.

"The sign of a successful education is to teach a child to obey until
he can freely authorize himself to disobey from time to time. Because
can one learn to disobey certain orders if one has not learned to
obey?

"Submission demeans," Marcelli explains. "Whereas obedience

allows a child to grow up." (He also says that children should watch a bit of television, so they have a shared culture with other kids.)

To follow Marcelli's whole argument about authority, it would help to have been raised in France, where philosophy is taught in high school. What I do understand is that part of the point of building such a firm *cadre* for kids is that they can sometimes leave the *cadre* and it will be there when they get back.

Marcelli is echoing another point I've heard a lot in France: without limits, kids will be consumed by their own desires. ("By nature, a human being knows no limits," Marcelli tells me.) French parents stress the *cadre* because they know that without boundaries, children will be overpowered by these desires. The *cadre* helps to contain all this inner turmoil and calm it down.

That could explain why my children are practically the only ones having tantrums in the park in Paris. A tantrum happens when a child is overwhelmed by his own desires and doesn't know how to stop himself. The other kids are used to hearing *non*, and having to accept it. Mine aren't. My "no" feels contingent and weak to them. It doesn't stop the chain of wanting.

Marcelli says that kids with a *cadre* can absolutely be creative and "awakened"—a state that French parents also describe as "blossoming." The French ideal is to promote the child's blossoming within the *cadre*. He says a small minority of French parents think that blossoming is the only important thing and don't build any *cadre* for their kids. It's pretty clear how Marcelli feels about this latter group. Their children, he says, "don't do well at all, and despair in every sense."

I'm quite taken with this new view. From now on I'm determined to be authoritative but not authoritarian. When I'm putting Bean to bed one evening, I tell her that I know she needs to do *bêtises* sometimes. She looks relieved. It's a moment of complicity.

"Can you tell that to Daddy?" she asks.

Bean, who, after all, spends her days in a French school, has a better grasp of discipline than I do. One morning I'm in the lobby of our apartment building. Simon is traveling, I'm alone with the kids, and we're running late. I need the boys to get into the stroller so I can rush Bean to school and then take them to the crèche. But the boys refuse to get into their double stroller. They want to walk, which will take even longer. What's more, we're in the courtyard of our building, so the neighbors can hear and even watch this whole exchange. I summon whatever precoffee authority I can muster and insist that they get in. This has no effect.

Bean has been watching me, too. She clearly believes that I should be able to galvanize two little boys.

"Just say 'one, two, three,'" she says, with considerable irritation. Apparently, this is what her teachers say when they want an uncoop-erative child to comply.

Saying one, two, three isn't rocket science. Some American parents certainly say it, too. But the logic behind it is very French. "This gives him some time, and it's respectful to the child," Daniel Marcelli says.[1] The child should be allowed to play an active role in obeying, which requires giving him time to respond.

In *It Is Permissible to Obey*, Marcelli gives the example of a child who seizes a sharp knife. "His mother looks at him and says to him, her face 'cold,' her tone firm and neutral, her eyebrows lightly furrowed: 'Put that down!'" In this example, the child looks at his mother but doesn't move. Fifteen seconds later, his mother adds, in a firmer tone, "You put it down right away" and then ten seconds later, "Do you understand?"

In Marcelli's telling, the little boy then puts the knife on the table. "The mother's face relaxes, her voice becomes sweeter, and she says to him, 'That's good.' Then she explains to him that it's dangerous and that you can cut yourself with a knife."

Marcelli notes that although the child was obedient in the end, he was also an active participant. There was reciprocal respect. "The child has obeyed, his mother thanks him but not excessively, her child recognizes her authority . . . For this to happen, there must be words, time, patience, and reciprocal recognition. If his mother had rushed over to him and snatched the knife from his hands, he wouldn't have understood much of anything."

It's hard to strike this balance between being the boss but also listening to a child and respecting him. One afternoon, as I'm getting Joey dressed to leave the crèche, he suddenly collapses in tears. I'm all charged up in my new "It's me who decides" mode. I have the fervor of a convert. I decide that this is like the incident with Adrien on the doctor's scale: I'm going to force him to get dressed.

But Fatima, his favorite caregiver at the crèche, hears the ruckus and comes into the changing room. She takes the opposite tack from me. Joey may throw fits all the time at home, but at the crèche it's quite unusual. Fatima leans into Joey and starts stroking his forehead.

"What is it?" she keeps asking him gently. She views this tantrum not as some abstract, inevitable expression of the terrible twos but as communication from a very small, blond, rational being.

After a minute or two, Joey calms down enough to explain—through words and gestures—that he wants his hat from his locker. That's what this whole scene had been about. (I think he'd tried to grab it earlier.) Fatima takes Joey down from the changing table, then watches as he goes to the locker, opens it, and takes out the hat. After that, he's *sage* and ready to go.

Fatima isn't a pushover. She has a lot of authority with the kids. She didn't think that just because she patiently listened to Joey, she was giving in to him. She just calmed him down, then gave him a chance to express what he wanted.

Unfortunately, there are endless scenarios and no one rule about what to do in every case. The French have a whole bunch of contradictory principles and few hard-and-fast rules. Sometimes you listen carefully to your kid. And sometimes you just put him on the scale. It's about setting limits, but also about observing your child, building complicity, and then adapting to what the situation requires.

For some parents, all this probably becomes automatic. But for now, I wonder if this balance will ever come naturally to me. It feels like the difference between trying to learn salsa dancing as a thirty-year-old and growing up dancing salsa as a child with your dad. I'm still counting steps and stepping on toes.

In some American homes I've visited, it's not uncommon for a child to be sent to his room during practically every meal. In France, there are lots of small reminders about how to behave, but being *puni* (punished) is a big deal.

Often, parents send the punished child to his room or to a corner. Sometimes, they spank him. I've seen French kids spanked in public only a few times, though friends of mine in Paris say they see it more frequently. At a staging of *Goldilocks and the Three Bears*, the actress playing mommy bear asks the audience what should happen to the baby bear, who's been acting up.

"*La fessée!*" (a spanking) the crowd of little kids shouts in unison. In a national poll,[2] 19 percent of French parents said they spank their kids "from time to time"; 46 percent said they spank "rarely"; and 2 percent said they spank "often." Another 33 percent said they never spank their kids.[3]

In the past, *la fessée* probably played a bigger role in French child rearing and in enforcing adults' authority. But the tide is turning. All the French parenting experts I read about oppose it.[4] Instead of spanking, they recommend that parents become adept at saying no. Like Marcelli, they say that "no" should be used sparingly. But once uttered, it must be definitive.

This idea isn't new. In fact, it comes all the way from Rousseau. "Give willingly, refuse unwillingly," he writes in *Émile*. "But let your refusal be irrevocable. Let no entreaties move you; let your 'no,' once uttered, be a wall of brass, against which the child may exhaust his strength some five or six times, but in the end he will try no more to overthrow it. Thus you will make him patient, equable, calm and resigned, even when he does not get all he wants."

In addition to the rapid-movement gene, Leo has also been born with the subversive gene.

"I want water," he announces at dinner one night.

"What's the magic word?" I ask sweetly.

"Water!" he says, smirking. (Strangely, Leo—who looks the most like Simon—speaks with a slight British accent. Joey and Bean both sound American.)

Building a *cadre* for your kids is a lot of work. In the early years, it requires much repetition and attention. But once it's in place, it makes life much easier and calmer (or so it seems). In moments of desperation I start telling my kids, in French, *"C'est moi qui décide"* (It's me who decides). Just uttering this sentence is strangely fortifying. My back stiffens a bit when I say it.

The French way also requires a paradigm shift. I'm so used to believing that everything revolves around the kids. Being more "French" means moving the center of gravity away from them and letting my own needs spread out a bit, too.

Feeling like I have some control also makes having three little kids a lot more manageable. When Simon is traveling one spring weekend, I let the kids drag carpets and blankets out on our balcony and create a kind of Moroccan lounge. I bring them hot chocolate, and they sit around sipping it.

When I tell Simon about this later, he immediately asks, "Wasn't it stressful?" It probably would have been a few weeks earlier. I'd have felt overpowered by them or too worried to enjoy it. There would have been shouting, which—since our balcony overlooks the courtyard—our neighbors would have heard.

But now that I'm the decider, at least a little bit, having three kids on the balcony with hot chocolate actually feels manageable. I even sit down and have a cup of coffee with them.

One morning I'm taking Leo to crèche by himself. (Simon and I have divided the morning duties.) As I'm riding down the elevator with Leo, I feel a sense of dread. I decide to tell him firmly that there will be no shouting in the courtyard. I present this new rule as if it has always existed. I explain it firmly, while looking into Leo's eyes. I ask him whether he understands, and then pause to give him a chance to reply. After a thoughtful moment, he says yes.

When we open the glass door and walk out into the courtyard, it's silent. There's no shouting or whining. There's just a very speedy little boy, tugging me along.

Chapter 14

let him live his life

One day, a notice goes up at Bean's school. It says that parents of students ages four to eleven can register their kids for a summer trip to the Hautes-Vosges, a rural region about five hours by car from Paris. The trip, *sans* parents, will last for eight days.

I can't imagine sending Bean, who's five, on an eight-day school holiday. She's never even spent more than a night alone at my mother's house. My own first overnight class trip, to SeaWorld, was when I was in junior high.

This trip is yet another reminder that while I can now use the subjunctive in French, and even get my kids to listen to me, I'll never actually be French. Being French means looking at a notice like this and saying, as the mother of another five-year-old next to me does, "What a shame. We already have plans then." None of the French parents find the idea of dispatching their four- and five-year-olds for a week of group showers and dormitory life to be at all alarming.

I soon discover that this school trip is just the beginning. I didn't go to sleepaway camp until I was ten or eleven. But in France, there are hundreds of different sleepaway *colonies de vacances* (vacation colonies) for kids as young as four. The younger kids typically go away for seven or eight days to the countryside, where they ride ponies, feed goats, learn songs, and "discover nature." For older kids, there are *colonies* that specialize in things like theater, kayaking, or astronomy.

It's clear that giving kids a degree of independence, and stressing a kind of inner resilience and self-reliance, is a big part of French parenting. The French call this *autonomie* (autonomy). They generally aim to give children as much autonomy as they can handle. This includes physical autonomy, like the class trips. It also includes emotional separation, like letting them build their own self-esteem that doesn't depend on praise from parents and other adults.

I admire a lot about French parenting. I've tried to absorb the French way of eating, of wielding authority, and of teaching my kids to entertain themselves. I've started speaking at length to babies and letting my kids just "discover" things for themselves, instead of pushing them to acquire skills. In moments of crisis and confusion, I often find myself asking: What would a French mother do?

But I have a harder time accepting certain parts of the French emphasis on autonomy, like the school trips. Of course I don't want my kids to be too dependent on me. But what's the rush? Must the push for autonomy start so young? And aren't the French overdoing it a bit? In some cases, the drive to make kids self-reliant seems to clash with my most basic instincts to protect my kids and to make them feel good.

American parents tend to dole out independence quite differently. It's only after I marry Simon, a European, that I realize I spent much of my childhood acquiring survival skills. You wouldn't know it from looking at me, but I can shoot a bow and arrow, right a capsized canoe, safely build a fire on someone's stomach, and—while treading water—convert a pair of blue jeans into an inflated life jacket.

As a European, Simon didn't have this survivalist upbringing. He never learned how to pitch a tent or steer a kayak. He'd be hard-pressed to know which end of a sleeping bag to crawl into. In the wild he'd survive about fifteen minutes—and that's only if he had a book.

The irony is, while I have all these faux pioneering skills, I learned them in tightly scheduled summer camps after my parents had signed disclaimers drawn up by lawyers in case I drowned. And that was before there were Webcams in classrooms and vegan, nut-free birthday cakes.

Despite their scouting badges and killer backhands, middle-class American kids are famously quite protected. "The current trend in parenting is to shield children from emotional or physical discomfort," the American psychologist Wendy Mogel writes in *The Blessing of a Skinned Knee*. Instead of giving kids freedom, the well-heeled parents Mogel counsels "try to armor [their kids] with a thick layer of skills by giving them lots of lessons and pressuring them to compete and excel."

It's not simply that Americans don't emphasize autonomy. It's that we're not sure it's a good thing. We tend to assume that parents should be physically present as much as possible, to protect kids from harm and to smooth out emotional turbulence for them. Simon and I have joked since Bean was born that we'll just move with her to wherever she attends college. Then I see an article saying that some American colleges now hold "parting ceremonies" for the parents of incoming freshmen, to signal that the parents need to leave.

French parents don't seem to have this fantasy of control. They want to protect their kids, but they aren't obsessed with far-flung eventualities. When they're traveling they don't, as I do, e-mail their husband once a day to remind him to bolt the front door and to make sure that all the toilet lids are closed (so a child can't fall in).

In France, the social pressure goes in the opposite direction. If a parent hovers too much or seems to micromanage his child's experiences, someone else is apt to urge him to back off. My friend Sharon, the literary agent with two kids, explains: "Here there's an argument about pushing a child to the max. Everyone will say, 'You have to let children live their lives.'"

The French emphasis on autonomy comes all the way from Françoise Dolto. "The most important thing is that a child will be, in full security, autonomous as early as possible," Dolto says in *The Major Stages of Childhood*. "The trap of the relationship between parents and children is not recognizing the true needs of the child, of which freedom is one. . . . The child has the need to feel 'loved in what he is becoming,' sure of himself in a space, day by day more freely left to his own exploration, to his personal experience, and in his relations with those of his own age."

Dolto is talking, in part, about leaving a child alone, safely, to figure out things for himself. She also means respecting him as a separate being who can cope with challenges. In Dolto's view, by the time a child is six years old, he should be able to do everything in the house—and in society—that concerns him.[1]

The French way can be tough for even the most integrated Americans to accept. My friend Andi, an artist who's lived in France for more than twenty years, says that when her older son was six she found out that he had an upcoming class trip.

"Everyone tells you how great it is, because in April there'll be a *classe verte* [literally, a green class]. And you say to yourself, 'Hmm, what's that? Oh, a field trip. And it's a week? It lasts a week?'" At her son's school, the trips are optional until first grade. After that, the whole class of twenty-five kids is expected to go on a weeklong trip with the teacher each spring.

Andi says that by American standards, she isn't a particularly clingy mother. However, she couldn't get comfortable with the "green class"—which was to be held near some salt marshes off the western coast of France. Her son had never even gone on a sleepover. Andi still corralled him into the shower each night. She couldn't imagine him going to bed without her tucking him in. She liked his teacher, but she didn't know the other adults who'd be supervising the trip. One was the teacher's nephew. Another was a supervisor from the playground. The third, Andi recalls, was just "this other person [the teacher] knows."

When Andi told her three sisters in the United States about the trip, "they completely freaked out. They said, 'You don't have to do that!' One's a lawyer, and she's like, 'Did you sign anything?'" Andi says they were mainly worried about pedophiles.

At an informational meeting about the trip, another American mom from the class asked the teacher how she would cope with a scenario in which an electrical wire accidentally fell in the water and a child then walked into the water. Andi says the French parents snickered. She was relieved that she hadn't asked the question, but she admits that it reflected her own "hidden neuroses."

Andi's own main concern—which she didn't dare raise at the meeting—was what would happen if her son became sad or upset during the trip. When this happens at home, "I try to help him identify his emotions. If he started crying and he didn't know why, I would say, 'Are you scared, frustrated, are you angry?' That was my thing. I was like, 'Okay, we're going to go through this together.'"

The French emphasis on autonomy extends beyond school trips. My heart regularly jumps when I'm walking around my neighborhood, because French parents will often let small kids race ahead of them on the sidewalk. They trust that the kids will stop at the corner and wait for them. Watching this is particularly terrifying when the kids are on scooters.

I live in a world of worst-case scenarios. When I run into my friend Hélène on the street and we stop to chat, she lets her three girls wander off a bit, toward the edge of the sidewalk. She trusts that they won't suddenly dash into the street. Bean probably wouldn't do that either. But just in case, I make her stand next to me and hold my hand. Simon reminds me that I once wouldn't let Bean sit in the stands to watch him play soccer, in case she got hit by the ball.

There are many small moments in France when I'd expect to help my kids along, but they're supposed to go it alone. By accident, I often run into the caregivers from the boys' crèche leading a group of toddlers down the street to buy the day's baguettes. It's not an official outing; it's just taking a few kids for a walk. Bean has been on school trips to the zoo or to a big park on the outskirts of Paris, which I learn about only by accident weeks later (when I happen to take her to the same zoo). I am rarely asked to sign waivers. French parents don't seem to worry that anything untoward might be happening on these trips.

When Bean has a recital for her dance class, I'm not even allowed backstage. I make sure she has a pair of white leggings, which is the only instruction that's been communicated to parents. I never speak to the teacher. Her relationship is with Bean, not with me. When we get to the theater, I just hand Bean over to an assistant, who shuttles her backstage.

For weeks Bean has been telling me, "I don't want to be a marionette." I wasn't sure what that meant, but it becomes clear as soon as the curtains open. Bean comes onstage in full costume and makeup, with a dozen other little girls, doing deliberately jolty arm and leg movements to a song called "Marionetta." Not deliberately, the girls are way out of sync with one another. They look like escaped marionettes who've had too much cognac.

But it's clear that Bean, without my knowledge, has memorized an entire ten-minute dance routine. When she comes out from backstage after the show, I gush about what a wonderful job she did. But she looks disappointed.

"I forgot to not be a marionette," she says.

French kids aren't just more independent in their extracurricular activities. They also have more autonomy in their dealings with one another. French parents seem slower to intervene in playground disputes or to mediate arguments between siblings. They expect kids to work these situations out for themselves. French schoolyards are famously free-for-alls, with teachers mostly watching from the sidelines.

When I pick up Bean from preschool one afternoon, she has just come from the schoolyard and has a red gash on her cheek. It's not deep, but it's bleeding. She won't tell me what happened (though she doesn't seem concerned, and she isn't in pain). Her teacher claims not to know what happened. I'm practically in tears by the time I question the director of the school, but she doesn't know anything about it either. They all seem surprised that I'm making such a fuss.

My mother happens to be visiting, and she can't believe this non-chalance. She says that a similar injury in America would prompt official inquiries, calls home, and lengthy explanations.

For French parents, such events are upsetting, but they aren't Shakespearean tragedies. "In France we like it when kids brawl a bit," the journalist and author Audrey Goutard tells me. "It's the part of us that's a bit French and a bit Mediterranean. We like that our children know how to defend their territory and quarrel a bit with other children. . . . We're not bothered by a certain violence between children."

Bean's reluctance to say how she got the gash probably reflects another aspect of the autonomy ethos. "Telling" on another child—known in French as *rapporter contre*—is viewed very badly. People theorize that this is because of all the lethal informing on neighbors that went on during World War II. At the annual meeting of my apartment's building association, many of whose members were alive during the war, I ask if anyone knows who's been tipping over our stroller in the lobby.

"We don't *rapporter*," an older woman says. Everyone laughs.

Americans don't like tattletales, either. However, in France, even among kids, having the inner resolve to suffer some scrapes and keep your lips sealed is considered a life skill. Even within families, people are entitled to their secrets.

"I can have secrets with my son that he can't tell his mother," Marc, the French golfer, tells me. I see a French movie in which a well-known economist picks up his teenage daughter at a Parisian police station after she's been brought in for shoplifting and possessing marijuana. On the drive home, she defends herself by saying that at least she didn't rat on the friend who was with her.

This don't-tell culture creates solidarity among kids. They learn to rely on one another and on themselves, rather than rushing to parents or school authorities for backup. There certainly isn't the same reverence for truth at any cost. Marc and his American wife, Robynne, tell me about a recent case in which their son Adrien, who's now ten, saw another student setting off firecrackers at school. There was a big inquiry. Robynne urged Adrien to tell the school authorities what he'd seen. Marc advised him to consider the other boy's popularity and whether he could beat up Adrien.

"You have to calculate the risks," Marc says. "If the advantage is not to do anything, he should do nothing. I want my son to analyze things."

I see this emphasis on making kids learn their own lessons when I'm renovating our apartment. Like all the American parents I know, I'm eager for everything to be rigorously childproof. I choose rubber flooring for the kids' bathroom, lest they slip on wet tile. I also insist that every appliance has a kidproof lock and that the oven door is the type that doesn't get hot.

My contractor, Régis, an earthy, roguish fellow from Burgundy, thinks I'm nuts. He says the way to "childproof" an oven is to let the kid touch it once and realize that it's hot. Régis refuses to install rubber floors in the bathroom, saying that they would look terrible. I concede, but only when he also mentions the apartment's resale value. I don't budge on the oven.

On the day that I read an English story to Bean's class at maternelle, the teacher gives a brief English lesson beforehand. She points to a pen and asks the kids to say the pen's color in English. In response, a four-year-old boy says something about his shoes.

"That has nothing to do with the question," the teacher tells him.

I'm taken aback by this response. I would have expected the teacher to find something positive to say, no matter how far off the subject the answer is. I come from the American tradition of, as the sociologist Annette Lareau describes it, "treating each child's thought as a special contribution."[2] By crediting kids for even the most irrelevant comments, we try to give them confidence and make them feel good about themselves.

In France, that kind of parenting is very conspicuous. I see this when I take the kids to the inground trampolines in the Tuileries gardens, next to the Louvre. Each child jumps on his own trampoline inside a gated area while parents watch from the surrounding benches. But one mom has brought a chair inside the gates and parked it directly in front of her son's trampoline. She shouts "Whoa!" each time he jumps. I know, even before I approach to eavesdrop further, that she must be an Anglophone like me.

I know this because, although I manage to restrain myself at the trampolines, I feel compelled to say "Whee!" each time one of my kids goes down a slide. This is shorthand for "I see you doing this! I approve! You're wonderful!" Likewise, I praise even their worst drawings and artwork. I feel that I must, to boost their self-esteem.

French parents also want their kids to feel good about themselves and "bien dans leur peau" (comfortable in their own skin). But they have a different strategy for bringing this about. It's in some ways the opposite of the American strategy. They don't believe that praise is always good.

The French believe that kids feel confident when they're able to do things for themselves, and do those things well. After children have learned to talk, adults don't praise them for saying just anything. They praise them for saying interesting things, and for speaking well. Sociologist Raymonde Carroll says French parents want to teach their children to verbally "defend themselves well." She quotes an informant who says, "In France, if the child has something to say, others listen to him. But the child can't take too much time and still retain his audience; if he delays, the family finishes his sentences for him. This gets him in the habit of formulating his ideas better before he speaks. Children learn to speak quickly, and to be interesting."

Even when French kids do say interesting things—or just give the correct answer—French adults are decidedly understated in response. They don't act like every job well done is an occasion to say "good job." When I take Bean to the free health clinic for a checkup, the pediatrician asks her to do a wooden puzzle. Bean does it. The doctor looks at the finished puzzle and then does something I'm not constitutionally capable of: practically nothing. She mutters the faintest "*bon*"—more of a "let's move on" than a "good"—then proceeds with the checkup.

Not only don't teachers and authority figures in France routinely praise children to their faces but, to my great disappointment, they also don't routinely praise children to their parents. I had hoped this was a quirk of Bean's rather sullen first-year teacher. The following year she has two alternating teachers. One is a dynamic, extremely warm young woman named Marina, with whom Bean has an excellent rapport. But when I ask Marina how things are going, she says that Bean is "*très compétente.*" (I type this into Google Translate, to make sure I haven't missed some nuance of *compétente* that might suggest brilliance. It just means "competent.")

It's good that my expectations are low when Simon and I have a midsemester meeting with Agnès, Bean's other teacher. She, too, is lovely and attentive. And yet she also seems reluctant to label Bean or make any general statements about her. She simply says, "Everything is fine." Then she shows us the one worksheet—out of dozens—that Bean had trouble finishing. I leave the meeting having no idea of how Bean ranks against her peers.

After the meeting, I'm miffed that Agnès didn't mention anything that Bean has done well. Simon points out that in France, that's not a teacher's job. Rather, Agnès's role is to discover problems. If the child is struggling, the parents need to know. If the child is coping, there's nothing more to say.

This focus on the negative, rather than on trying to boost kids'— and parents'—morales with positive reinforcement, is a well-known (and often criticized) feature of French schools. It's almost impossible to get a perfect score on the French *baccalauréat*, the final exams at the end of high school. A score of 14:20 (14 out of a possible 20) is considered excellent, and 16:20 is almost like getting a perfect score.[3]

Through friends I meet Benoît, who's a father of two and a professor at one of France's elite universities. Benoît says his high-school-aged son is an excellent student. However, the most positive comment a teacher ever wrote on one of his papers was *des qualités* (some good qualities). Benoît says French teachers don't grade their students on a curve, but rather against an ideal, which practically no one meets.[4] Even for an outstanding paper, "the French way would be to say 'correct, not too bad, but this and this and this and this are wrong.'"

By high school, Benoît says there's little value placed on letting students express their feelings and opinions. "If you say, 'I love this poem because it makes me think of certain experiences I had,' that's completely wrong. . . . What you're taught in high school is to learn to reason. You're not supposed to be creative. You're supposed to be articulate."

When Benoît took a temporary posting at Princeton, he was surprised when students accused him of being a harsh grader. "I learned that you had to say some positive things about even the worst essays," he recalls. In one incident, he had to justify giving a student a D. Conversely, I hear that an American who taught at a French high school got complaints from parents when she gave grades of 18:20 and 20:20.

The parents assumed that the class was too easy and that the grades were "fake."

All this criticism can intimidate kids. A girlfriend of mine who went to French schools until she moved to Chicago for high school, remembers being shocked by how American students spoke up confidently in class. She says that unlike in her French schools, students weren't immediately criticized for being wrong or for asking dumb questions. Another friend, a French physician who lives in Paris, tells me excitedly about the new yoga class she's taking, taught by an American woman. "She keeps telling me how well I'm doing and how beautiful I am!" she says of the teacher. In her many years of French schooling, my friend had probably never gotten so much praise.

In general, the French parents I know are a lot more supportive than French teachers. They do praise their kids and give them positive reinforcement. Even so, they don't slather on praise, the way we Americans do.

I'm starting to suspect that French parents may be right in giving less praise. Perhaps they realize that those little zaps of pleasure kids get each time a grown-up says "good job" could—if they arrive too often—simply make kids addicted to positive feedback. After a while, they'll need someone else's approval to feel good about themselves. And if kids are assured of praise for whatever they do, then they won't need to try very hard. They'll be praised anyway.

Since I'm American, what really convinces me is the research. Praise seems to be yet another realm in which French parents are doing—through tradition and intuition—what the latest scientific studies suggest.

In their 2009 book *NurtureShock*, Po Bronson and Ashley Merryman write that the old conventional wisdom that "praise, self-esteem and performance rise and fall together" has been toppled by new research showing that "excessive praise . . . distorts children's motivations; they begin doing things merely to hear the praise, losing sight of the intrinsic enjoyment."

Bronson and Merryman point to research showing that when heavily praised students get to college, they "become risk-averse and lack perceived autonomy." These students "commonly drop out of classes rather than suffer a mediocre grade, and they have a hard time picking a major. They're afraid to commit to something because they're afraid of not succeeding."[5]

This research also refutes the conventional American wisdom that when kids fail at something, parents should cushion the blow with positive feedback. A better tack is to gently delve into what went wrong, giving kids the confidence and the tools to improve. French schools may be a bit harsh, especially in the later years. But this is exactly what Bean's French teachers were doing, and it certainly reflects what French parents believe.

The French seem to proceed through parenting using a kind of scientific method, to test what works and what doesn't. In general, they are unmoved by ideas about what *should* work on their kids and clear-sighted about what actually does work. What they conclude is that some praise is good for a child, but that if you praise her too much, you're not letting her live her life.

Over the winter holidays I bring Bean back to the United States. At a family gathering, she starts putting on a one-child show, which mostly involves acting like a teacher and giving the grown-ups orders. It's cute but, frankly, not brilliant. Yet gradually, every adult in the room stops to watch and to remark on how adorable Bean is. (She wisely drops in some French phrases and songs, knowing that these always impress.)

By the time the show is over, Bean is beaming as she soaks up all the praise. I think it's the highlight of her visit. I'm beaming, too. I interpret the praise for her as praise for me, which I've been starving for in France. All through dinner afterward, everyone talks—within earshot of both of us—about how terrific the show was.

This is great on vacation. But I'm not sure I'd want Bean to get that kind of unconditional praise all the time. It feels good, but it seems to come bundled with other things, including letting a child constantly interrupt because she's bursting with a sense of her own importance. It might also throw off Bean's internal calibration of what's truly entertaining and what's not.

I've accepted that if we stay in France, my kids probably won't ever learn to shoot a bow and arrow. (God forbid they're ever attacked by eighteenth-century American Indians.) I've even toned down my praise a bit. But adjusting to the overarching French view on autonomy is a lot harder. Of course I know that my children have an emotional life that's separate from mine, and that I can't constantly protect them from rejection and disappointment. Nevertheless, the idea that they have their lives and I have mine doesn't reflect my emotional map. Or maybe it just doesn't suit my emotional needs.

Still, I have to admit that my kids seem happiest when I trust them to do things for themselves. I don't hand them knives and tell them to go carve a watermelon. They mostly know when things are way beyond their abilities. But I do let them stretch a bit, even if it's just to carry a breakable plate to the dinner table. After these small achievements, they're calmer and happier. Dolto is most certainly right that autonomy is one of a child's most basic needs.

She also may be right about age six being the threshold. One night, I'm sick with the flu and keeping Simon awake with my coughing. I retreat to the couch in the middle of the night. When the kids march into the living room at about seven thirty A.M., I can hardly move. I don't start my usual routine of putting out breakfast.

So Bean does. I lie on the couch, still wearing my eyeshades. In the background I hear her opening drawers, setting the table, and getting out the milk and cereal. She's five and a half years old. And she's taken my job. She's even subcontracted some of it to Joey, who's organizing the silverware.

After a few minutes, Bean comes over to me on the couch. "Breakfast is ready, but you have to do the coffee," she says. She's calm, and very pleased. I'm struck by how happy—or more specifically how *sage*—being autonomous makes her feel. I haven't praised or encouraged her. She's just done something new for herself, with me as a witness, and is feeling very good about it.

Dolto's idea that I should trust my children, and that trusting and respecting them will make them trust and respect me, is very appealing. In fact, it's a relief. The clutch of mutual dependency and worry that often seems to bind American parents to their kids feels inevitable at times, but it never feels good. It doesn't seem like the basis for the best parenting.

Letting children "live their lives" isn't about releasing them into the wild or abandoning them (though French school trips do feel a bit like that to me). It's about acknowledging that children aren't repositories for their parents' ambitions or projects for their parents to perfect. They are separate and capable, with their own tastes, pleasures, and experiences of the world. They even have their own secrets.

My friend Andi ended up letting her older son go on that trip to the salt marshes. She says he loved it. It seems he didn't need to be tucked in every night; it was Andi who needed to do the tucking. When it was time for Andi's younger son to start taking the same class trips, she just let him go.

Maybe I'll get used to these trips, though I haven't signed up Bean for one yet. My friend Esther proposes that we send our daughters off together to a *colonie de vacance* next summer, when they'll be six years old. I find this hard to imagine. I want my kids to be self-reliant, resilient, and happy. I just don't want to let go of their hands.

the future in french

My mother has finally accepted that we live across an ocean from her. She's even studying French, though it's not going as well as she'd like. An American friend of hers, who lived in Panama but spoke little Spanish, suggests a technique: Say a Spanish sentence in the present tense, then shout the name of the intended tense. "I go to the store . . . *pasado!*" means that she went to the store. "I go to the store . . . *futuro!*" means that she'll go later.

I've forbidden my mother to do this when she comes to visit. To my astonishment, I now have a reputation to protect. I have three kids in the local school and courteous relations with neighborhood fishmongers, tailors, and café proprietors. Paris finally cares that I'm here.

I still haven't swooned for the city. I get tired of the elaborate exchanges of *bonjour* and of using the distancing *vous* with everyone but colleagues and intimates. Living in France feels a bit too formal and doesn't bring out my freewheeling side. I realize how much I've changed when, on the metro one morning, I instinctively back away from the man sitting next to the only empty seat, because I have the impression that he's deranged. On reflection, I realize my only evidence for this is that he's wearing shorts.

Nevertheless, Paris has come to feel like home. As the French say,

I've "found my place." It helps that I've made some wonderful friends. It turns out that behind their icy facades, Parisian women need to mirror and bond, too. They're even hiding a bit of cellulite. These friendships have turned me into a bona fide Francophone. I'm often surprised, midconversation, to hear coherent French sentences coming out of my own mouth.

It's also exciting watching my kids become bilingual. One morning, as I'm getting dressed, Leo points to my brassiere.

"What's that?" he asks.

"A bra," I say.

He immediately points to his arm. It takes me a second to understand: the French word *bras* (with a silent *s*) means "arm." He must have learned this word at his crèche. I quiz him and discover that he knows most of the other main body parts in French, too.

What has really connected me to France is discovering the wisdom of French parenting. I've learned that children are capable of feats of self-reliance and mindful behavior that, as an American parent, I might never have imagined. I can't go back to not knowing this—even if we end up living elsewhere.

Of course, some French principles are easier to implement when you're actually on French soil. When other children aren't having midday snacks at the playground, it's easier not to give your child a snack either. It's also easier to enforce boundaries for your own kids' behavior when everyone around you is enforcing more or less the same boundaries (or as I often ask Bean, "Do they let you do this in school?").

But much about "French" parenting doesn't depend on where you live, or require access to certain types of cheese. It's as accessible in Cleveland as in Cannes. It mostly requires a parent to shift how she conceives of her relationship to her children and what she expects from them.

Friends often ask whether I'm raising my kids to be more French or American. When I'm with them in public, I usually think they're somewhere in between: badly behaved compared with the French kids I know and pretty good compared with the Americans.

They don't always say *bonjour* and *au revoir*, but they know that they're supposed to. Like a real French mother, I'm always reminding them of it. I've come to see this as part of an ongoing process called their *éducation*, in which they increasingly learn to respect other people, and learn to wait. This *éducation* seems to be gradually sinking in.

I'm still striving for that French ideal: genuinely listening to my kids but not feeling that I must bend to their wills.[1] I still declare, "It's me who decides" in moments of crisis, to remind everyone that I'm in charge. I see it as my job to stop my kids from being consumed by their own desires. But I also try to say yes as often as I can.

Simon and I have stopped discussing whether we'll stay in France. If we do, I'm not sure what's in store as our children get older. By the time French kids become teenagers, their parents seem to give them quite a lot of freedom and to be matter-of-fact about their having private lives, and even sex lives. Perhaps that gives the teenagers less reason to rebel.

French teenagers seem to have an easier time accepting that *maman* and *papa* have private lives, too. After all, the parents have always acted as if they do. They haven't based life entirely around their children. French kids do plan to move out of their parents' homes eventually. But if a Frenchman in his twenties still lives with his parents, it isn't quite the humiliating tragedy that it is in America. They can let one another live their lives.

The summer before Bean starts kindergarten I realize that the French way of parenting has really gotten under my skin. Practically all of her French friends are spending weeks of their summer vacations with their grandparents. I decide that we should send Bean to stay in Miami with my mother. My mom will be visiting us in Paris anyway, so they can fly back together.

Simon is against it. What if Bean gets madly homesick and we're an ocean away? I've found a day camp with daily swimming lessons. Because of the timing, she'll have to start the camp midsession. Won't it be difficult for her to make friends? He suggests we wait a year, until she's older.

But Bean thinks the trip is a spectacular idea. She says she'll be fine alone with her grandmother, and that she's excited about the camp. Simon finally acquiesces, perhaps calculating that with Bean away, he'll get to spend more time in cafés. I'll fly to Miami to bring her home.

I give my mother just a few instructions: no pork, lots of sunblock. Bean and I spend a week fine-tuning the contents of her carry-on bag for the airplane. We have a moment of melancholy, when I promise to call every day.

And I do. But as soon as Bean arrives in Miami, she is so absorbed in her adventure that she won't stay on the phone for more than a minute or two. I rely on reports from my mom and her friends. One of them writes in an e-mail to me, "She ate sushi with us tonight, taught us some French, told us about some pressing issues concerning her friends from school, and went off to bed with a smile on her face."

After just a few days, Bean's English—which was once mid-Atlantic-mysterious with a British twist—now sounds almost fully American. She says "car" with a full, flat "ahr." However, she's definitely milking her status as an expatriate. My mom says they listened to her language tapes in the car and that Bean declared, "That man doesn't know French."

Bean does try to figure out what's happened in Paris while she was away. "Is Daddy fat? Is Mommy old?" she asks us, after about a week. My mom says Bean keeps telling people when I'll arrive in Miami, how long I'll stay, and where we'll go after that. Just as Françoise Dolto predicted, she needs both independence and a rational understanding of the world.

When I tell friends about Bean's trip, their reactions split straight down national lines. The North Americans say that Bean is "brave" and ask how she's coping with the separation. None are sending kids her age off for ten-day stints with their grandparents, especially not across an ocean. But my French friends assume that detaching a bit is good for everyone. They take for granted that Bean is having fun on her own and that I'm enjoying a well-deserved break.

As the kids become more independent, Simon and I are getting along better. He's still irritable, and I'm still irritating. But he's decided that it's okay to be cheerful sometimes and to admit that he enjoys my company. Every once in a while, he even laughs at my jokes. Weirdly, he seems to find Bean's sense of humor hilarious.

"When you were born, I thought you were a monkey," he tells her playfully one morning.

"Well, when you were born, I thought you were a caca," she replies. Simon laughs so hard at this, he's practically in tears. It seems I've just never hit on his preferred category of humor: scatological surrealism.

I haven't started making potty jokes, but I have made other concessions. I micromanage Simon less, even when I come out in the morning and he's serving the kids unshaken orange juice. I've figured out that, like them, he craves autonomy. If that means a glass full of pulp for me, so be it. I no longer ask what he's thinking about. I've learned to cultivate—and appreciate—having some mystery in our marriage.

Last summer, we went back to the seaside town where I first noticed all those French children eating happily in restaurants. This time, instead of having one child with us, we have three. And instead of trying to manage in a hotel, we wisely rent a house with a kitchen.

One afternoon, we take the kids out for lunch at a restaurant near the port. It's one of those idyllic French summer days, when white-washed buildings glow in the midday sun. And strangely, all five of us are able to enjoy it. We order our food calmly, and in courses. The kids stay in their seats and enjoy their food—including some fish and vegetables. Nothing lands on the floor. I have to do a bit of gentle coaching. It's not as relaxing as dining out alone with Simon. But it really does feel like we're on vacation. We even have coffee at the end of the meal.

bébé
day by day

introduction

When I wrote a book about what I'd learned raising three kids in France, I wasn't sure that anyone besides my mother would read it. Actually, I wasn't even convinced that she would make it all the way through (she tends to prefer fiction).

But to my surprise, many nonrelatives read the book, too. For a while there were lots of angry articles about it. Who was I to insult "American" parenting—if there really is such a thing? Surely there are lots of little French brats? Had I only researched rich Parisians? Was I extolling socialism—or worse, bottle feeding?

I'm the sort of person who hears any criticism of herself and immediately thinks: that's so true! But then I started getting e-mails from regular American parents like me. (I've posted many of these e-mails on my Web site.) I quickly cheered up. They didn't think I'd falsely accused Americans of having a parenting problem. Like me, they were living that problem, and they were eager to hear about an alternative.

Some parents told me that the book validated what they had already been doing privately—and often guiltily. Others said they'd tried the book's methods on their kids, and that these really did work. (No one was more relieved to hear this than me.) Many asked for more tips and specifics, or for a version of the book—*sans* my personal backstory and voyage of discovery—that they could give as a kind of manual to grandparents, partners, and babysitters.

This is that book. The 100 "keys to French parenting" are my attempt to distill the smartest and most salient principles I've learned from French parents and experts. You don't have to live in Paris to apply them. You don't even have to like cheese. (Though you should have a look at the recipes at the end. They're a sample of what kids in French day cares eat, and they're delicious for grown-ups, too.)

I think there's wisdom in all 100 keys. But they're not my inventions or my personal proclamations. Some of the ideas might appeal to you. Others won't. They're not all right for everyone. The French are very clear that every child is different and that you should break the rules sometimes. But as you read the keys, you'll start to notice that behind many of the individual tips are a few guiding principles. One of these principles was radical for me, as an American: if family life is centered entirely on children, it's not good for anyone, not even for the kids.

I think American parents have already figured this out. By now we've seen the statistics showing that as a new intensive style of parenting has taken hold—one that's popped up seemingly out of nowhere in the last twenty years—marital satisfaction has fallen. Parents are famously less happy than nonparents, and they become even less happy with each additional child. The most depressing study of middle-class American families I read described how parents have gone from being authority figures to being "valet[s] for the child." Given the amount of short-order cooking and schlepping that goes on, I would add "personal chefs" and "chauffeurs," too.

The clincher is that we're starting to doubt whether this demanding way of parenting is even good for kids. Some experts call the first generation of children to graduate from this brand of child rearing "teacups" because they're so fragile and warn that the way we're defining success is making them unhappy.

Obviously, French parents don't do everything right. And they don't all do the same things. The keys describe France's national conventional wisdom. It's what French parenting books, magazines, and experts widely say that you should do; and what most of the middle-class parents I know actually do, or at least believe they should be doing. (Though, a Parisian friend of mine said she planned to give a copy to her brother, so he could "become more French.")

A lot of "French" wisdom feels like common sense. I've gotten letters from readers describing the overlaps between French parenting and Montessori, or the teachings of a Hungarian-born woman named Magda Gerber. Others assured me it's what we Americans did before Reaganomics, the psychotherapy boom, and that study saying that poor kids don't hear enough words when they're little. (Let's just say that the American upper-middle class massively overcompensated.)

But some French ideas have a power and elegance that's all their own. French parents to a great extent believe that babies are rational, that you should combine a little bit of strictness with a lot of freedom, and that you should listen carefully to children but not do everything they say. Their ability to move kids beyond "kid foods" is remarkable. Above all, the French think that the best parenting happens when you're calm. What's really neat is that, in France, you have an entire nation, in real time, trying to follow these principles. It's a country-sized experiment.

The main reason why French parenting is relevant to us now is that it's a kind of mirror image of what's been happening in America. We tend to think we should teach kids cognitive skills, such as reading, as soon as possible. They focus on "soft" skills like socializing and empathy in the early years. We want kids to be stimulated a lot; they think downtime is just as crucial. We often hesitate to frustrate a child; they think a child who can't cope with frustration will grow up miserable.

We're focused on the outcomes of parenting; they think the quality of the eighteen years or so you spend living together counts for a lot, too. We tend to think long-term interrupted sleep, routine tantrums, picky eating, and constant interruptions are mostly inevitable when you have little kids. They believe these things are—please imagine me saying this in a French accent—*impossible*.

Since I'm a journalist, what really sold me on the French principles was the data. Many things that French parents do by intuition, tradition, or trial and error are exactly what the latest research recommends. The French take for granted that you can teach little babies how to sleep through the night; that patience can be learned; that too much praise can be counterproductive; that you should become attuned to a baby's rhythms; that toddlers don't need flash cards; that tasting foods makes you like those foods—all things that science is telling us, too. (To keep the keys simple, I've listed many of the relevant studies in the bibliography.)

Please take this book as inspiration, not doctrine. And be flexible. As French parents often tell me, "You have to keep changing what you do." Kids change quickly. As they do, you can keep the same guiding principles, but apply them differently. I hope this book helps make that possible. Rather than giving lots of specific rules, it's more like a toolbox to help parents figure things out on their own. As the old saying goes: Don't give a man a *filet de saumon à la vapeur*. Just teach him how to fish.

And don't worry about socialism. American parenting is evolving, as it always does. But whatever our next phase is, it won't be French (or Chinese or Icelandic). It'll be our own home brew. I'm happy to toss in some ideas. My mother, at least, thinks I'm on to something.

Chapter 1

a croissant
in the oven

All pregnant women worry. You're making a human being, after all. Some of us can barely make dinner. But in America, worrying can become an Olympic sport. We feel we must weigh whether each bite of food we eat is in the baby's best interest. All this angst doesn't feel pleasant. But often, it does feel necessary. We're signaling that there's nothing we won't sacrifice for our unborn child.

The French don't valorize a pregnant woman's anxiety. Instead, in the word cloud of French pregnancy, terms like *serenity, balance,* and *Zen* keep popping up. Mothers-to-be are supposed to signal their competence by showing how calm they are and by making it clear that they still experience pleasure. This small shift in emphasis makes a big difference.

1. Pregnancy Is Not an Independent Research Project

French mothers-to-be might read a baby book or two. But they don't consider this required reading or feel that they must pick a parenting philosophy. There is an important difference between being prepared and being the person who recites the names of chromosomal disorders at dinner.

Making a baby is more mysterious and meaningful than anything you've ever done. You can dwell in the enormity of that without trying to micromanage it, and without anointing a personal guru. The most important voice to have inside your head is your own.

2. Calm Is Better for the Baby

If you're not persuaded to be calm for your own sake, do it for your unborn child. French pregnancy magazines say that the fetus senses his mother's moods. He's jolted by too much stress and soothed when pleasure hormones cross the placenta. Experts urge pregnant women to reduce worry by discussing their concerns with a doctor or therapist and by pampering themselves with pedicures, romantic nights out (preferably with the baby's father), and lunch with friends. In the French telling, the resulting *zen maman* pops out a *zen bébé*, and a calm pregnancy sets the tone for calm parenting.

3. Don't Panic About Sushi

France's future *mamans* try to keep the risks in perspective. They know that some things—like cigarettes and alcohol—are categorically hazardous to the unborn child. French doctors now advise going cold turkey on both (though some women still have the occasional *coupe de champagne*). But other things are dangerous only if they happen to be contaminated. Sushi, salami, uncooked shellfish, and unpasteurized cheese are in this category.

Please don't rush out and eat oysters (or any of the above). Listen to your doctor. But remember that accidentally eating unpasteurized Parmesan cheese with your pasta is not grounds for a nervous break-down.

4. The Fetus Doesn't Need Cheesecake

Pregnancy isn't the culinary free-for-all you've been saving up for through all those food-deprived years of courtship and marriage. French guides say that when your body shouts for brioche, you should distract it by eating an apple or a piece of cheese. Women's long-term strategy is to enjoy the occasional bowl of *mousse au chocolat*, instead of banish-ing it entirely. This quells the beast and makes them less likely to go overboard on such foods later. This way of eating—moderation instead of deprivation—could explain why a recent French pregnancy book was called *Emergency: She Wants Strawberries*.

5. Eat for One (and a Bit)

Plan to emerge from pregnancy with your allure intact. Take your doc-tor's weight-gain limits seriously. (The French limits are lower than American ones, and Frenchwomen treat them like holy edicts.) Re-member that it will be much easier to lose the baby weight if you haven't gained too much while pregnant. One French guide says that a moderately active pregnant woman needs an additional two hun-dred to five hundred calories per day, but warns that anything more "inevitably turns into fat." This needn't feel austere. Crucially, French-women don't eat merely to nourish the fetus. They also believe that they're entitled to enjoy themselves.

6. Don't Borrow Your Husband's Shirts

Dressing like a shapeless blob is bad for morale (yours and your mate's; possibly even the baby's). Invest strategically in a few flattering maternity clothes. Then convert cardigans and leggings from your closet into pregnancy gear and brighten your face with lipstick and colored scarves. Attention to these details signals that you are not graduating from "*femme*" to "*maman*." You'll be both.

7. Stay Sexual

French pregnancy magazines don't just mention that it's okay to have sex. They spell out exactly how to do it—including lists of pregnancy-safe sex toys (nothing with batteries), aphrodisiacs (mustard, cinnamon, and chocolate), and detailed instructions on how to maneuver yourself into third-trimester positions. Accompanying fashion spreads show pregnant women in lacy maternity lingerie with come-hither looks. Some of this is aspirational. Pregnant Frenchwomen don't morph into sex goddesses; they have the same fluctuating libidos as the rest of us. But they don't assume that they've crossed into a realm where even the appearance of intimacy is optional. They know that if you put your seductive powers in the deep freeze, it's harder to thaw them out later.

8. Epidurals Aren't Evil

The French don't view childbirth as a heroic journey in pain tolerance, or early proof of the trials a mother is willing to undergo for her child. Frenchwomen don't typically launch their babies into the world amid a frenzy of micromanagement in which they specify the lighting, the guest list, and who gets to "catch" the baby when it comes out.

There are midwives, prenatal baby whisperers, and even some home births in France. The French don't think there's anything wrong with giving birth the way you want to. But they maintain that the point is to get the baby safely from your uterus into your arms. While some things may be better *au naturel* (breasts and maple syrup come to mind), others are better with a giant dose of drugs. Even Frenchwomen who subsist on organic food and plan to breastfeed well into preschool are delighted when the anesthesiologist arrives.

9. Don't Stand on the Business End

Dads: Unless you are actually delivering the baby, don't stand at the "end of the tunnel." Yes, there's the miracle of life to witness. Of course you want to seem welcoming to your child. But consider meeting him half a second later, in order to preserve your partner's feminine mystique. It gets messy down there. As the French saying goes: Not all truths should be told.

Chapter 2

bébé einstein

The French believe that babies aren't helpless blobs. They treat even newborns like tiny, rational people who understand language and can learn things (when they're taught gently and at their own pace). This isn't as far-fetched as it sounds. American scientists have proved that babies aren't blank slates; they can make moral judgments and do basic math. Who knows what baby superpowers they'll discover next? We should at least remember that when we talk, they might be listening.

10. Give Your Baby a House Tour

Like anyone entering her new home for the first time, your baby wants to get oriented and know where she'll be sleeping. When you bring her back from the hospital, show her around. This is it: home base! Later, make a practice of saying good-bye to her when you're going out and telling her when you'll be back. Help her make sense of the world by telling her Grandma is Daddy's (or Mommy's) mother, and what that new sound is outside. The French believe that when they speak to a baby, they're not just reassuring her with the sound of a parent's voice; they're conveying important information. They think that explaining things to an upset baby can calm her down.

11. Observe Your Baby

When you ask a new French mom to explain her parenting philosophy, she'll often shrug and say: "I just observe my baby." She means that she literally spends a lot of time watching what the baby does. This is more important—and less obvious—than it sounds. The mother is trying to tune in to the baby's experience, and learn to read and follow her cues. (American scientists call this sensitivity and say it's one of the most important qualities in a caregiver.) The idea is that you want to be there when the baby needs you. But when she's happily singing and drooling on the play mat, try to just let her be. You are striving to achieve what the French call *complicité*—mutual trust and understanding, even with someone who regularly spits up on you.

12. Tell Your Baby the Truth

France's most famous parenting expert, Françoise Dolto, said that children don't need family life to be perfect. But they do need it to be coherent, and not secret. She insisted that babies can sense when there's a problem in the home and need the same comforting confirmation we all do: "You're not nuts! Something really is wrong!" Dolto said that from six months old, parents should tell the baby if they're getting divorced. When a grandparent dies, parents should gently explain this and briefly bring the child to the funeral. An adoptee needs to hear about her birth mother, even if her adoptive mother simply says: "I don't know her, but you knew her." The French believe that from the time a child is small, parents can make situations easier to accept just by making them clear.

13. Be Polite

French parents tend not to speak down to their infants in singsongy baby talk. However they do pay them the courtesy of saying hello, "please," and "thank you." If the baby understands you, it's never too early to start modeling good manners. And this early *politesse* sets the tone for calm and respectful relations later.

14. Don't Stimulate Her All the Time

Of course you should talk to your baby, show her things, and read her books. But a baby, like anyone else, needs downtime. She doesn't want to be constantly watched and spoken to. She needs time to assimilate all the new information she's been taking in. (Her parents need it, too.) Let interactions and conversations follow a natural rhythm. Give the baby time to roll around in a safe space and be free.

15. Nudge Her onto a Schedule

For the first few months, French parents usually feed babies on demand. After that, they take a few things for granted:

- The baby should eat at more or less the same times each day.
- A few big feeds are better than lots of small ones.
- The baby should adjust to the family's regular eating rhythm.

With these ideas in mind, you can gradually stretch out the amount of time between feedings. Distract the baby from pangs of hunger by taking her for a walk or strapping her into a carrier. At the beginning, you might gain only a few minutes a day. But she'll get used to waiting a bit. Eventually she'll get to three hours between feeds, and before long to four. Soon she'll be on more or less the same eating rhythm she'll be on for the rest of her life: breakfast, lunch, and dinner, plus an afternoon snack. (This roughly corresponds to 8:00 A.M., noon, 4:00 P.M., and 8:00 P.M., but the schedule isn't observed with military precision.)

16. Baby Formula Isn't Poison

French mothers know that breast is best. But they don't view breast-feeding as a measure of the mom, or keep nursing through Dantesque trials of pain and inconvenience. Many pragmatically point out that they themselves are healthy, despite having drunk a lot of powdered formula—the old, worse formula (there are other factors, but still). Some guilt is encroaching in France. But Frenchwomen still tend to think it's unhealthy and unpleasant to breastfeed under moral duress. They believe that whether and how long to nurse should be your private decision, not your play group's. The best reason to breastfeed, they say, is if you and your baby enjoy it.

17. Make Vegetables a Child's First Food

If your baby's first food is bland rice cereal, she'll probably take to it. But why not start with something more exciting? From about six months, French parents feed babies flavor-packed pureed spinach, carrots, seeded zucchini, and other vegetables. They soon move on to fruits, small amounts of meat, and different types of fish. They're trying to launch their children on a lifelong relationship with these flavors and introduce them to the pleasures of eating.

Chapter 3

....

rock-a-bye bébé

ere's a French paradox: French babies often sleep through the night by three or four months old, or even sooner. Yet their parents don't make them "cry it out" for hours on end.

This isn't a coincidence, a mystery, or the result of adding Cognac to their milk. If you believe that little babies can learn things, then you can teach them things. And one of the things you can teach them, early on, is how to sleep.

18. Understand the Science of Sleep

Your baby is unique and adorable and will one day be accepted to a high school of performing arts. There will undoubtedly be a biopic about his life, in which an aging Gwyneth Paltrow plays you, his elderly but still ravishing mother. However, as French parents know, even your own baby is subject to the laws of science. And one of these laws is that all healthy babies, even yours, sleep in brief cycles. At the end of each cycle, babies often wake up and cry a bit.

The key to sleeping for longer stretches is for the baby to learn how to connect his sleep cycles on his own. He needs to be able to wake up after one cycle, then plunge into the next one without anyone else having to get out of bed. Grown-ups—except for the insomniacs and menopausal among us—manage this same feat every night.

Connecting sleep cycles is a skill. A few lucky babies are born with it. Most have to practice before they master it.

19. Babies Are Noisy Sleepers

Infants make a lot of noise when they sleep. They whine. They move their arms like traffic cops. This does not mean they are awake. If you instantly race in to their rooms or pick them up each time they make a peep, you will sometimes wake them up.

20. Do "The Pause"

We know that babies often cry when they're learning to connect their sleep cycles. We also know that they can make a noise like an angry frog and yet still be asleep. So from the time the baby is a few weeks old, pause a bit when he cries at night.*

You are waiting to see if, this time, he will have a breakthrough moment and plunge into the next sleep cycle on his own, without anyone else's help. If you immediately rush in and pick him up, he won't have a chance to develop this skill.

Maybe the baby isn't ready to connect his cycles yet. But if you don't pause, you won't know, and neither will the baby. He'll think he needs you to put him back to sleep at the end of each cycle. Rushing

---

* When you get to know your baby's cries better, you might come to recognize his get-me-out-of-this-wet-diaper cry. When you hear that one, you don't need to pause—just change him.

in may make you feel like a devoted and sacrificial parent. But in effect you're treating your baby like a helpless blob who is not ready to learn and grow.

You needn't pause for very long. Some French parents wait five minutes or so. Others wait a bit more, or less. They're not letting the baby cry it out. If after these few minutes he's still crying, they reason that he must need something. Then they pick him up.

21. Get Baby in the Mood to Sleep

The Pause is necessary but not sufficient to teach babies how to sleep. The French believe you should also have rituals that set the tone for bedtime. Keep the baby near daylight during the day, even when he's napping. Signal to him that the big nighttime sleep is approaching by giving him a bath, changing him into pajamas, singing him a lullaby, and actually saying "good night." Once he's calm and relaxed, but preferably still awake, put him to bed in a dark room at night. Spending cozy time together before bed matters. You want to send him off to sleep feeling secure enough that he can separate from you for a little while and still be okay.

22. Try the Talking Cure

Why talk to everyone else about how your baby sleeps except the baby himself? Tell him it's bedtime. Explain that the whole family needs rest. Say that if he wakes up in the night, you're going to pause a few minutes before you come in to him, because you want him to be able

to fall back asleep on his own. Tell him how nice it will be for everyone—including him—when he no longer needs to wake up at 3:00 A.M.
One French baby book says that after a baby sleeps through the night
for the first time, his parents should tell him how pleased and proud
they are. Doing this also helps lock in the baby's newfound ability.

23. Sleeping Well Is Better for the Baby

French parents don't sleep-teach babies just for their own convenience.
They also believe that sleeping well is in a child's best interest. Research backs them up: a child who sleeps poorly can become hyperac-
tive and irritable, have trouble learning and remembering things, and
have more accidents. (My personal studies suggest that the same is true
for sleep-deprived parents.)

And sleep contains an important symbolic lesson for babies: learning
to sleep is part of learning to be part of the family. Babies eventually
need to adapt to what others need, too. Three months—the age when
many French babies sleep through the night—happens to be about
when French maternity leave ends, and many *mamans* need to be fresh
for work in the morning.

24. Don't Expect Any
of This to Work Immediately

It probably won't. But stick with it and stay confident that your baby
will, as the French say, "do his nights." Convey this confidence to your
baby (it helps!). Believe that if you keep gently and patiently teaching

your baby how to sleep well, he will eventually learn—often just when
your own sleep-deprivation experiment starts to feel unbearable.

25. If You Miss the Window for the Pause, Let Baby Cry It Out

The gentle sleep-teaching method of The Pause works best in the baby's first four months. When parents miss this window, French experts
often suggest doing some form of crying it out—leaving the baby to
cry for a longer period. Talk to the baby about this, too. It generally
succeeds within a few nights.

······························

Chapter 4

bébé

gourmet

magine a planet where family mealtimes are pleasant, children eat the same foods as their parents, and few kids get fat. That planet is France. But none of this happens automatically. French parents set out to teach their kids how to eat well, and they work at it assiduously. Their efforts pay off four times a day. The moral of the French food story is: treat your child like a little gourmet, and he will (gradually) rise to the occasion.

26. There Are No "Kid" Foods

You can find chicken nuggets, fish fingers, and pizza in France. But these are occasional foods for kids, typically not daily fare (the same goes for French fries—known locally as *frites*). Parents almost never let their kids become picky eaters who survive on mono-diets of pasta and white rice. Starting from a very young age, French kids mostly eat the same foods as their parents. The weekly lunch menu at Paris's state-run day care consists of four-course meals (including a cheese course) that look like something you might order in a bistro (see the sample weekly crèche menu on page 375).

27. There's One Snack a Day

I used to find it hard to imagine kids going from breakfast to lunch without as much as a raisin in between. But I've discovered that this feat is possible and even pleasant. French kids typically eat only at mealtimes and at the afternoon snack, called the *goûter* (pronounced gew-tay).

It turns out that if the child doesn't snack much, she's hungry by mealtimes, so she eats more. There's also something calming about not regarding every moment as a potential eating opportunity. Everyone can get on with other things. And once you're in the swing of this one-snack system, the *goûter* becomes a special little occasion every day. It's usually some combination of sweets, dairy, and fruit. Often there's some chocolate. One classic *goûter* is a chocolate sandwich—a piece of dark chocolate in a baguette. It might come with a box of juice.

28. Don't Solve a Crisis with a Cookie

Not producing an Oreo whenever a child whines can have far-reaching benefits. First, you're not rewarding her outbursts, so you're not encouraging her to whine again. Second, you're teaching her not to eat just because she's upset. She'll thank you when she's thirty and can still fit into her high school jeans.

29. *You Are the Keeper of the Fridge*

In France, kids don't have the right to open the refrigerator and take whatever they want. They have to ask their parents first. This doesn't just cut down on the snacking in the house. It also cuts down on the chaos.

30. *Let Kids Cook*

The five-year-old French girl who lives next door to us measures and mixes the oil, vinegar, mustard, and salt for the family's vinaigrette all by herself. It's no coincidence that she loves salad. We all feel more invested in foods that we've had a hand in preparing. (Just think how much you want everyone to taste your casserole at Thanksgiving.)

I've seen French two-year-olds sit at the kitchen counter tearing up spinach. Three-year-olds learn to peel cucumbers, cut tomatoes with a blunt-tipped knife, and mix the batter for crepes. Parents oversee this process and don't mind a little mess. Plus there's no better time to find out what happened to your kindergartner at school than when you are peeling the shells off hard-boiled eggs together.

When the cooking is done, eat as the French typically do: together, at the table, with the television off.

31. Serve Food in Courses, Vegetables First

Family meals don't need to be fancy. You don't need to light candles or drape a white napkin over your arm. Just bring out some vegetables first, before anything else. If your kids haven't been snacking all day, they will be hungry and more likely to eat them. (The same strategy works at breakfast with cut-up fruit.) A vegetable starter doesn't have to be elaborate. It can be a bowl of peas in pods (all the better to shell them), some cut-up cherry tomatoes with salt and olive oil, or sautéed broccoli. Just put a serving on each child's plate, and wait.

32. Everyone Eats the Same Thing

In France, children don't decide what they'll have for dinner. There are no choices or customizations. There's just one meal, the same one for everyone. It's safe to try this at home. If a child doesn't eat something, or barely eats it, react neutrally. Do not offer her something else instead. If she is just emerging from a kids' food ghetto, ease her into it by making family meals that everyone likes, then gradually introducing new dishes.

Above all, stay positive and calm. Give the new rules time to settle. Remember that you're crediting your child with being able to eat the same foods as you. Accompany the new rules with some new freedoms, like letting her cut the quiche, or sprinkle the Parmesan cheese herself. When you eat in a restaurant, let her order what she wants, within reason.

33. You Just Have to Taste It

Most kids like ice cream instantly (though mine strangely complained that it was "too cold"). However, many other foods take some warming up to. Their very newness puts kids off. It's only through trying these foods lots of times that kids start to like them.

This is the cornerstone of the way the French feed their children. Kids have to take at least one bite of every dish that's on the table. I'm sure there are French families who don't consider this rule to be sacred and infallible, but I have yet to meet them.

Present the tasting rule to your child as if it's a law of nature—like gravity. Explain that our tastes are shaped by what we eat. If she's nervous about tasting something for the first time, let her just pick up a piece and sniff it (often a little nibble will follow). One new food per meal is enough. Serve it alongside something you know she likes.

Oversee this process without acting like a prison guard. Be calm and even playful about it. After she takes the requisite bite, acknowledge this. React neutrally if she says she doesn't like it. Never offer a replacement food. Remember, you're playing the long game. You don't want her to eat an artichoke once, under duress. You want her to gradually learn to like artichokes.

34. Keep Foods in the Rotation

Even if a certain food isn't a hit, make sure it keeps coming back. Put broccoli in soup, melt some cheese on it, or stir-fry it. Broccoli might never be your daughter's favorite food. But with each taste, it will get closer to becoming part of her repertoire. She'll come to regard it as normal. Once it's solidly established, keep it in the mix. Ultimately, your child won't love all foods. But she'll give each one a chance.

35. You Choose the Foods, She Chooses the Quantities

A child knows (or should learn to know) when she's had enough. Serve smallish portions, and don't pressure her to finish. Wait and see if she asks for seconds before serving more. If she asks for a third helping of pasta, offer her a yogurt or some cheese instead. Sweeten the deal by letting her add some honey or a spoonful of jam to plain yogurt. After that, let her choose a fresh fruit or a fruit puree (like those small containers of unsweetened applesauce).

The goal isn't to cajole enough nutrients into a child's mouth at every sitting. It's to guide her into becoming an independent eater who enjoys food and regulates her own appetite. If she doesn't eat enough at one meal, she'll catch up at the next one. If she's always snacking, she'll never learn to eat at mealtimes.

36. Variety, Variety

The French are nuts about variety. They serve kids lots of different foods, prepared lots of different ways. They aim for a variety of textures and colors, too. This has many benefits:

- Kids get a variety of nutrients. They're more likely to eat a balanced diet if they eat lots of different foods.

- It makes mealtimes more peaceful. If your kids are used to different foods, you don't have to be terrified that a picky eater will erupt at the sight of an herb in her soup.
- It's more social. You can take your child anywhere and she'll find something she likes. You won't have to keep apologizing to hosts who don't serve plain pasta. You build complicity with your child as you roll with it together.
- It's more pleasurable for the child. Her world expands as she discovers different tastes, smells, and textures.
- It shows your confidence in your child. If you treat her like a budding food adventurer, she'll eventually live up to your expectations. Whereas if you treat her like a finicky eater who can handle only grilled cheese and the occasional banana, that's what she'll become.

37. Drink Water

In France, chilled or lukewarm water is the de facto drink at lunch and dinner (and anytime in between). Parents typically don't take drink orders; they just put a pitcher of water on the table. (This quickly becomes a habit.) Juice is for breakfast and for the occasional afternoon snack. Sugary drinks are for special occasions like parties.

38. Looks Matter

Everyone is more drawn to food that looks appetizing. In Parisian restaurants, almost as much thought goes into presenting food as into cooking it. That can be your principle at home, too. Put takeout on serving plates. Garnish a monotone dinner with cherry tomatoes or some grated carrots. Enlist kids to arrange raw vegetables on a platter, or assemble colorful sandwich melts, which you then broil in the oven. From two or three years old, all kids can eat on ceramic plates and drink out of small glasses, as French kids do.

39. Talk About Food

French people talk a lot about food. That's part of how they convey to kids that eating isn't just for nutrition—it's a full-on sensory experience. Food guides suggest getting beyond "I like it" / "I don't like it" and instead suggest asking questions such as: Are the apples sour or sweet? How does mackerel taste different from salmon? Which is better—red-leaf lettuce or arugula?

Treat food as an endless conversation starter. When the cake collapses or the stew is a disaster, laugh about it together.

At the supermarket, take a walking tour of the produce department, and let your kid choose some fruits and vegetables (one of my sons likes to ride in the shopping cart wielding a giant leek).

Above all, keep the food chat positive. If your child abruptly announces that she doesn't like pears anymore, calmly ask what she's decided to like instead.

40. Have the Day's Nutritional Balance in Mind

French parents carry around a little mental map of what their kids eat each day. They expect them to get most of their protein at lunchtime, whereas dinner will center on grains and vegetables. Kids typically eat sugary foods for dessert with lunch or at the afternoon *goûter*. Dinnertime dessert is usually yogurt or cheese and fruit. ("What you eat in the evening just stays with you for years," one French mother explained to me.)

41. Dinner Shouldn't Involve Hand-to-Hand Combat

A French nutritionist says her best advice is this: Don't let your child see how desperately you want him to eat his vegetables.

Don't puff up with exaggerated food cheer either. Play it cool. Those haricots verts you've just placed on the table are not the Second Coming. The tone you're aiming for at mealtimes is cheerful nonchalance. Just be calmly positive about food. Tell kids that meals are a time for the whole family to be together and enjoy one another's company.

42. Eat Chocolate

Don't treat candy like it's kryptonite or try to pretend that refined sugar doesn't exist. That will just make kids more likely to go overboard when they finally get their hands on some. Instead, teach them that sweets are occasional pleasures to enjoy in controlled doses. French kids eat small helpings of chocolate or cookies on a regular basis, usually at the afternoon *goûter*. They often eat cake on weekends, just not too much. On birthdays and at school parties, parents tend to give kids free rein. We all need some time away from the regular rules.

43. Keep Meals Short and Sweet

Dinner is not a hostage situation. Don't expect young kids to stay at the table for longer than twenty or thirty minutes. When they ask to be liberated, let them go. With age comes longer meals.

In restaurants, leaving the table usually isn't an option. Plan these outings carefully. Make sure that children arrive hungry and not exhausted. Bring some books or drawing supplies. Before you go inside, explain even to little children that special rules apply—one of which is that they can choose what they'll eat. Remind them to be *sage*—calm and in control of themselves. (Unlike the English equivalent, "Be good," this implies a certain wisdom and capacity for self-control.)

Chapter 5

sooner isn't better

t is tempting to think of early childhood as the start of a marathon in which the finish line is admission to a university (winners get to go to the Ivy League). In this analogy, you'd want your kids off to a fast start—to begin talking, reading, and doing math as soon as possible. You'd give them flash cards, brain-building toys, and maybe a special contraption to help them learn to walk.

The French want their kids to be successful, too. (They have their own version of the Ivy League, called the *grandes écoles*.) But they probably wouldn't use the marathon analogy. They don't tend to think there's any point in rushing little kids through developmental milestones, or teaching them skills like reading and math before they are most ready for them. French preschoolers learn some letters, but they don't actually learn to read until the equivalent of first grade—about age six. (Teenagers in Finland have some of the highest average reading and math scores in the Western world, and kids there don't learn to read until they're seven.)

The latest American research validates this slower approach. It turns out that it's more important to teach preschoolers skills like concentration, getting along with others, and self-control (more about self-control in chapter 6). These abilities—more than math worksheets or preliteracy training—create a strong basis for later academic success. And as the French can affirm, avoiding the baby marathon is a lot more pleasant for both parents and kids.

44. Don't Teach Your Toddler How to Read

Yes, it's technically possible to teach three-year-olds how to recognize words. But what's the rush? You don't want to take time away from teaching children the things they most need to learn at that age, like how to be organized, articulate, and empathetic. French preschools teach kids how to have conversations, finish projects, and tackle problems. In my daughter's Parisian kindergarten class one day, the assignment was for twenty-five illiterate five-year-olds to give talks on "justice" or "courage." When these kids are six, they'll learn to read in much less time than it would take to teach them at three.

45. Don't Rush the Developmental Stages

The French have a saying: "You can't go faster than the music." They believe that a child will roll over, rise up, get potty-trained, and start to talk when he's good and ready. Parents should lovingly encourage and support him—not turn his childhood into boot camp. Anyway, being a little kid shouldn't be hard work. There's enough time for that later.

46. Teach the Four Magic Words

We Americans have "please" and "thank you." The French have those plus two more: "hello" and "good-bye." They're especially zealous about making a child say *bonjour* as soon as he walks into someone's house. He doesn't get to slouch in under the cover of his parents' greeting.

French parents view *bonjour* as a critical lesson in empathy. Saying it forces a child out of his selfish bubble and makes him realize that other people have needs and feelings, too—such as the simple need to be acknowledged. *Bonjour* also sets the tone for him to observe other rules of civility. If he says *bonjour*, he's less likely to draw on the walls afterward. He's been counted as a person; a little person, but a person nonetheless.

47. Let Kids "Awaken" and "Discover"

Centuries of great French art, cooking, and design have left their mark on French parenting. Today's French parents teach kids about sensory pleasures like tasting new foods, "discovering" their bodies through movement (Americans might call this exercise), or "awakening" to new sensations like splashing in a pool (this comes long before French children actually learn to swim). Awakening often doesn't require much hard work from parents. It can come from rolling around on a picnic blanket and studying the grass. It probably helps forge some neural pathways. But the real point is to teach children how to enjoy just being in the world.

48. Encourage Insouciance

A few music classes are fine. But try to give little kids lots of free time just to play. "When the child plays, he constructs himself," one of my daughter's Parisian day-care teachers explained. (By design, the day care gives kids large quantities of unstructured time.) The latest science seems to side with the French. A roundup of neuroscience research couldn't say enough about the benefits of exploratory play: it teaches kids persistence, relationship skills, and creative problem solving; it improves their attention spans and their confidence; and it gives them a chance to master activities. But playing isn't just developmentally important; it's also fun.

49. Let Your Child Socialize with Other Kids

You know how you crave adult company after being alone with a three-year-old all day? Well, just imagine how that three-year-old feels—in reverse. French mothers want to spend time with their offspring. But they also think it's crucial that kids socialize with people who are equally enchanted by fire engines and princess paraphernalia. They want their children to learn how to make friends, to wait their turns, and to get along in a group. In general, middle- and upper-middle-class working parents would rather put their children in high-quality day care than leave them at home alone with a nanny.

50. Back Off at the Playground

French parents believe that once a child can walk on his own and safely climb up the slide, their job is to watch from the sidelines as he plays. At French playgrounds, you don't see parents narrating a child's every move, going down the slide behind their kids, or automatically leaping to their child's defense in every dispute. They give him a chance to work out conflicts on his own.

Resist the urge to cross wobbly wooden bridges or to provide constant commentary and encouragement. Just sit on a bench, watch, and recharge. That way you'll be a lot more joyful and patient when he does need you.

51. Do Extracurriculars for Pleasure

You're not building a bionic child. Do not give him violin lessons or read him the twelfth book of the day merely to help him gain hypothetical IQ points. Choose activities that your child enjoys, then do them at a natural pace. Read the child-development studies if you want, but don't let them plan your child's day.

52. *It's Not Just About Outcomes*

....

Yes, it's a competitive world. Of course you want to position your offspring to beat out that trilingual rug rat next door. But childhood is not merely preparation for the future. The quality of the nearly two decades you're spending together matters, too. Learn to identify and enjoy what the French call *moments privilégiés*, little pockets of joy or calm when you simply appreciate being together.

....

Chapter 6

wait a minute

One reason why French family life often feels calm is that parents emphasize patience. They don't treat waiting and related skills—like coping with frustration and delaying gratification—as innate qualities that kids are born with (or without). They believe these can be learned. French parents aim to teach their kids patience, the same way they will later teach them how to ride a bicycle.

Also, they find the alternative intolerable. French parents can imagine a world in which they could never finish a phone call or a cup of coffee, and where kids collapse each time they're denied a candy bar. They've seen children who regularly go from calm to hysterical in seconds and make everyone miserable in their wakes. They don't want to live in that world or think it's inevitable to do so. And they don't think that living there would make children happy either.

53. Give Kids Lots of Chances to Practice Waiting

The secret to patience isn't expecting a child to be a stoic who freezes and silently waits. Scientists have found that kids become good at waiting once they learn how to distract themselves—by inventing a little song or burping at themselves in the mirror, for instance. This makes the waiting bearable.

French parents have discovered this, too. They know that they don't even have to teach a child how to distract himself. If they simply say "wait" a lot (*attend* in French) and make a child practice waiting on a daily basis, she'll figure out how to distract herself. But if they drop everything the instant she complains that she's bored, or if they get off the phone when she interrupts, the child isn't going to get good at waiting. She's going to get good at whining.

54. *Slow Down Your Response Times*

Embrace a French pace of life. When you're busy scrambling eggs and your daughter asks you to inspect her tower of toilet paper rolls, explain nicely that you'll be there in a few minutes. At dinner, don't leap up to grab a napkin the moment she demands it (or, better yet, put the napkins on a low shelf so she can get one herself). When you're busy, politely point out to your child what you're doing, and ask her to take it in.

This doesn't just make life calmer. It's also what the French call an obligatory passage for the child, when she learns that she's not the center of the universe. Parents believe that a child who doesn't realize this—and who feels she's entitled to anything she wants—won't see any reason to grow up.

The French have reasonable expectations. They wouldn't ask a young child to sit through Shakespeare (or Molière). They just want her to be able to wait a few seconds, or a few minutes. Slowing things down even this little bit will make her better at coping with boredom, and take the panicky edge off things. Patience is a muscle. The more a child plays on her own, the better she gets at it.

55. Treat Kids as if They Can Control Themselves

Play to the top of a child's intelligence. Expect her not to grab things and to be able to put all her LEGOS back in their box. Get down on the floor and gently tell a toddler who's pulling books off the shelf that she should stop, and show her how to put them back. When she tosses grapes on the floor, show her how to keep them on her plate. Do this patiently and face-to-face. A child needs to learn the limits, but she also needs love. "It takes both love and frustration for the child to construct himself," one expert explains. If you give the child just love without limits, she'll soon become a little tyrant (the French call this an *enfant roi*—a child king).

56. Don't Let Your Child Interrupt You

When a child interrupts (assuming she's not hemorrhaging), French parents believe that you should calmly say some version of "I'm in the middle of speaking to someone. Please wait and I'll be with you in a moment." Then make good on that promise. Continue your conversation, but when you've finished, turn back to the child and listen to her. Have her wait her turn to speak at the dinner table, too, and teach her at least to say "excuse me" if it's urgent.

Remember that you're not just trying to enjoy the simple pleasure of completing a thought. You're also teaching your child to respect others and to be aware of what's happening around her. One French-woman says that when her son interrupts, she has him look at the person she's speaking to so that he fully registers what's going on. "It's a way of living together," she explains. All this practice won't prevent your child from ever interrupting again. But she'll gradually get more in touch with the rhythm of the room.

57. Don't Interrupt Your Child

Everyone in the house has a right to be absorbed in something without being interrupted. When a child is happily caught up in an activity, parents should try not to come charging over with a question or a change of plans. When people aren't bursting in on one another, the whole pace of family life slows down a notch.

58. Observe the French Food Rules

French food rituals offer a daily exercise in teaching children how to delay gratification. Kids eat most meals in courses, rather than all at once. They taste foods, even ones they don't like—a form of coping with frustration. They wait to eat at mealtimes. If they get some chocolate in the morning, they typically don't eat it until the afternoon *goûter*. With practice, all of this gets much easier; in fact, it becomes natural and not arduous at all.

59. *Let Them Eat Cake*

Baking is a regular weekend activity for many French families, starting practically from the time kids can sit alone in a chair. The measuring and sequencing are excellent lessons in patience. So is the fact that once the cake is made, families usually wait until the *goûter* to eat it. And everybody—parents included—aims to eat reasonable portions (they're trying to model restraint for their kids).

60. *View Coping with Frustration as a Crucial Life Skill*

French parents don't worry that they'll damage a child by frustrating her. *Au contraire*, they think a child can't be happy if she needs to have things instantly, and if she's constantly subject to her own whims. They believe that kids get pride and pleasure from being able to choose how they respond to things.

Teaching kids to handle frustration also makes them more resilient later on. Young children who are good at delaying gratification are more likely to grow into teenagers who can handle setbacks, and who are good at concentrating and reasoning. Consider it a French paradox: trying to make kids happy all the time will make them less happy later on.

61. Cope Calmly with Tantrums

French parents are just as flummoxed and distressed by tantrums as the rest of us. They don't have a magic recipe to make the crying stop. What they generally agree on is: you shouldn't concede to an unreasonable demand. ("Above all, don't give in," one father tells me.) Tantrums don't change the rules.

This doesn't mean that you should be cold. French parents say that kids are understandably angry when they can't have or do something. The parents try to show sympathy ("Who wouldn't want to have a cookie just before lunch?") and to let kids express their discontent. Some parents say they ask the child what she thinks a good solution is, given the constraints. If the child can calm down enough to talk, she'll often have some reasonable ideas—like having the same cookie as an afternoon snack.

Sometimes, giving an upset child more autonomy can change the mood and calm her down. Let her help you prepare dinner or serve herself. Be in touch with her rhythms. Don't expect an overtired child to go grocery shopping or out to dinner.

When the tantrum happens at home and goes on for too long, parents typically send the child to her room and tell her to come out when she's calm again. "If it's too loud I say, 'Go yell in your room.' But I understand that it makes her very angry," the mother of a five-year-old explains. Typically, "she goes into her room and yells, then she comes back out and does what I asked," this mom claims. If a child manages to come out calmly, parents respond positively and then everyone moves on.

In short, be calm and sympathetic without giving in.

62. Be Patient About Teaching Patience

Your child won't become an expert delayer in a day. Learning to wait is part of what the French call her *éducation*—an ongoing process of teaching her skills and values, which has nothing do with school. Be consistent. Whenever you start to waver, consider the alternative.

Chapter 7

free to be
tu and me

When a mother hovers over her child too much in France, someone is apt to say: "Just let him live his life!" French parents do a lot for their kids, but they don't try to clear away all obstacles, physical and emotional. Instead, they strive to treat children as independent beings who can, more and more as they get older, cope with challenges on their own.

This autonomy develops at a reasonable pace. Little French kids don't drive cars or operate heavy machinery. Parents supervise closely and judge when the child is ready to take the next step. But they believe that autonomy is crucial for children. When you treat kids as capable and trustworthy, they respond by taking on more responsibility and behaving better. And giving kids a bit of space can actually bring you closer.

63. Give Kids Meaningful Chores

Don't underestimate what children can do, with some guidance. It's quite normal for French three- and four-year-olds to help load the dishwasher after dinner, for instance. (Moms I know report no more than a few broken plates.) A friend of mine's six-year-old says her favorite activity is taking out the garbage all by herself. She also proudly

describes the time when her mom stood outside a small shop and let
her go inside alone to buy some lemons.

When done on a regular basis, these small acts of autonomy are very
meaningful. Kids who play an active role in the household become
more self-reliant and learn that adults are not just there to serve them.
Weirdly, children also find these activities fun. Obviously, the thrill
won't last forever. But the idea that their contribution to the family
matters probably will.

64. Build a Cadre

The *cadre* (meaning "frame" or "framework") is the mental image that
French parents have about how best to raise kids. They strive to be very
strict about a few key things—that's the frame. But inside the frame,
they aim to give kids as much freedom as they can handle.

Parents decide which things they will be strict about. Parisians I've
met often choose respect for others, how much screen time kids are
allowed, and anything dealing with food. French children categorically
aren't allowed to hit their parents.

You can apply the *cadre*'s cocktail of strictness and freedom to lots
of different situations. Some that I've heard from French parents are:

- At bedtime you have to stay in your room, but inside your
  room you can do whatever you want.
- You can watch only two hours of television this weekend, but
  you choose when to use these two hours and you choose the
  DVD or the show you want to watch.
- You have to taste a bit of everything at a meal, but you don't
  have to eat it all.

- When we go out, I can veto your outfit if it's inappropriate, but at home you can wear what you want.
- Most of the time you can't eat sweets, but you can at the afternoon snack.
- I don't buy nonnecessities on demand, but you can buy them with your pocket money. (French kids usually start getting monthly pocket money at about age seven. The typical amount corresponds to the child's age; e.g., a seven-year-old gets seven euros—about nine and a half dollars—per month.)

65. Everybody Needs a Curse Word

There's a special one for French preschoolers: *caca boudin* (pronounced caca booh-dah). This literally translates as "poop sausage," but it's an all-purpose word that can mean "you wish," "bollocks," or "whatever." No one teaches his child to say *caca boudin*. Kids just pick it up from one another. Their parents might cringe a bit when they hear the phrase, but they tend not to ban it. Instead, they teach kids to wield it appropriately. Some tell their children they can say *caca boudin* only in the bathroom, or when they're alone with their friends. They can't say it to teachers, or at dinner. Kids are subject to lots of rules. Sometimes they just need to say *caca boudin*.

66. Hand Your Kids Over

If you can get a grandparent or trusted relative on board, let your child spend some time away from you. (French five-year-olds go on multiday class trips without any parents along, just teachers. During school holidays, they'll often spend a week or two alone with their grandparents.) Give your surrogate a few basic instructions, and try to project cheerful confidence when you're saying good-bye. Don't worry that Grandma will do things differently from you; your child mostly just needs tenderness, attention, and a bit of food. Start out with an overnight stay, then move up to a long weekend. "If everything goes well, he'll come back smarter," a French child psychiatrist explains* about kids aged three to five. "You'll find him changed, he will have learned to behave like a big boy. He'll gain in independence." I won't even start on the benefits to his parents.

67. Don't Become a Referee

The French ideal is for adults to avoid becoming the arbiters of all disputes—whether between siblings, playmates, or new acquaintances in the sandbox. A father tells me that when his five-year-old twins argue, he asks them to suggest a solution. (They usually think of something, he says.) Teachers say they back off at recess, to give kids some much-needed freedom ("If we intervene all the time, they go a little nuts," one day-care minder explained).

French experts say that sibling rivalry is inevitable and that the arrival of a new baby is a genuine shock for an older child. In the latter case, "you must console him, help him express himself, reassure him, tell him that you understand his anxiety, his sorrow, his jealousy, show him that it's normal for him to have these feelings," one parenting book says.

---

* In an article in a French parenting magazine titled "He's Going Away Without You, It's Good for Him!"

68. Keep the Risks in Perspective

French parents know about choking hazards, allergies, and pedophiles. They take reasonable precautions. But they try not to obsess over far-flung scenarios. Instead of internalizing all worry, they believe that parents should speak to children about risks and teach them how to protect themselves. A French expert suggests explaining to a child as young as one that cars exist and that they're dangerous; thus he cannot cross a street without an adult.

There's a crucial difference between shielding a child from danger and cutting him off from the world. Remember that children gain confidence from overcoming difficulties and relying on their own resources. As one French writer warns, "To grow up without risk is to risk not growing up."

69. Don't Raise a Praise Addict

A French mother tells me that instead of saying "Bravo" when her five-year-old does something well, she sometimes prefers to ask, "Are you proud of yourself?" Like many French parents, she believes that children don't build self-esteem from being relentlessly assured that they're doing a good job. They build it from doing new things by themselves, and doing them well. Indeed, praising a child too much can be damaging. He'll become so eager to maintain your high opinion that he won't want to risk trying something new. Or he'll do things merely to get the brief high that comes from hearing "Bravo," but will lose motivation when you're not there to say it. Of course you should be encouraging (you don't want to underpraise either). Just don't overdo it.

70. *Encourage Kids to Speak Well*

....

Once a child can speak fluently, French parents and teachers don't automatically coo at everything he says. When he's wildly off topic, they say so, and steer him back. At the dinner table, they pay more attention when he says clever things and expresses himself well. This is meant to be constructive. They aim to turn the child into a good conversationalist, not a bore who blathers on. (He might get away with that at his grandmother's, but it will be less charming later on dates.)

71. *Expect the "Déclic"*

....

The *déclic* (deh-kleek) is an aha moment when a child figures out how to do something important on his own. Something clicks. For young children, it can be the period when they become potty trained or work out how to make friends. For teenagers, it's the moment or period when they become motivated to do well at school, or when they stop working to satisfy their parents and start working because they want to succeed for themselves. It's a welcome sign of maturity and autonomy. French parents often wait and hope for their children to have a *déclic*. Non-French parents do, too. It's helpful to have a name for it.

72. Let Children Have a "Jardin Secret"

The French believe that everyone is entitled to a "secret garden"—a private realm. It's part of being an independent person. Even very involved parents accept that their children need privacy—particularly as they grow older—and will have some secrets. They don't expect to know every detail of their children's lives. They do expect to know that, generally, everything is okay.

73. Respect a Child's Space, and He'll Respect Yours, Too

Autonomy is something fundamental that your child needs. (Françoise Dolto said that by age six, a child should be able to do everything at home that concerns him.) Granting him autonomy—as he's ready—shows that you trust and respect him. It's an appeal to his higher self. Give him this, and he's more likely to respect what you need, too. Ideally, as the French say, everyone in the family should get to live his life.

Chapter 8

cherchez la femme

French mothers strive for a very particular kind of balance in their lives. It's not a keeping-plates-in-the-air balance. It's more like a balanced meal (you wouldn't want to eat just potatoes). The French ideal is that no one part of your life—not being a wife, a worker, or a mom—should eclipse the other parts. Even the most devoted *maman* expects to devote energy and passion to things other than her children.

France has all kinds of social services that make it easier to do this. But it also has a different approach to womanhood, guilt, and free time. The reigning view in France is that if the child is a woman's only goal, everyone suffers, including the child. Not all French moms manage to maintain just the right *équilibre*. But crucially, they keep it in mind.

74. Guilt Is a Trap

For American mothers, guilt can be like a tax you pay for being away from your child. It buys you some free time. As long as you feel guilty about leaving her, you can escape for a few hours. (Sociologists call this leisure time spent worrying "contaminated time.")

French moms understand the temptation to feel guilty. But they don't want to spoil their precious free time. Instead of embracing guilt, they try to push it away. When they meet up for drinks, they remind one another that "the perfect mother doesn't exist" and take pride in being able to detach from their children and relax. "When I'm there, I give them one hundred percent, but when I'm off, I'm off," a mother of three explains.

75. Show Kids That You Have a Life Apart from Them

It's not enough for French mothers to have pleasures and interests apart from their children. They also want their kids to know about these things. They believe it's burdensome for a child to feel that she's the sole source of her mother's happiness and satisfaction. (A Parisian mother I know told me she was going back to work partly for her daughter's sake.)

Frenchwomen want other adults to see that they have nonmom lives, too. Even if they've spent the day folding tiny socks, they strive to resist talking at length about their children's toilet habits. They know that if you act (and dress) as if you have a fascinating inner life, you may soon find that you actually do—and that you feel more balanced as a result.

There are pragmatic reasons for having a life of your own. Some Frenchwomen drop out of the workforce when they have kids, but many don't. Even those in stable marriages calculate that not making their own money leaves them financially vulnerable in case of divorce. And they believe that, sans paycheck, they'll lose status and decision-making power at home and become less interesting to people outside of it.

76. Don't Attend Children's Birthdays

They're for kids. In Paris, from about age three, birthday parties and playdates are usually drop-offs. Parents don't feel they must supervise another adult's supervision of their child, or stick around to reassure the child herself. They make sure she's in good hands, and then they leave. Usually they're invited back for coffee or cocktails at the end. It's a practical way of coping with the fact that all parents are extremely busy, and that—while we're delighted that our kids get along—we're not all actually friends.

77. Lose the Baby Weight

For Frenchwomen, there's no better proof that they haven't morphed from *femme* to *maman* than getting back their prebaby figures, or some reasonable facsimile thereof. Parisiennes often aim to do this by three months postpartum.

It helps that they don't gain too much weight while they're pregnant and that they're not permanently exhausted from night wake-ups. Many French moms also follow a nondeprivation diet as a matter of course. During the week they eat smallish portions, have the main meal at lunchtime, don't snack between meals, and avoid bread, pasta, and sugary foods. But on weekends (or on one weekend day) they eat freely. In other words, they don't vow never to eat lasagna or croissants again; they just save these for special occasions. Frenchwomen are in step with recent research showing that people have more self-control when they don't permanently exclude certain foods; they just tell themselves that they'll have them later. Studies also recommend closely monitoring your weight (Frenchwomen call this paying attention).

78. Don't Dress Like a Mom

Unless a Frenchwoman is actually holding a child, it's usually hard to tell if she's a mother. There's no telltale look or type of pants. They don't sex it up to overcompensate. But they don't walk around wearing sweatpants and scrunchies either. Instead, they seek an elegant middle ground. Frenchwomen don't feel selfish for caring about their appearance. (In the French edition of *Marie Claire*, a mother of three confesses that she's sometimes so busy *she wears unmatched bras and panties*.) Looking good improves morale and makes you feel more balanced. It just does.

79. Don't Become a "Taxi Mother"

Parisian mothers think it's perfectly reasonable to weigh the impact on their own quality of life when making choices for their children. A Frenchwoman who spends most of her free time shuttling her kids between extracurricular activities isn't seen as a devoted mom—she's viewed as someone who has dramatically lost her balance. Her sacrifice isn't even considered good for the kids. Yes, they may benefit from studying judo and taking piano lessons. But they also need to have unstructured time at home. A French psychologist says there's a crucial difference between being responsive and attentive to your child and becoming a "vending machine" who's always on.

80. You Can Be Happier Than Your Least Happy Child

Really you can. It doesn't mean that you're a bad person. It means that you're a separate person with your own needs and temperament. French mothers are deeply affected by their children's feelings. But they believe it's best to respond to an upset child with objectivity and calm. You're modeling the way you'd like your child to feel.

Chapter 9

finding
your couple

F rench experts say that in the first few months after the baby is born, his parents should—indeed must—give themselves over to his care. The family is in the *fusionelle* phase. Some call this, presidentially, the first hundred days.

But sometime around the three-month mark, parents are supposed to gradually make room for their own relationship again. There's no fixed schedule. No one expects them to abandon the baby and jump on a flight to Bali. It's more of a rebalancing in which they "relearn the contours of intimacy"—both physically and emotionally, and make space in the family home where they can be a couple too.

81. Your Baby Doesn't Replace Your Husband

He's cuddly, he's adorable, and your mother loves him. But your child shouldn't permanently nudge your partner out of the picture. "The family is based on the couple. If it exists only through children, it withers," a French psychologist explains. In some families, the three-month mark is when the baby starts sleeping in his own room. (Until then he may have been in a bassinet in his parents' room, or even in their bed.) Long-term cosleeping is very rare in France, in part because it keeps things between Mom and Dad from getting back to normal.

The French famously believe that all healthy people—old people, ugly people, even new parents—have sex drives. A leading French parenting magazine says that if your libido hasn't returned by four to six months postpartum, you should seek professional help.

82. Your Bedroom Is Your Castle

Guard it carefully. Your child doesn't have the right to barge in whenever he wants. For starters, you need sleep. Explain to him that in the morning he must play in his room until it's very bright outside (or teach him to read a digital clock, and explain that he can't come in until the first number is an eight—or a seven on school days).

It's also important for him to understand—through tender gestures and closed doors—that there's a part of his parents' lives that doesn't involve him. "My parents' room was a sacred place, different from the rest of the house," one Frenchwoman recalls. "You didn't just walk in, you had to have a good reason. Between them there was an obvious pleasure that implied something unknown for us, the children." If your child believes he already has it all—that there's no mysterious adult world to aspire to—why should he bother growing up?

83. Be Clear-Eyed About How Hard Kids Are on a Relationship

The French swoon for babies, but they also talk about "le baby-clash"— the risk of couples separating in the first two years after the birth, from the shock of becoming coparents and of losing their freedom. Experts don't have a magic solution, but say it's helpful to see this coming ("It's not us honey, it's *le baby-clash!*") and to discuss problems with each other. Reigniting intimacy helps, too, as does clearly divvying up baby duties.

84. Pretend to Agree

No matter how misguided your partner's proclamations about the household rules are, don't contradict him in front of the kids. Wait and speak to him in private. He should do the same for you. You'll build complicity with your spouse. And since the rules aren't up for discussion, they'll have more force. You'll both seem more authoritative to the children, and they'll be reassured by the impression that there's something solid at the family's core.

85. 50/50 Isn't the Gold Standard

Feeling entitled to absolute equality in housework and child care can be a recipe for resentment and rage. Fifty-fifty rarely happens. Try tempering your feminist theory with some old-fashioned French pragmatism. Frenchwomen would love their partners to do more, but many make peace with a division of labor that isn't equal but that more or less works. They try to weigh equality against having a husband who's calm and destressed after his Saturday morning soccer match. And they've discovered that there's less conflict when everyone has his or her own tasks to perform at home—even if the actual hours involved aren't equal. Paradoxically, if you're less angry, you might want to have more sex, and he might do more around the house as a result.

86. *Treat Men Like a Separate Species*

Take the edge off inequality even more by treating men the way that many Frenchwomen do—as adorably hapless creatures who, in most cases, are biologically incapable of keeping track of the kids' inoculation schedules. Of course they come home with the wrong kind of cereal and with strawberries that look as if they've been beaten with a mallet. They're men! They just can't help it. (One Frenchwoman told me, with mock exasperation, that her husband makes only his side of the bed.) Frenchwomen advise trying not to throw a tantrum when you come home from a business trip to find your home besieged by dirty laundry. Assume that the poor fellow was doing his best.

87. *Men, Praise Mom for Her Mastery of the Mundane*

Centuries of expert courtship have taught Frenchmen that you cannot overpraise a woman. They try to compensate for their shortcomings at home by marveling at the dull and time-consuming tasks their partners perform and by confessing that such multitasking is beyond them. (When said gallantly, this sounds less patronizing than you'd expect.) If the woman doesn't have a paying job, Frenchmen are wise enough never to ask: What did you *do* all day?

88. Maintain Some Mystery About Yourself

Don't have an extramarital affair, or do terrible things in secret (it may surprise you to know that ordinary French citizens rarely cheat; it's French presidents who tend to be terribly unfaithful). But keep a bit of mystery in your marriage, à la française. Let there be innuendo, knowing glances, and things left unsaid. It's okay to flirt with others, too. Realize that—unlike in Hollywood scripts—you can feel energized by these interactions without their leading inexorably to adultery and death.

89. Make Evenings Adult Time

After the stories, songs, and cuddles, French parents are firm about bedtime. They believe that having some kid-free time in the evenings is not an occasional privilege; it's a fundamental human right. Ditto with spending the occasional evening out or escaping for a restorative long weekend à deux. The French don't have an equivalent of "date night." When they can, they just go out—the way our parents used to. They consider a solid and loving marriage to be essential to the happy functioning of the whole family. Explain this honestly to the kids; they'll get it.

90. Don't Put a Teepee in Your Living Room

The French know that it's hard to enjoy adult time when you're staring at a miniature kitchen. They typically don't let children's toys and games reside permanently in the living room. Make a family ritual of putting them back in the kids' rooms before bedtime. Have a (non-Technicolor) box in the living room where you can hide stray LEGOS and doll extremities. Don't let baby-proofing be your dominant interior design motif.

Chapter 10

just say

"non"

A battle cry of French parenting is: It's me who decides (*C'est moi qui décide*). Parents say—and occasionally shout—this phrase to remind everyone who's in charge or to shift the balance of power back in their favor. Just uttering it is fortifying. (Try saying it, even in French. You'll feel your back stiffen.)

To be the decider, you don't have to be an ogre. French parents don't want to turn their kids into obedient robots. But they still agree with Jean-Jacques Rousseau's contention, made 250 years ago, that perpetual negotiations are bad for kids. "The worst education is to leave him floating between his will and yours, and to dispute endlessly between you and him as to which of the two will be the master."

91. Say "No" with Conviction

The French didn't invent *non*. But they're especially good at saying it. They don't worry that blocking a child will limit his creativity or crush his spirit. They believe that kids blossom best inside limits, and that it's reassuring to know that a grown-up is steering the ship.

The French *non* is convincing partly because parents don't say it constantly. They believe that a few strategically administered *no*'s have a better chance of registering with kids than a blizzard of them. They're consistently strict about a few key things.

But the real secret is the unambivalent delivery. Kids can tell when you really mean no and you won't back down. You don't have to shout it. Just look directly at the child, kneeling down if you have to, and explain the rule with calm confidence. This takes some practice, when you get your *no* right, you'll feel it. You won't just sound more authoritative to your child; you will actually believe yourself to be the boss.

92. Say "Yes" as Often as You Can

The French believe that another key to having authority with your child is to say yes as often as you can. (One expert points out that *authority* has the same root as *authorize*.) It takes some recalibrating to make your default answer become *yes*. But doing this has a calming effect. The child feels more respected, and she gets to satisfy her need to do things for herself. Of course, total freedom would be overwhelming. The ideal French scenario is that the child asks permission to do something, and the parent grants it.

93. Explain the Reason Behind the Rule

When you say no, you should always explain why not. You're not trying to scare your child into obeying you. Rather, you want to create a world that's coherent and predictable to him, and to show that you respect his autonomy and intelligence.

If a situation is dangerous, act first and give your reason afterward. Always be matter-of-fact: you don't want your explanation to sound like a negotiation (it's not). Sometimes it helps to refresh kids on the rules. One French mom says that as soon as she walks into the supermarket, she reminds her two girls that they're there to buy necessities for the house, not toys or candy. She says she's been so consistent about applying this, the girls don't even ask for these extras anymore. (They can choose to buy them with their pocket money.)

When speaking to kids, French parents will often use the language of rights: "You don't have the right to bite Pierre." This implies that there's a coherent system of rules and that the child *does* have the right to do other things.

94. Sometimes Your Child Will Hate You

French psychologists say that kids' desires are practically endless. Your job as a parent is to stop this chain by sometimes saying no. The child will probably get angry when you do this. She might even temporarily hate you. This isn't a sign that you're a terrible parent. "If the parent isn't there to stop him, then he's the one who's going to have to stop himself or not stop himself, and that's much more anxiety-provoking," one psychologist explains. In other words, if you need your child to like you all the time, you simply cannot do your job. Be strong and your child will, as the French say, "find her place."

95. Dedramatize

This word comes up a lot in France when it comes to dealing with upset or cranky kids of all ages. The idea is that you should drain some intensity from conflictual moments by responding calmly to them, or by lightening the mood with a joke.

Avoid castigating your child in front of others. One French mom told me she suspected that her teenage daughter was smoking cigarettes during a sleepover, but she waited until the friend left the next morning before mentioning it. "If you make a scene, your child will stop talking to you," she explained.

Aim to have authority without losing your connection with the child. If you're so angry that you need time to cool off, then say so. "I don't think the world of children is so far from the world of adults. They're capable of understanding everything," this mom said.

96. You're Not Disciplining, You're Educating

The next time your child speaks with a mouth full of pasta, remember that you're gradually teaching her table manners, in the same way that you would teach her to do math. In other words, the learning doesn't happen all at once. As the French say, you're not disciplining, you're giving the child an *éducation*, an ongoing process that starts when kids are very young. Unlike discipline, *éducation* (which has nothing to do with school) is something parents imagine themselves to be doing all the time. Reminding yourself of this will help you feel less disrespected and angry when the occasional slice of cucumber lands on your lap.

Don't jump on your child for every offense. The French call a small act of naughtiness a *bêtise* (pronounced beh-teeze). Having this word helps keep the crime in perspective. When your child jumps on the couch or swipes a piece of bread off the counter before dinner, she's just done a *bêtise*. All kids do them sometimes. Save your punishments for the felonies. It will help her learn what's important.

97. Do the Big Eyes

In France, one suitable response to a *bêtise* is to give a child "the big eyes." It's a disapproving, owl-like look that serves as a warning. It means that you saw what she did, and she should watch her step. "The important thing is that she knows she's breaking a rule," one mother told me.

98. Give Kids Time to Comply

You're running a family, not a military battalion. Don't expect your child to jump as soon as you issue an order. Explain what you'd like her to do, then watch and wait for her to comply. Obviously you're applying pressure. But you also want to give her autonomy over how and at what speed she complies. It's more likely to be an effective long-term lesson if she feels that she has some say in the matter, too.

99. Punish Rarely, but Make It Matter

To be *puni* in a French family is a big deal. It's not something that usually happens every night at dinner. Experts say a punishment should be administered immediately and matter-of-factly, without malice. Parents typically send a naughty child to her room to "marinate," or think on it, and tell her to come out when she's calm and ready to talk. For older kids, the punishment is often a few days without TV, computers, video games, or a cell phone. Parents say they're careful to warn children before punishing them, and to follow through on their threats. They also try to be fair on the other end—by returning the phone on the promised day. After a conflict, they say it's the parent's role to reestablish the connection, for instance by suggesting that they play a favorite game together. They teach the child that after the storm comes calm.

100. Sometimes There's Nothing You Can Do

Know when to fold 'em. There are times when nothing works, and you have to wait it out. Remember, you're on a long-term mission to educate. You don't have to win every battle.

favorite recipes from the parisian crèche

These dishes are eaten by children aged three and under who attend Paris's public day cares. They're typically cooked from scratch by in-house chefs at each center, then served as part of four-course meals composed of an appetizer, a main course and side dish, a cheese course, and then a fruit dessert (kids under twelve months have just two courses). A crèche nutritionist has adapted the quantities for family dining; each recipe serves two adults and two children.

Appetizers and Side Dishes

Carottes Râpées à l'Orange

Grated Carrots with Orange

This dish can be prepared just before serving or allowed to marinate overnight.

3 carrots

2 tablespoons canola oil

Juice of 1 orange

⅛ clove crushed garlic

Pinch of salt

Grate the carrots.

Mix the oil, juice, garlic, and salt in a small bowl.

Pour this mixture over the grated carrots and toss.

Velouté d'Artichaut à la Crème

Creamy Artichoke Soup

1 large Idaho or russet potato

2 shallots, finely chopped

2 tablespoons olive oil

6 canned or bottled artichoke bottoms, diced

Water (about 2 cups)

Salt

2 tablespoons crème fraîche (or sour cream)

Herbs (parsley, basil, or cilantro), chopped

Wash and peel the potato. Dice it into large pieces.

In a large pan or casserole dish, sauté the shallots in a little olive oil.

Add the potatoes and the artichokes. Sauté them for 2 to 3 minutes.

Cover the vegetables with water, add some salt, and cook for about 40 minutes (or 20 minutes in a pressure cooker).

After cooking, add the cream and mix well. If you prefer a smooth consistency, use a hand mixer to blend the soup.

Keep the soup warm until you're ready to eat it. Add a pinch of chopped herbs before serving.

Brocoli Braisé

Braised Broccoli

1 pound broccoli, fresh or frozen
Salt
1 tablespoon unsalted butter

Steam fresh broccoli for 4 to 5 minutes, or submerge it in boiling water for 5 to 6 minutes. Steam frozen broccoli for 8 to 10 minutes, or submerge it in boiling water for 10 to 12 minutes. The broccoli should be firm, not mushy. Save some of the cooking water. Drain the broccoli well and add a few pinches of salt.

Melt the butter in a pan. Sauté the broccoli in the butter over medium heat for 5 minutes, until it's tender. If the broccoli is still too firm, moisten it with a bit of the cooking water.

Main Courses

Potage Complet Lentilles
Complete-Meal Lentil Soup

2 shallots, chopped

Olive oil

2 cups lentils

2 medium potatoes, peeled, washed, and chopped into
medium-sized pieces

5 cups cold water

1 clove garlic, chopped

Black pepper

½ teaspoon cumin

2 medium carrots, peeled

Salt

¼ cup crème fraîche or sour cream (optional)

2 ounces boneless chicken breasts, finely diced

Parsley, chopped

In a large saucepan, sauté the shallots in some olive oil, add
the lentils and potatoes, and cover with the cold water. Add
the garlic, black pepper, cumin, and carrots.

Bring to a boil and simmer, covered, over medium heat for 45 minutes, or until the potatoes and lentils are soft. Add more water if needed. Season with salt. Stir the crème fraîche into the lentils (you can mix in less cream if you want, or just add a dollop to each bowl before serving). While the lentils are cooking, use a sauté pan to brown the chicken in a little olive oil. Pour the soup into bowls, then add some chicken and a pinch of parsley to each.

Saumon à la Créole

Salmon Creole

This dish has become a staple in Parisian crèches thanks to the many in-house chefs who hail from the French Caribbean.

1 medium onion, chopped

1 ½ tablespoons sunflower or olive oil

14 ½ ounces diced tomatoes, canned or fresh

½ teaspoon thyme, chopped

1 bay leaf

Parsley, chopped

Salt and pepper

4 medium-sized salmon fillets, fresh or frozen

Juice of 1 lemon

Preheat the oven to 425°F.

In a large pan, sauté the onion in the oil.

Add the tomatoes, thyme, bay leaf, parsley, and salt and pepper. Cover and let simmer for 15 minutes.

Place the salmon fillets in an ovenproof pan. (If you're using frozen fillets, first defrost them in a microwave oven.)

Squeeze the lemon juice over the salmon, then spoon the tomato mixture on top of that. Bake in the oven for 20 to 30 minutes, or until thoroughly cooked. Before serving remove the bay leaf and any bones, and add a pinch of fresh parsley or chives to each plate. Serve the salmon with rice and a side of vegetables (braised broccoli, for instance).

Flan de Courgettes

Zucchini Flan

3 medium-sized zucchini

2 shallots, finely chopped

2 tablespoons olive oil

4 eggs

A bit less than 1 cup crème fraîche (or sour cream)

¼ teaspoon salt

¼ teaspoon ground nutmeg

¾ cup grated cheese (Gruyère or Swiss)

Preheat the oven to 350°F.

Wash and peel the zucchini. Cook them whole, either by steaming them for 9 minutes or by submerging them in boiling water for 15 minutes.

Drain the zucchini well. Cut them into thin round slices.

Sauté the shallots in the olive oil.

In a bowl, mix the eggs, crème fraîche, shallots, salt, and nutmeg. Don't overmix.

Line a square or rectangular pan with parchment paper (if you have it).

Arrange a layer of zucchini in the bottom of the pan.

Spoon the egg mixture over the zucchini until it's completely covered. Add another layer of zucchini and cover with the egg mixture again. Keep doing this until you've used up all the ingredients.

Sprinkle the cheese over the top and bake for 30 to 40 minutes.

Optional (but highly recommended): top each serving of zucchini flan with a bit of warm tomato coulis (see recipe below).

Tomato Coulis

4 large ripe tomatoes (or about 11 ounces canned diced
    tomatoes)
3 tablespoons olive oil
1 clove garlic, peeled and left whole
½ teaspoon thyme, chopped
½ teaspoon parsley, chopped
1 bay leaf
½ tablespoon sugar
Salt and pepper

For fresh tomatoes: Cut the skin at the base of the tomatoes and plunge them into boiling water for 30 seconds

.so you can easily remove the skin. Peel, seed, and dice them.

Heat the oil in a saucepan. Add the garlic, thyme, parsley, bay leaf, tomatoes, sugar, and salt and pepper. Cover and simmer on low heat for 20 to 30 minutes.

Remove the garlic clove and bay leaf before serving.

Desserts

Purée de Poire et Banane

Pear and Banana Puree

2 large or 3 small soft pears
2 bananas
Juice of ½ lemon
¼ cup water

Wash and peel the pears and bananas. Cut them into pieces.

In a medium-sized saucepan, cook them with the lemon juice and water for 15 to 20 minutes over low heat. Mix occasionally with a spoon.

Take the mixture off the heat and allow it to cool for a few minutes.

When it's no longer steaming, pour it into small cups. Cover and refrigerate them until mealtime.

Pomme au Four à la Cannelle

Baked Apple with Cinnamon

**4 apples (any cooking apples, including Granny Smith
or Golden Delicious)**
1⅓ tablespoons unsalted butter
4 teaspoons sugar
Cinnamon

Preheat the oven to 350°F.

Wash and core the apples (leave a bit of core at the bottom
if you can).

Put a knob of butter and a teaspoon of sugar in the center
of each apple. Sprinkle some cinnamon over the top.

Put about ⅛ inch of water in a baking dish (to keep the
apples from sticking), and place the apples on top.

Cook for 20 to 30 minutes, until the center of the apples
melt.

Remove the apples from the water. Serve them warm or
cold.

Gâteau Chocolat

Chocolate Cake

Butter and flour to grease the pan

5 ounces dark baking chocolate

7 tablespoons unsalted butter (a bit less than 1 stick)

6 tablespoons powdered sugar

6 tablespoons flour

3 large or 4 small eggs, separated

Salt

Optional: whipped cream or crème fraîche

Preheat the oven to 350°F. Grease and flour a 9-inch round cake pan.

In a saucepan over very low heat, slowly melt the chocolate and butter.

Remove the chocolate mixture from the heat. While mixing with a wooden spoon, sprinkle in the powdered sugar, then the flour. Add the egg yolks one by one and stir.

In a separate bowl, beat the egg whites with a pinch of salt until they form stiff peaks.

Slowly fold the egg whites into the chocolate mixture. Do not overmix.

Immediately pour the batter into the pan. Bake for 30 minutes.

Let the cake cool. Serve with a dollop of whipped cream.

sample
weekly lunch menu
from the
parisian crèche

	Appetizer	*Main Course*
monday		
UNDER 12 MONTHS		mashed boneless filet of hake with lemon sauce
12 TO 18 MONTHS	tomato salad with lemon and herbs	chopped boneless filet of hake with lemon sauce
18 MONTHS TO 3 YEARS	tomato salad with lemon and herbs	boneless filet of hake with lemon-butter sauce
tuesday		
UNDER 12 MONTHS		mashed turkey with basil sauce
12 TO 18 MONTHS	cream of leek soup	chopped turkey with basil sauce
18 MONTHS TO 3 YEARS	cream of leek soup	chopped turkey with basil sauce
wednesday		
UNDER 12 MONTHS		mashed slow-cooked lamb with carrot and tomatoes
12 TO 18 MONTHS	grated red cabbage with soft white cheese (fromage blanc)	chopped slow-cooked lamb with carrots and tomatoes
18 MONTHS TO 3 YEARS	grated red cabbage with soft white cheese (fromage blanc)	slow-cooked lamb with carrots and tomatoes
thursday		
UNDER 12 MONTHS		finely chopped ham
12 TO 18 MONTHS	Macedonian salad (green beans, carrots, celery, and flageolet beans in a lemon sauce)	chopped ham
18 MONTHS TO 3 YEARS	wheat, tomato, and green pepper salad	gratin of endives and ham
friday		
UNDER 12 MONTHS		mashed filet of boneless salmon in lemon-dill sauce
12 TO 18 MONTHS	finely grated organic carrot salad	chopped filet of boneless salmon in lemon-dill sauce
18 MONTHS TO 3 YEARS	grated organic carrot salad	filet of boneless salmon in lemon-dill sauce

Side Dish	Cheese	Dessert
organic spinach puree		sugarless apple-strawberry puree
organic spinach puree	Coulommiers cheese (a soft cow's milk cheese that resembles Brie)	sugarless apple-strawberry puree
organic spinach with béchamel sauce	Mimolette cheese (a hard orange cow's milk cheese)	sugarless apple-strawberry puree
puree of zucchini		sugarless pear and organic apple puree
puree of zucchini	Chanteneige cheese (a spreadable white cheese)	fresh kiwi
ratatouille with rice	Chanteneige cheese	fresh kiwi
puree of mushrooms		banana-rhubarb compote with sugar
puree of mushrooms	white Tomme cheese (a firm cow's milk cheese)	banana-rhubarb compote with sugar
couscous	white Tomme cheese	banana-rhubarb compote with sugar
puree of fresh endives		puree of cooked clementine and organic apples
puree of fresh endives	Roquefort cheese	fresh clementine
	Roquefort cheese	fresh clementine
puree of broccoli		puree of cooked organic apples
puree of broccoli	chèvre (goat's milk cheese)	baked organic apples
twist pasta with butter	chèvre (goat's milk cheese)	baked organic apples

acknowledgments

I am extremely grateful to my agent, Suzanne Gluck, and to Ann Godoff and Virginia Smith Younce at the Penguin Press.

My profound thanks go to Sapna Gupta for her astute reading of the manuscript. Adam Kuper gave me advice and encouragement when I needed it most. Pauline Harris provided expert help with research. Ken Druckerman didn't just comment on the early chapters; he also accepted packages on my behalf.

Thank you to Marianne Velmans at Transworld, and to Sarah Hutson, Kate Samano, Cathryn Summerhayes, Aislinn Casey, Sofia Groopman, and Jane Fleming Fransson. Merci to my posse of mother readers: Christine Tacconet, Brooke Pallot, Dietlind Lerner, Amelia Relles, Sharon Galant, and the heroic Hannah Kuper, who read the chapters on pregnancy while having contractions herself.

I am grateful to nutritionist Sandra Merle at the Direction des Familles et de la Petite Enfance in Paris, for providing the recipes; to Claire Smith, who worked tirelessly to test them; and to baby Kate and others, who were made to eat them.

I am especially indebted to the many French families who let me hang around with them, and to the people whose introductions made all that hanging around possible: Cécile Agon, Benjamin Benita, Véronique Bouruet-Aubertot, Ingrid Callies, Aurèle Cariès, Christophe Delin, Christophe Dunoyer, Andrea Ipaktchi, Laurence Kalmanson, Solange Martin, Gail Negbaur, William Oiry, Robynne Pendariès, Lucie Porcher, Jonathan Ross, Frédérique Souverain, Hélène Toussaint, Emilie Walmsley, and Esther Zajdenweber.

Thanks to crèche Cour Debille and crèche Enfance et Découverte, especially Marie-Christine Barison, Anne-Marie Legendre, Sylvie Metay, Didier Trillot, Alexandra Van-Kersschaver, and Fatima Abdullarif. Special gratitude goes to the family of Fanny Gerbet.

For their general support, often in the form of food or shelter, thanks to Marsha Druckerman, Shana Druckerman, Adam Ellick, Adelyn Escobar, Joanne Feld, Steve Fleischer, Nancy and Ronald Gelles, Mark Gevisser, Valerie Picard, Lithe Sebesta, Kari Snick, Jeffrey Sumber, Patrick Weil, and Scott Wenger. Thank you to Benjamin Barda and my colleagues on the rue Bleue for their camaraderie, parenting tips, and lessons on how to enjoy lunch.

It's much easier to write a parenting book when you're blessed with extraordinary parents—Bonnie Green and Henry Druckerman. It's also a gift to be married to someone who's better at what I do than I am. I couldn't have written this book without the encouragement and tolerance of my husband, Simon Kuper. He critiqued every draft, and in so doing, made me a better writer.

Finally, thank you to Leo, Joel, and Leila (rhymes with sky-la). This is what Mommy was doing in her office. I hope that one day you'll think it was worth it.

notes

french children don't throw food

1. *French parents are very concerned about their kids* In a 2002 survey by the International Social Survey Program, 90 percent of French adults agreed or strongly agreed with the statement "Watching children grow up is life's greatest joy." In the United States it was 85.5 percent; in the United Kingdom it was 81.1 percent.

2. *"more attention to the upbringing of children than can possibly be good for them"* Joseph Epstein, "The Kindergarchy: Every Child a Dauphin," *The Weekly Standard*, June 9, 2008. Epstein may also have coined the word "kindergarchy."

3. *benefit from more stimulation, too* Judith Warner describes this in *Perfect Madness: Motherhood in the Age of Anxiety* (New York: Riverhead Books, 2005).

4. *has plunged since its peak in the early 1990s* According to the FBI's Uniform Crime Report, the rate of violent crimes in the United States fell 43 percent between 1991 and 2009.

5. *when I discover a research study* Alan B. Krueger, Daniel Kahneman, Claude Fischler, David Schkade, Norbert Schwarz, and Arthur A. Stone, "Time Use and Subjective Well-Being in France and the U.S.," *Social Indicators Research* 93 (2009): 7–18.

6. *only the Irish have a higher birth rate* According to 2009 figures from the OECD, France's birth rate is 1.99 per woman; Belgium's is 1.83; Italy's is 1.41; Spain's is 1.4; and Germany's is 1.36.

Chapter 2: paris is burping

1. *in France it's 1 in 6,900* From a report called *Women on the Front Lines of Health Care: State of the World's Mothers 2010*, published by Save the Children in 2010. The figures are from an appendix in the report titled "The Complete Mothers' Index 2010."
2. *about 87 percent of women have epidurals, on average* "Top des Maternités." www.maman.fr/top_des_maternites-1-1.html.

Chapter 3: doing her nights

1. *A meta-study of dozens of peer-reviewed sleep papers* Jodi Mindell et al., "Behavioral Treatment of Bedtime Problems and Night Wakings in Young Children: An American Academy of Sleep Medicine Review," *Sleep* 29 (2006): 1263–76.
2. *The authors of the meta-study point to a paper* Teresa Pinella and Leann L. Birch, "Help Me Make It Through the Night: Behavioral Entrainment of Breast-Fed Infants' Sleep Patterns," *Pediatrics* 91, 2 (1993): 436–43.

Chapter 4: wait!

1. *Most could wait only about thirty seconds* Mischel's experiments were recounted by Jonah Lehrer in *The New Yorker*, May 18, 2009.
2. *'Hold on, I'm talking to Papa'* Walter Mischel cautions that even if young French children are good at waiting, that doesn't mean that they'll become successful adults. Many other things affect them, too. And while Americans typically don't expect small children to wait well, they trust that the same children will somehow acquire this skill later in life. "I believe an undisciplined child isn't doomed to become an undisciplined adult," Mischel says. "Just because a kid is throwing around food at age seven or eight, at a restaurant . . . doesn't mean that the same child isn't going to become a superb businessperson or scientist or teacher or whatever fifteen years later."
3. *ended up eating it* Mischel found that kids can easily learn to distract themselves. In a subsequent marshmallow test, experimenters told the children that instead of thinking about the marshmallow, they should think about something happy like "swinging on a swing with Mommy pushing" or to pretend it was just a *picture* of a marshmallow. With

this instruction, overall waiting times increased dramatically. Waiting times improved even though kids knew that they were trying to trick themselves. The moment the experimenter walked back into the room, children who had been busy self-distracting for fifteen minutes gobbled up the marshmallow.

4. *now includes snacks* Jennifer Steinhauer, "Snack Time Never Ends," *The New York Times*, January 19, 2010.

5. *But the French moms said it was very important* Marie-Anne Suizzo, "French and American Mothers' Childrearing Beliefs: Stimulating, Responding, and Long-Term Goals," *Journal of Cross-Cultural Psychology* 35, 5 (September 2004): 606–26.

6. *an enormous U.S. government study of the effects child care* National Instutute of Child Health & Human Development (NICHD), Study of Early Child Care and Youth Development, 1991–2007. www.nichd.nih.gov/research/supported/seccyd/Pagesoverview.aspx.

7. *American kids doing quite a lot of* **n'importe quoi** A 2006 study of white, middle-class Canadian couples found that when the kids were around—which was very often—it was impossible for parents to have quality time together. One participant said that while speaking to his wife, "we would be interrupted on a minute-to-minute basis." The authors concluded, "For any experience of being a couple together, they simply had to get away from the children." Vera Dyck and Kerry Daly, "Rising to the Challenge: Fathers' Role in the Negotiation of Couple Time," *Leisure Studies* 25, 2 (2006): 201–17.

8. *A French psychologist writes* The psychologist is Christine Brunet, quoted in *Journal des Femmes*, February 11, 2005.

9. *"an obligatory passage"* Anne-Catherine Pernot-Masson, quoted in *Votre Enfant*.

Chapter 5: tiny little humans

1. *as far away as Normandy or Burgundy* Élisabeth Badinter, *L'amour en plus: Histoire de l'amour maternel* (Paris: Flammarion, 1980), 56–63.

2. *to replace the mother in the family store* Ibid.

3. *writes a French social historian* Ibid.

4. *because doing so gives the children pleasure* Marie-Anne Suizzo, "French and American Mothers' Childrearing Beliefs: Stimulating,

Responding, and Long-Term Goals," *Journal of Cross-Cultural Psychology* 35, 5 (September 2004): 606–26.

5. *"I don't know where she got her answers"* Dolto: *Une vie pour l'enfance*, *Télérama hors série*, 2008.

6. *but that she later created* Dolto decided that she wanted a career after seeing formerly well-off women from her neighborhood come begging at her school because they'd lost their husbands in World War I. "I saw the decrepitude of bourgeois widows who didn't have a profession," she explained.

7. *In a letter to her written in 1934* Françoise Dolto, *Lettres de jeunesse: Correspondance 1913–1938* (Paris: Gallimard, 2003).

8. *she would ask her young patients* Recollection of the psychoanalyst Alain Vanier, reported in *Dolto: Une vie pour l'enfance*, *Télérama hors série*, 2008.

9. *"some of them are small. But they communicate"* The psychologist is Muriel Djéribi-Valentin. She was interviewed by Jacqueline Sellem for an article titled "Françoise Dolto: An Analyst Who Listened to Children," which appeared in *l'Humanité* in English and was translated by Kieran O'Meara, www.humaniteinenglish.com/article1071.html.

10. *give the baby a tour of the house* Marie-Anne Suizzo found that 86 percent of Parisian mothers she interviewed "specifically stated that they talk to their infants to communicate with them." Marie-Anne Suizzo, "Mother-Child Relationships in France: Balancing Autonomy and Affiliation in Everyday Interactions," *Ethos* 32, 3 (2004): 292–323.

11. *writes Yale psychologist Paul Bloom* Paul Bloom, "The Moral Life of Babies," *The New York Times Magazine*, May 3, 2010.

12. *that eight-month-olds understand probabilities* Alison Gopnik writes that these new studies "demonstrate that babies and very young children know, observe, explore, imagine and learn more than we would ever have thought possible." Gopnik is a psychologist at the University of California at Berkeley and author of *The Philosophical Baby*.

Chapter 6: day care?

1. *and turn them into "Americans"* Abby J. Cohen, "A Brief History of Federal Financing for Child Care in the United States," *The Future of Children: Financing Child Care* 6 (1996).

2. ***don't have to work, or can afford nannies.*** Eventually, the latter part of preschool was assimilated into the American public-school system. But day care remained staunchly private. Middle-class parents and experts believed that mothers should look after young children. The state wasn't supposed to intrude on that stage of family life, except when "a family—or the country itself—is in crisis," Abby Cohen writes.

The Great Depression was one such crisis. By 1933, the American government had set up emergency nursery schools, but this was explicitly done to create jobs. Cohen notes that a 1930 report by the White House's Conference on Children said, "No one should get the idea that Uncle Sam is going to rock the baby to sleep." Most of the schools were shut down once the worst of the Depression passed.

When the United States entered World War II, another child-care crisis erupted: Who would look after Rosie the Riveter's babies? Between 1942 and 1946 the federal government built child-care centers serving children whose mothers had gone to work in the defense industry. Most were in California, where much of the war production was taking place. Initially, the centers charged just fifty cents a day.

When the war ended, the government said that it was shutting down the centers so mothers could go back to keeping house. Some mothers protested. First Lady Eleanor Roosevelt wrote, "Many thought [the centers] were purely a war emergency measure. A few of us had an inkling that perhaps they were a need that was constantly with us, but one that we had neglected to face in the past." Some centers got funding for a few more years, but most eventually shut down.

A new push for the U.S. government to help parents pay for child care—and even provide some of it—began to galvanize in the 1960s. There was a wave of new research about how disadvantages very early in life persist when kids are older. Head Start was created to fund schools for very poor three- to five-year-olds.

Of course, middle-class mothers wanted their kids to have the advantages of early education, too. And with more women working, child care was increasingly a problem. In 1971, Congress passed the Comprehensive Child Development Act. The act was meant to professionalize the child-care workforce, build lots of new child-care centers, and make quality child care available and affordable. President Nixon vetoed the act, claiming (in a veto written by his adviser Pat Buchanan) that it favored "communal approaches to child-rearing over the family centered approach." It was a brilliant invocation of both Cold War fears about communism and the long-standing idea that mothers should look after children themselves.

In the 1980s, this ambivalence about day care took on a new form: alleged sex-abuse rings set in home- and center-based day-care facilities. In a series of high-profile cases, day-care owners and employees were charged with pedophilia, sometimes even involving devil worship and journeys into underground labyrinths. Many of these charges turned out to be bunk, and key convictions were overturned because testimony from the children involved had been coerced by overzealous prosecutors. Journalist Margaret Talbot wrote that even the most outrageous charges seemed credible in the early 1980s because Americans were nervous about mothers of young children going to work: "It was as though there were some dark, self-defeating relief in trading niggling everyday doubts about our children's care for our absolute worst fears—for a story with monsters, not just human beings who didn't always treat our kids exactly as we would like; for a fate so horrific and bizarre that no parent, no matter how vigilant, could have ever prevented it," she said.

3. *are typically open from six* A.M. *to six thirty* P.M. When there were sex-abuse cases at some CDCs in the 1980s, the House Subcommittee on Military Personnel and Compensation held hearings to investigate the whole system. It found the same problems faced by private-sector day care: high staff turnover, low pay, and sometimes nonexistent inspections, according to Gail L. Zellman and Anne Johansen in "Examining the Implementation and Outcomes of the Military Child Care Act of 1989." In response, Congress passed the Military Child Care Act in 1989. This contained exactly the sort of rules that American day-care advocates had been clamoring for: specialized training for caregivers, experts overseeing each center, and no-notice inspections four times a year.

4. *American parents remain ambivalent about day care* In 2003, 72 percent of Americans agreed that "too many children are being raised in

day-care centers these days," up from 68 percent in 1987, according to the Pew Research Center.

5. *perfect conviction that the children understand* A 2009 report by the Paris mayor's office said that caregivers shouldn't speak badly about a child's parents, origins, or appearance, even if the child is an infant, and even if the remark is made to someone else. "The implicit message in this type of reflection is always perceived intuitively by the children. The younger they are, the more they understand what is contained behind the words," the report says.

6. *but must be trained in-house* OECD, "Starting Strong II: Early Childhood Education and Care," 2006.

7. *the way kids develop and behave later in life* NICHD Study of Early Child Care and Youth Development.

8. *One of the study's researchers* Jay Belsky, "Effects of Child Care on Child Development: Give Parents Real Choice."

Chapter 7: bébé au lait

1. *do some breastfeeding* OECD, "France Country Highlights, Doing Better for Children," 2009.

2. *a third are still nursing exclusively at four months* WHO Global Data Bank on Infant and Young Child Feeding, 2007–2008.

3. *weighing yourself daily* "The more carefully and frequently you monitor yourself, the better you'll control yourself," Roy F. Baumeister and John Tierney write in *Willpower: Rediscovering the Greatest Human Strength* (New York: The Penguin Press, 2011).

4. *they will eat those foods later* Ibid.

5. *there's no reason to feel bad about that* In a 2004 study, when French and American mothers ranked the importance of "always put[ting] the baby's needs before one's own," American mothers gave it 2.89 out of 5; French mothers gave it 1.26 out of 5. Marie-Anne Suizzo, "French and American Mothers' Childrearing Beliefs: Stimulating, Responding, and Long-Term Goals," *Journal of Cross-Cultural Psychology* 35, 5 (September 2004): 606–26.

6. *a fashion spread in a French mothers' magazine* Violaine Belle-Croix,

"Géraldine Pailhas, des visages, des figures," *Milk Magazine*, September 13, 2010.

7. *is also required to keep her looking and feeling seductive* "French women know that an inner life is a sexy thing. It needs to be nurtured, developed, pampered . . . ," Debra Ollivier writes in *What French Women Know: About Love, Sex, and Other Matters of the Heart and Mind* (New York: G. P. Putnam's Sons, 2009).

Chapter 8: the perfect mother doesn't exist

1. **Just 71 percent of Americans and Britons said this** Given the baby boom and the shortage of spots in *crèches*, the French state pays some mothers about five hundred euros a month to look after their own kids until the youngest is three. Mothers are also entitled to work part-time for the first three years.

2. *to make child care less pleasant for mothers* American mothers found child care twice as unpleasant as French mothers. Alan B. Krueger, Daniel Kahneman, Claude Fischler, David Schkade, Norbert Schwarz, and Arthur A. Stone, "Time Use and Subjective Well-Being in France and the U.S.," *Social Indicators Research* 93 (2009): 7–18.

3. **Annette Lareau observed among white and African American middle-class parents** Annette Lareau, *Unequal Childhoods: Class, Race, and Family Life* (Berkeley: University of California Press, 2003).

4. *she's also supposed to attend* **the practices** Annette Lareau writes that most of the middle-class families she observed were frenetically busy, with parents working full-time, then shopping, cooking, overseeing baths and homework, and driving kids back and forth to activities. "Things are so hectic that the house sometimes seems to become a holding pattern between activities," she writes. From "Question and Answers: Annette Lareau, *Unequal Childhoods: Class, Race, and Family Life*," http://sociology.sas.upenn.edu/sites/sociology.sas.upenn.edu/files/Lareau_Question&Answers.pdf.

5. *"they might lose!"* Elisabeth Guédel Treussard, "Pourquoi les mères françaises sont supérieures," *French Morning*, January 24, 2011.

6. *more time on child care than parents did in 1965* Robert Pear, "Married and Single Parents Spending More Time with Children, Study Finds," *The New York Times*, October 17, 2006.

Chapter 9: caca boudin

1. *child care is the top expense* The Basic Economic Security Tables for the United States 2010, published by Wider Opportunities for Women, 2010, www.wowonline.org/documents/BESTIndexforTheUnitedStates 2010.pdf.

2. *"passionately, madly, not at all"* Debra Ollivier, What French Women Know: About Love, Sex, and Other Matters of Heart and Mind (New York: G. P. Putnam's Sons, 2009).

Chapter 11: i adore this baguette

1. *marital satisfaction has fallen* Jean M. Twenge, W. Keith Campbell, and Craig A. Foster, "Parenthood and Marital Satisfaction: A Meta-Analytic Review," Journal of Marriage and Family 65, 3 (August 2003): 574–83.

2. *mothers find it more pleasant to do housework than to take care of their kids* In a well-known 2004 study, working mothers in Texas said child care was one of their most unpleasant daily activities. They preferred housework. Daniel Kahneman et al., "A Survey Method for Characterizing Daily Life Experience: The Day Reconstruction Method," Science, December 3, 2004.

3. *their unhappiness increases with each additional child* Jean M. Twenge et al., "Parenthood and Marital Satisfaction."

4. *A paper on middle-class Canadians* Vera Dyck and Kerry Daly, "Rising to the Challenge: Fathers' Role in the Negotiation of Couple Time," Leisure Studies 25, 2 (2006): 201–17.

5. *have a bigger gap than we do between what men and women earn* In the overall 2010 Global Gender Gap Index, created by the World Economic Forum, the United States ranked nineteenth and France ranked forty-sixth.

6. *men doing household work and looking after children* According to Institut national de la statistique et des études économiques (Insee).

7. *and 25 percent more time on child care* According to the U.S. Bureau of Labor Statistics, news release, June 22, 2010, "American Time Use Survey—2009 Results," www.bls.gov/news.release/archives/atus_06222010.pdf.

8. *"it's hard for me to cool back down"* In a 2008 study, 49 percent of

employed American men said they did as much or more child care as
their partners. But just 31 percent of women saw it this way. Ellen
Galinsky, Kerstin Aumann, and James T. Bond, *Times Are Changing:
Gender and Generation at Work and at Home.*

9. *leaving Simon in Paris with the boys* Alan B. Krueger et al., "Time Use
and Subjective Well-Being in France and the U.S." French women
spent about 15 percent less time doing housework than the American
women did.

10. *about twenty-one more vacation days each year* Ibid.

11. *A 2006 French study* Denise Bauer, Études et Résultats, "Le temps des
parents après une naissance," Direction de la recherche, des études,
de l'évaluation et des statistiques (DREES), April 2006, www.drees
.sante.gouv.fr/le-temps-des-parents-apres-une-naissance,4413.html.

Chapter 12: you just have to taste it

1. *Just 3.1 percent of French five- and six-year-olds are obese* Nathalie
Guignon, Marc Collet, and Lucie Gonzalez, "La santé des enfants en
grande section de maternelle en 2005–2006," Drees études et resultats,
September 2010.

2. *10.4 percent of kids between two and five are obese* Centers for Disease
Control and Prevention, "Prevalence of Obesity Among Children
and Adolescents: United States, Trends 1963–1965 Through 2007–
2008."

3. *"health is seen as the main reason for eating"* Lemangeur-ocha.com,
"France, Europe, the United States: What Eating Means to Us: Interview with Claude Fischler and Estelle Masson," posted online, January 16, 2008.

Chapter 13: it's me who decides

1. *"and it's respectful to the child," Daniel Marcelli says* In an interview
with *Enfant Magazine*, "Comment réussir à se faire obéir?" October
2009, 78–82.

2. *In a national poll* "Les Français et la fessée" by the polling agency
TNS Sofres/Logica for Dimanche Ouest France, November 11, 2009.

3. *said they never spank their kids* Fifty-five percent also said that they
oppose spanking.

4. *All the French parenting experts I read about oppose it* Marcel Rufo, a well-known child psychiatrist based in Marseille, says: "There are two generations of parents . . . those of yesterday who were spanked and hit and who say, 'We weren't traumatized by it.' And then there are the parents of today, who I think are much better, because they're more about understanding the child than about prohibiting things. The role of the parent is to give his view to the child, to explain things to him. The child will accept them." *Le Figaro Magazine*, November 20, 2009, www.lefigaro.fr/actualite-france/2009/11/20/01016-20091120 ARTFIG00670-deux-claques-pour-la-loi-antifessee-.php.

Chapter 14: let him live his life

1. *everything in the house—and in society—that concerns him* When French and American mothers were asked to rank the importance of "Not let[ting] the baby become too dependent on his or her mother," American mothers ranked the statement 0.93 out of a possible 5. French mothers ranked it 3.36. Marie-Anne Suizzo, "French and American Mothers' Childrearing Beliefs: Stimulating, Responding, and Long-Term Goals," *Journal of Cross-Cultural Psychology* 35, 5 (September 2004): 606–26.

2. *"treating each child's thought as a special contribution"* Raymonde Carroll writes in *Cultural Misunderstandings* that American parents "avoid as much as possible criticizing their children, making fun of their tastes, or telling them constantly 'how to do things.'"

3. *is almost like getting a perfect score* Getting 16:20 is a "rare and outstanding achievement," according to a report prepared by the University of Cambridge exam board for British Universities. Reported in "A Chorus of Disapproval," *The Economist*, September 30, 2010, www.economist.com/node/17155766.

4. *against an ideal, which practically no one meets* This creates a problem for social scientists when they try to compare life in the United States and France. "Americans tend to be more emphatic when reporting their well-being," say the authors of that study of women in Ohio and Rennes. Americans were more likely to choose extremes like "very satisfied" and "not at all satisfied," whereas Frenchwomen avoided these. The researchers adjusted their findings to account for this.

5. *"because they're afraid of not succeeding"* Po Bronson and Ashley Merryman, *NurtureShock: New Thinking About Children* (New York: Twelve, 2009), http://abcnews.go.com/GMA/Books/story?id=8433586&page=7.

the future in french

1. *that I must bend to their wills* "For Françoise Dolto, a desire is not a need, it shouldn't necessarily be satisfied, but we should listen to it and speak about it, which makes all the difference," says Muriel Djéribi-Valentin, in "Françoise Dolto: An Analyst Who Listened to Children," *l'Humanité* in English.

bibliography

ABCs of Parenting in Paris. 5th edition. Emily James, managing ed. Paris: MESSAGE Mother Support Group, 2006. www.messageparis.org.

Antier, Edwige. "Plus on lève la main sur un enfant, plus il devient agressif." *Le Parisien.* November 15, 2009.

Auffret-Pericone, Marie. "Comment réussir à se faire obéir?" *Enfant.* October 2009, 91–96.

Badinter, Elisabeth. *L'Amour en Plus: Histoire de l'amour maternel.* Paris: Flammarion Lettres, 1980.

———. *The Conflict: How Modern Motherhood Undermines the Status of Women.* New York: Metropolitan Books, 2012.

———. *Le Conflit: La femme et la mère.* Paris: Flammarion Lettres, 2010.

Baumeister, Roy F., and John Tierney. *Willpower: Rediscovering the Greatest Human Strength.* New York: Penguin Press, 2011.

Belsky, Jay. "Effects of Child Care on Child Development: Give Parents Real Choice." March 2009. Text of speech given at Conference of European Ministers of Family Affairs, Prague, February 2009.

Bennhold, Katrin. "Where Having It All Doesn't Mean Having Equality." *The New York Times,* October 11, 2010.

Bloom, Paul. "Moral Life of Babies." *The New York Times Magazine,* May 3, 2010. http://www.nytimes.com/2010/05/09/magazine/09babies-t.html?pagewanted=all.

Bornstein, Marc H., Catherine S. Tamis-LeMonda, Marie-Germaine Pecheux, and Charles W. Rahn. "Mother and Infant Activity and

Interaction in France and in the United States: A Comparative Study." *International Journal of Behavioral Development* (1991): 21–43.

Bronson, Po, and Ashley Merryman. *NurtureShock: New Thinking About Children*. New York: Twelve, 2009.

Brunet, Christine, and Nadia Benlakhel. *C'est pas bientôt fini ce caprice? Les calmer sans s'énerver*. Paris: Albin Michel, 2005.

Calhoun, Ada. "The Battle over 'Cry It Out' Sleep Training." Salon.com, March 17, 2010.

Carroll, Raymonde. *Cultural Misunderstandings: The French-American Experience*. Chicago: University of Chicago Press, 1990.

CIA. *The World Factbook*. https://www.cia.gov/library/publications/the-world-factbook/.

Cimpian, Andrei, Holly-Marie C. Arce, Ellen M. Markman, Carol S. Dweck. "Subtle Linguistic Cues Affect Children's Motivation." *Association for Psychological Science* 18, 4 (2007).

Cohen, Abby J. "A Brief History of Federal Financing for Child Care in the United States." *The Future of Children: Financing Child Care* 6 (1996): 26–40.

Cohen, Michel. *The New Basics*. New York: Harper Paperbacks, 2004.

Clerget, Stéphane, and Danièle Laufer. *La mère parfaite, c'est vous*. Paris: Hachette Littératures, 2008.

Delahaye, Marie-Claude. *Livre de bord de la future maman*. Paris: Marabout, 2007.

De Leersnyder, Hélène. *L'enfant et son sommeil*. Paris: Robert Laffont, 1998.

Direction de la recherche, des études, de l'évaluation et des statistiques (DREES). *Le temps des parents après une naissance*. April 2006.

Dolto, Françoise. *Les étapes majeures de l'enfance*. Paris: Gallimard, 1994.

———. *Lettres de jeunesse: Correspondance 1913–1938*, Paris: Gallimard, 2003.

———. *Lorsque l'enfant Paraît, Tome 1*. Paris: Éditions du Seuil, 1977.

Dolto, Françoise, and Danielle Marie Lévy. *Parler juste aux enfants*. Paris: Gallimard, 2002.

Dyck, Vera, and Kerry Daly. "Rising to the Challenge: Fathers' Role in the Negotiation of Couple Time." *Leisure Studies* 25, 2 (2006): 201–17.

Eisenberg, Arlene, Heidi E. Murkoff, and Sandee Hathaway. *What to Expect: The Toddler Years*. London: Simon and Schuster, 1996.

Epstein, Jean. "Parents, faites-vous confiance!" Interview. www.aufeminin. com. October 7, 2009.

Famili.fr. "Devenir parents et rester amants?" http://www.famili.fr/,devenir -parents-et-rester-amants,599,280849.asp.

———. "La reprise de la sexualité après bébé." http://www.famili.fr/,la -reprise-de-la-sexualite-apres-bebe,438,10193.asp.

Franrenet, Sandra. "Quelles punitions pour nos fripons?" http://madame .lefigaro.fr/societe/quelles-punitions-pour-nos-fripons-280211-137257 . February 28, 2011.

Galinsky, Ellen, Kerstin Aumann, and James T. Bond. *Times Are Changing: Gender and Generation at Work and at Home.* Report. New York: Families and Work Institute, 2009.

Gallais, Marie. "Impossible de s'occuper seule." *Parents,* October 2012, 99–100.

Gerkens, Danièle. "Comment rendre son enfant heureux?" Interview with Aldo Naori. *Elle,* February 26, 2010.

Girard, Isabelle. "Pascal Bruckner at Laurence Ferrari: Le mariage? Un acte de bravoure." *Le Figaro—Madame,* September 11, 2010.

Gravillon, Isabelle, et al. "Nos enfants sont-ils trop protégés?" *Enfant Magazine,* September 2012, 56–57.

Guiliano, Mireille. *French Women Don't Get Fat.* New York: Alfred A. Knopf, 2005.

Haberfeld, Ingrid. "Quel est l'impact du stress sur la grossesse?" *Parents,* April 2012, 60–61.

Hausmann, Ricardo, Laura D. Tyson, and Saadia Zahidi. "The Global Gender Gap Report 2010." Geneva, Switzerland: World Economic Forum, 2010.

Heckman, James J. "Schools, Skills and Synapses." http://www.heckmane-quation.org/content/resource/presenting-heckman-equation.

Henry, Dominique. "Il part sans vous, et c'est bon pour lui!" *Famili,* August/September 2012, 104–6.

Hulbert, Ann. *Raising America: Experts, Parents, and a Century of Advice About Children.* New York: Vintage Books, 2004.

Institute National de la statistique et des études économiques (INSEE). Evolution des temps sociaux au cours d'une journée moyenne, 1986 and 1999. http://www.insee.fr/fr/themes/tableau.asp?ref_id=natccf05519.

Kahneman, Daniel, and Alan B. Krueger. "Developments in the Measurement of Subjective Well-Being." *Journal of Economic Perspectives* 20, 1 (2006): 3–24.

Kamerman, Sheila. "Early Childhood Education and Care: International Perspectives." Testimony prepared for the United States Senate Committee on Health, Education, Labor, and Pensions, Washington, D.C., March 27, 2001.

———. "A Global History of Early Childhood Education and Care." Background paper. UNESCO, 2006.

Krueger, Alan B., ed. *Measuring the Subjective Well-Being of Nations: National Accounts of Time Use and Well-Being*. Chicago: University of Chicago Press, 2009.

Krueger, Alan B., Daniel Kahneman, Claude Fischler, David Schkade, Norbert Schwarz, and Arthur A. Stone. "Time Use and Subjective Well-being in France and the U.S." *Social Indicators Research* 93 (2009): 7–18.

———. "Questions and Answers About Unequal Childhoods." http://sociology.sas.upenn.edu/a_lareau2.

Lareau, Annette. *Unequal Childhoods: Class, Race and Family Life*. Berkeley: University of California Press, 2003.

Lemangeur-ocha.com. "France, Europe, the United States: What Eating Means to Us: Interview with Claude Fischler and Estelle Masson," posted online January 16, 2008.

Mairie de Paris. "Mission d'information et d'évaluation sur l'engagement de la collectivité parisienne auprès des familles en matière d'accueil des jeunes enfants de moins de trois ans." June 15, 2009.

Marbeau, J. B. F. *The Crèche or a Way to Reduce Poverty by Increasing the Population*. Trans. Vanessa Nicolai. Montreal, 1994 (original work published 1845). PDF of translation supplied by Larry Prochner, University of Alberta.

Marcelli, Daniel. *Il est permis d'obéir*. Paris: Albin Michel, 2009.

Marchi, Catherine. "12 conseils pour faire le Bonheur de votre enfant." *Parents*, August 2010, 52–54.

Melmed, Matthew. Statement submitted to the Committee on Education and Labor, U.S. House of Representatives, Hearing on Investing in Early Education: Improving Children's Success. Washington, D.C., January 23, 2008.

Merle, Sandra. Interview with the author, September 20, 2012.

Military.com. "Military Child Care." http://www.military.com/benefits/resources/family-support/child-care.

Mindell, Jodi, et al. "Behavioral Treatment of Bedtime Problems and Night Wakings in Young Children: AASM Standards of Practice." *Sleep* 29 (2006): 1263–76.

Mischel, Walter. *A History of Psychology in Autobiography.* Edited by G. Lindzey and W. M. Runyan. Washington, D.C.: American Psychological Association, 2007.

————. Interview with the author, July 20, 2010.

Mogel, Wendy. *The Blessing of a Skinned Knee.* New York: Scribner, 2001.

Mon Enfant à l'école maternelle. http://cache.media.education.gouv.fr/file/Espace_parent/35/9/Guide_pratique_des_parents_ecole_maternelle_227359.pdf.

Murkoff, Heidi, Arlene Eisenberg, and Sandee E. Hathaway. *What to Expect When You're Expecting.* New York: Workman, 2002.

National Institutes of Health. "Child Care Linked to Assertive, Noncompliant, and Aggressive Behaviors: Vast Majority of Children Within Normal Range." July 16, 2003.

Ochs, Elinor, and Carolina Izquierdo. "Responsibility in Childhood: Three Developmental Trajectories." *Ethos* 37, no. 4 (2009): 391–413.

Ollivier, Debra. *What French Women Know: About Love, Sex, and Other Matters of the Heart and Mind.* New York: G. P. Putnam's Sons, 2009.

Organisation for Economic Co-operation and Development. "Éducation et Accueil des Jeunes Enfants." May 2003.

Parker, Kim. "The Harried Life of the Working Mother." Pew Research Center. October 1, 2009. http://pewresearch.org/pubs/1360/working-women-conflicted-but-few-favor-return-to-traditional-roles.

Pernoud, Laurence. *J'élève mon enfant.* Paris: Editions Horay, 2007.

Pew Global Attitudes Project. "Men's Lives Often Seen as Better: Gender Equality Universally Embraced, but Inequalities Acknowledged." July 1, 2010.

Pinella, Teresa, and Leann L. Birch. "Help Me Make It Through the Night: Behavioral Entrainment of Breast-Fed Infants' Sleep Patterns." *Pediatrics* 91, 2 (1993): 436–43.

Pleux, Didier. "Enfants tyrans: Un peu de bon sens!" Interview by Doctissimo.fr. http://www.doctissimo.fr/html/psychologie/mag_2003/mag1024/ps_7167_enfants_tyrans_bon_sens_itw.htm.

Prochner, Larry. "The American Creche: 'Let's Do What the French Do, but Do It Our Way.'" *Contemporary Issues in Early Childhood* 4, 3 (2003): 267–85.

Programme National Nutrition Santé. *La santé vient en mangeant et en bougeant.* 2004.

Richardin, Sophie. "Surfez sur les vagues du désir!" *Neuf Mois*, February 2009, 49–53.

Rossant, Lyonel, and Jacqueline Rossant-Lumbroso. *Votre Enfant: Guide à l'usage des parents.* Paris: Robert Laffont, 2006.

Rousseau, Jean-Jacques. *Émile, or On Education.* Translated by Allan Bloom. New York: Basic Books, 1979.

———. *Emile, or On Education.* Sioux Falls, S.D.: NuVision Publications LLC, 2007. http://www.nuvisionpublications.com/Print_Books.asp?ISBN=159547840X.

Sawica, Leslie, coordinator. *Le guide des nouvelles mamans.* Free booklet prepared with support from the French health ministry. 2009.

Senior, Jennifer. "All Joy and No Fun." *New York*, July 12, 2010.

Sethi, Anita, Walter Mischel, J. Lawrence Aber, Yuichi Shoda, and Monica Larrea Rodriguez. "The Role of Strategic Attention Deployment in Development of Self-Regulation: Predicting Preschoolers' Delay of Gratification from Mother-Toddler Interactions." *Developmental Psychology* 36, 6 (November 2000): 767–77.

Skenazy, Lenore. *Free-Range Kids.* San Francisco: Jossey-Bass, 2009.

Steingarten, Jeffrey. *The Man Who Ate Everything.* New York: Vintage Books, 1997.

Suizzo, Marie-Anne. "French and American Mothers' Childrearing Beliefs: Stimulating, Responding, and Long-Term Goals." *Journal of Cross-Cultural Psychology* 35, 5 (September 2004): 606–26.

———. "French Parents' Cultural Models and Childrearing Beliefs." *International Journal of Behavioral Development* 26, 4 (2002): 297–307.

———. "Mother-Child Relationships in France: Balancing Autonomy and Affiliation in Everyday Interactions." *Ethos* 32, 3 (2004): 292–323.

Suizzo, Marie-Anne, and Marc H. Bornstein. "French and European American Child-Mother Play: Culture and Gender Considerations." *International Journal of Behavioral Development* 30, 6 (2006): 498–508.

Talbot, Margaret. "The Devil in the Nursery." *The New York Times Magazine*, January 7, 2001.

Thirion, Marie, and Marie-Josèphe Challamel. *Le sommeil, le rêve et l'enfant: De la naissance à l'adolescence*. Paris: Albin Michel, 2002.

Thompson, Caroline. Interview with the author, April 20, 2010.

Turkle, Sherry. *Psychoanalytic Politics: Jacques Lacan and Freud's French Revolution*. New York: The Guilford Press, 1992.

———. "Tough Love." Introduction. In Françoise Dolto, *When Parents Separate*. Boston: David R. Godine, 1995.

Twenge, Jean M., W. Keith Campbell, and Craig A. Foster. "Parenthood and Marital Satisfaction: A Meta-Analytic Review." *Journal of Marriage and Family* 65, 3 (August 2003): 574–83.

UNICEF. "Child Poverty in Perspective: An Overview of Childhood Well-Being in Rich Countries." Innocenti Report Card 7, 2007. UNICEF Innocenti Research Center, Florence, Italy.

U.S. Bureau of Labor Statistics. American Time-Use Survey Summary, 2009 results.

Vaineau, Anne-Laure. *5 conseils pour éviter le baby-clash*. http://www.psychologies.com/Famille/Etre-parent/Equilibre-du-couple/Articles-et-Dossiers/5-conseils-pour-eviter-le-baby-clash.

Warner, Judith. "How to Raise a Child." *The New York Times*, July 27, 2012. http://www.nytimes.com/2012/07/29/books/review/teach-your-children-well-by-madeline-levine.html?pagewanted=all.

———. *Perfect Madness: Motherhood in the Age of Anxiety*. New York: Riverhead Books, 2005.

Winter, Pam. *Engaging Families in the Early Childhood Development Story; Neuroscience and Early Childhood Development: Summary of Selected Literature and Key Messages for Parenting*. Education Services Australia Ltd. As the legal entity for the Ministerial Council for Education, Early Childhood Development and Youth Affairs, 2010.

Zellman, Gail L., and Anne Johansen. "Examining the Implementation and Outcomes of the Military Child Care Act of 1989." Research brief. Santa Monica, Calif.: Rand Corporation, 1998.

Zigler, Edward, Katherine Marsland, and Heather Lord. *The Tragedy of Child Care in America*. New Haven and London: Yale University Press, 2009.

index

AVAILABLE FROM PENGUIN

Lust in Translation
Infidelity from Tokyo to Tennessee

It's an adulterous world out there. Yet, compared to the citizens of just about every other nation, Americans are the least adept at having affairs, have the most trouble enjoying them, and suffer the most in their aftermath, and journalist Pamela Druckerman has the facts to prove it.

Voyeuristic and packed with eyebrow-raising statistics and interviews, *Lust in Translation* is a world tour of infidelity that will give new meaning to the phrase "practicing monogamy."

PENGUIN
BOOKS